The Cry of the Earth and the Cry of the Poor

The Cry of the Earth and the Cry of the Poor

Hearing Justice in John's Gospel

Kathleen P. Rushton

scm press

© Kathleen P. Rushton 2020

Published in 2020 by SCM Press
Editorial office
3rd Floor, Invicta House,
108–114 Golden Lane,
London EC1Y 0TG, UK

www.scmpress.co.uk

SCM Press is an imprint of Hymns Ancient & Modern Ltd (a registered charity)

Hymns Ancient & Modern® is a registered trademark of
Hymns Ancient & Modern Ltd
13A Hellesdon Park Road, Norwich,
Norfolk NR6 5DR, UK

All rights reserved. No part of this publication may be reproduced,
stored in a retrieval system, or transmitted,
in any form or by any means, electronic, mechanical,
photocopying or otherwise, without the prior permission of
the publisher, SCM Press.

Kathleen P. Rushton has asserted her right under the Copyright, Designs and
Patents Act 1988 to be identified as the Author of this Work.

Scripture quotations, unless otherwise stated, are from the New Revised
Standard Version of the Bible, copyright 1989 by the Division of Christian
Education of the National Council of the Churches of Christ in the USA.
Used by permission. All rights reserved.

British Library Cataloguing in Publication data
A catalogue record for this book is available
from the British Library

978-0-334-05905-9

To my religious congregation
Nga Whaea Atawhai o Aotearoa
Sisters of Mercy New Zealand.

Contents

Abbreviations	ix
Acknowledgements	xi
Introduction	xiii
Overview of the Gospel of John	xxiii

Part 1 The Prologue — 1

From the Beginning to Word Made Flesh
    The Prologue: 1.1–5, 9–18 — 3

Part 2 The Ministry of Jesus (1.19 — 12.50) — 17

Bethany Across the Jordan
    A Man Whose Name was John: 1.6–8, 15, 19–34 — 19
    The First Disciples of Jesus: 35–51 — 26
Cana
    A Wedding: 2.1–12 — 33
Jerusalem
    Jesus in the Temple: 2.13–25 — 41
    A Pharisee Named Nicodemus: 3.1–21 — 46
Samaria
    Living Water: 4.5–42 — 56
Jerusalem
    Cry of the Marginalized: 5.1–47 — 65
Galilee
    'Come, Eat of My Bread': 6.1–69 — 72
Jerusalem
    'Rivers of Living Water': 7.37–39 — 85
    Jesus, the Scribes, the Pharisees and the Woman: 8.1–11 — 90
    The Beggar Born Blind: 9.1–41 — 95
    The Good Shepherd: 10.1–30 — 102

Bethany
    Martha, Mary and Lazarus: 11.1–45 — 109
    Mary Anoints Jesus: 12.1–8 — 115
Jerusalem
    'The Hour' Approaches: 12.12–16, 20–33 — 121

Part 3 The 'Hour' of Jesus: The Last Night, Passion and Resurrection 13.1—21.25 — 129

Jerusalem
    The Last Supper: 13.1—17.26 — 131
        Jesus Washes Feet: 13.1–17 — 133
        First Part of the Last Supper Discourse: 13.31—14.31 — 140
        Second Part of the Last Supper Discourse: 15.1—16.4a — 152
        Third Part of the Last Supper Discourse: 16.4b–15 — 162
        Jesus Prays: 17.1–26 — 170
    The Passion and Death of Jesus: 18.1—19.42 — 176
    Appearances of the Risen Jesus: 20.1–31 — 189
Galilee
    Appearance of the Risen Jesus to Seven Disciples: 21.1–25 — 200

Appendix 1: Gospel of John: Sunday and Main Feasts
    Liturgical Year Readings — 207
Appendix 2: Key Words in the Gospel of John — 212

Glossary — 215
Bibliography — 218
Scripture Index — 227
Index of Names and Subjects — 236

Abbreviations

BCE 'Before the Common Era', an inclusive term used rather than 'BC' (Before Christ).
CE   'Common Era' is a term used of the shared Jewish and Christian era (alternative to the exclusive term AD, *Anno Domini*, 'in the year of Our Lord').
LS   Pope Francis, 2015, *Laudato Si': An Encyclical Letter on Ecology and Climate Change*, Strathfield NSW: St Paul's Publications.
RCL Revised Common Lectionary
RL   Roman Lectionary
WCC World Council of Churches

Acknowledgements

This book came about through the support of many people. While my gratitude extends beyond those who can be named here, I express my appreciation for the support I have received from the following people and groups. David Shervington of SCM Press approached me to extend a 2016 Society of Biblical Literature paper I gave on 'Jesus and Justice in John's Gospel' into a book. It has been a delight to work with David, Rachel Geddes, Hannah Ward and staff. His invitation enabled me to return to work I began on the cosmological framework of prologue as a Cardinal Hume Visiting Scholar at Margaret Beaufort Institute of Theology, Cambridge, UK in 2011. My preference for writing in ways that make sound biblical scholarship accessible has been supported and extended by the staff and readers of *Tui Motu InterIslands* (Dunedin, Aotearoa New Zealand), for which I have contributed a monthly reflection on Sunday Gospel readings since 2009. I thank the present editor, Dr Ann Gilroy RSJ, for permission to use and to extend articles published there. I acknowledge previous editors Michael Hill IC and Kevin Twomey OP.

People from Christian traditions using the Revised Common Lectionary who have attended my quarterly Rosary House Spiritual Life Sunday Gospel Series, and the Christchurch Ecumenical Lay Preachers with whom I have been privileged to work, led me to address both the Roman and Revised Common Lectionaries. Staff and students of the Ecumenical Institute for Distance Theological Education (closed 2014) and the Catholic Institute of Aotearoa New Zealand have supported and extended me. I am grateful for the friendship of colleagues of the Aotearoa New Association of Biblical Studies, the Oceania Biblical Studies Association and the Australian Catholic Biblical Association. In particular I acknowledge Dr Elaine Wainwright RSM and colleagues working from an ecological perspective. I remember with gratitude the friendship and support of the late Dr Judith McKinlay, who died on 9 February 2019. So many have enriched my journey, including those I am privileged to accompany in spiritual direction and my spiritual director companions of Whakakōingo o te Ngākau: The Yearning Heart Group. I acknowledge my Parish of St Joseph's, Papanui, Christchurch, where I experience faith, hope and God's mission at the level of neighbourhood and street.

A three-month residential scholarship at Vaughan Park Anglican Retreat Centre, Long Bay, Auckland in 2017 enabled me to begin working on this book amid the warm hospitality and space of their glorious coastal location. At the beginning of this project, Bishop Charles Drennan gave helpful perspectives from his experience. Dr Margaret Maclagan read a first draft and Dr Veronica Lawson RSM read two drafts. Their insightful comments resulted in a much-improved final text. Mary Catherwood RSM, Jane Higgins, Paul Dalziel and Jenny Carter encouraged me in ways beyond what words can express. With gratitude I acknowledge the aroha and support of my religious congregation Nga Whaea Atawhai o Aotearoa Sisters of Mercy New Zealand. I acknowledge Mercy Global Presence which links congregations/institutes, individual Sisters of Mercy and Associates, partners in Mercy, and Mercy International Association in creative and energizing ways to focus on the displacement of persons and degradation of Earth. I am ever grateful for being surrounded by the love of my three sisters, two brothers and our extended family.

Kathleen P. Rushton RSM

Introduction

'I came that they may have life, and have it abundantly' (John 10.10). These words of Jesus seem to me to be at the heart of John's Gospel and related integrally to a reading that seeks to highlight Jesus and justice so as 'to hear *both the cry of the earth and the cry of the poor*' (*Laudato Si'* §49).[1] As I shall explain later, in John it is more helpful to rephrase 'the cry of the poor' as 'the cry of the marginalized'. This book offers interpretations of those passages in John's Gospel proclaimed in Sunday lectionaries (Roman and Revised Common). To differing degrees, three strands guide my approach. First, while respecting the shape of this Gospel, my main focus is to offer a framework to hear *both the cry of the earth and the cry of the marginalized* when this gospel is proclaimed in the three-year lectionary cycle so as to work towards taking transformative steps towards ecological and social justice. The body of this book deals with this. Second, I aim to offer a contribution to spiritual ecumenism that is about prayer and mission. My third strand aims to help sustain Christians in the huge task of addressing two of the most pressing issues of our time, namely, degradation of earth and the displacement of the poor, by integrating Scripture study within the contemplative tradition of the Church.

To hear *both the cry of the earth and the cry of the marginalized*

Reports and predictions about the need for climate justice reach us every day. Climate change, human exploitation and use of the resources of the planet, such as fossil fuels and the destruction of the forests and wetlands, call us to work for climate justice.[2] Environmental issues are connected with, and inseparable from, issues of justice affecting peoples across the globe and especially those in poverty. The scope and complexity of the ecological and social justice issues facing people can result in powerlessness and hopelessness. The Christian gospel offers hope for ways forward at this critical time.

Writing in the World Council of Churches (WCC) publication *Economy of Life*, Rogate Mshana and Athena Peralta stress that 'The mission of the ecumenical movement today is about transforming the world into a place of justice and peace for all God's creation ... [in a] participatory search for alternatives that are centred on the people and the Earth.'[3] Likewise, in *Laudato Si'*, for Pope Francis, 'we have to realize that a true ecological approach *always* becomes a social approach; it must integrate questions of justice in debates on the environment, so as to hear *both the cry of the earth and the cry of the poor*' (§49, italics his). This interconnected focus is found in the prophetic linking of the groaning of creation and the cries of people in poverty (Jer. 14.2–7). The urgency of the situation means that, 'For a Christian believer, committed to love for God's creation and to respect for the dignity of every human person, responding to this issue will be necessarily a central dimension of the life of faith.'[4]

'That they may all be one' (John 17.21)

My work with groups was on the Roman Lectionary until I became aware of participants who used the Revised Common Lectionary.[5] The same trend emerged with readers of my written reflections. Soon after my shift to address both lectionaries, I was on my way home from Sunday Eucharist when I found myself bowing my head spontaneously as I passed the nearby Methodist and Anglican churches. Engrained in me since childhood is the practice of making a sign of reverence when I pass a Catholic church. In a moment of grace, I realized that from their lecterns, the same gospel reading, give or take a few verses, was proclaimed as I had heard at Mass.

The prayer of Jesus on the eve of his suffering and death came to me, 'that they may all be one' (17.21). In *A Handbook of Spiritual Ecumenism*, Walter Kasper writes, '[It] is significant that Jesus did not primarily express his desire for unity in a teaching or in a commandment but in a prayer. Unity is a gift from above ...'[6] Ecumenical work is essentially a spiritual task because it is participation in this prayer of Jesus, a gift of the Holy Spirit, and has its origins in the loving communion of the Trinity. My ecumenical approach may be stretching for some readers and not part of their experience. I align my work with the spiritual ecumenism of prayer and mission (Kasper and Williams) and receptive ecumenism (Murray) as a way forward in the present doctrinal impasse and the trend of denominations retreating from ways in which they worked previously towards implementing the prayer of Jesus.[7] The Scriptures are a fundamental source for public and private prayer, and a bond of unity for all Christians. In the quest for spiritual ecumenism and as separated Christians grow in awareness of what they have in common, the three-year lectionary cycle is a significant shared resource. All belong to the household (*oikos*) of God. There are further links. The words 'ecology' and 'ecumenism' (*oikoumenē*), along with 'economics', which is so linked with *hearing both the cry of the earth and the cry of the marginalized*, are derived from this Greek word.[8]

The contemplative tradition of the Church

My approach is inspired by two great movements of our age – hunger for a spirituality that embraces meditation and contemplation, and a concern for the environment that is linked inextricably with social justice. In the case of the former, many are unaware of the contemplative tradition within Christianity. This book aims to integrate these movements with the study of Gospel passages proclaimed in public worship. I teach biblical studies within the *lectio divina* cycle, which I shall explain later. In addition, I am a spiritual director. Most of my directees are Anglican or Protestant who sought out a Catholic sister because of their perception that such a one holds to the contemplative tradition of the Church. My approach is also influenced by over four decades of involvement in ecumenical movements for justice. I have experienced committed people dropping out of such movements, and some leave their Christian church because of burnout and disillusionment.

In the next chapter, I shall offer an overview of John's Gospel under the three contexts or worlds of the biblical text that Sandra Schneiders summarizes as, 'While history lies *behind* the text and theology is expressed *in* the text, spirituality is *called forth by* the text as it engages the reader.'[9] At this point, I want to draw attention to spirituality – spirituality for transformation to participate with Jesus to finish the works of God for social and ecological justice.

I assume I share four things with my reader: participation in the public prayer of a worshipping community; a desire to reflect on the Scriptures; some understanding of twenty-first-century cosmologies and evolutionary biology; and a desire to hear *both the cry of the earth and the cry of the marginalized* in an unfinished evolving universe. In such a journey, 'it is we human beings above all who need to change … A great cultural, spiritual and educational challenge stands before us, and it will demand that we set out on a long path of renewal' (*LS* §202). In this change, we enter into the moral drama of life with understanding and empathy as well as allowing it to enter us.[10] This is about absorbing, taking time to allow and adjust to good news and new reality. We sit with what we may resist. We appropriate the reality of injustice, absorbing its impact. Feelings and thoughts arise by 'sitting with' it. The experience reshapes us. Working with it leads us out of ourselves and often moves our hands and feet to act. For Dean Brackley, 'sitting with reality, allowing it to work on us, working through the feelings and the thoughts it stirs is what we mean by *contemplation*.'[11]

Out of our need to be in touch with the rich complexity of reality, contemplation arises naturally. In this sense, contemplation is the opposite of flight from reality. Why is contemplation so essential? Brendan Byrne suggests that people approach life with one of two attitudes. One can live adopting an 'exploitative' attitude to everything outside oneself. All people and creation are approached from the standpoint of referring to one's own advantage. On the other hand, a 'contemplative' attitude ensures reverence and respect for the autonomy and uniqueness of every person and all creation outside oneself.[12] Besides contemplating reality, we need to contemplate words of wisdom, especially sacred Scripture, which 'purifies, orients, supplements, and extends our knowledge' without taking away from our powers.[13] According to Karen Armstrong, 'we seem to be losing the art of scripture in the modern world ... [which is] about reading it for transformation.'[14] This book is a resource for a spirituality of social and ecological justice; such a 'spirituality is *called forth by* the text as it engages the reader'.[15]

To read, meditate, pray, contemplate and also act enables us to discover an underlying spiritual rhythm in daily life in a very ancient art known as *lectio divina* (sacred reading), which goes back to the fourth century CE and was practised by all Christians, centuries before the divisions of the last 500 years. In this tradition, Christians experienced God in ongoing creation especially by 'attunement' to 'the presence of God in that special part of God's creation, which is the Scriptures'. The Christian life 'was understood as a gentle oscillation between the poles of *practice* and *contemplation*'.[16] Above I alluded to the danger that the complexity of the ecological and social justice issues can result in an overwhelming sense of powerlessness. Approaching the Sunday readings through this contemplative practice offers a way to recover the contemplative rest of Sunday, which,

> like the Jewish Sabbath, is meant to be a day which heals our relationships with God, with ourselves, with others and with the world ... so the day of rest, centred on the Eucharist [or worship], sheds light on the whole week, and motivates us to greater concern for nature and the poor. (*LS* §237)

We slow down to be attentive as we read, and reread, a text (*lectio*). Silence is needed 'to hear' the voice of our relational God who hears *the cry of the earth and the cry of the marginalized*. Then in meditation (*meditatio*), once a word or a phrase or a passage speaks to us in a personal way, we must take it in and 'ruminate' on it. This is a time to look up any references or notes of our Bible and to write notes. Further study may be needed. This book is offered as one resource. Then, because in reading and meditation the text has been engaged at the level of heart and experience, prayer (*oratio*) arises, which is loving dialogue with God, who speaks in and through the sacred text (see my diagram below). We allow the word to touch and change us so that our horizon expands in solidarity to include the earth and the marginalized. This leads to contemplation (*contemplatio*); we rest in the presence of God. Those who have been in love know that there are times when words are unnecessary. So, with God, we let go of our words, entering a time of being in the presence of God. The process of *lectio divina* is not concluded until it arrives at action (*actio*). What has been learnt from the sacred text is applied to daily life, relationships, work, creation and solidarity with the poor, as with Jesus we are invited to complete the works of God (John 5.36). The rediscovery of contemplation enables the human person to enter into the heart of the mystery of biblical faith, which is 'the ability to live without knowing' with the unanswered questions.[17] Contemplation creates within us a discerning vision of reality as God sees it, and forms within us 'the mind of Christ' (1 Cor. 2.16).

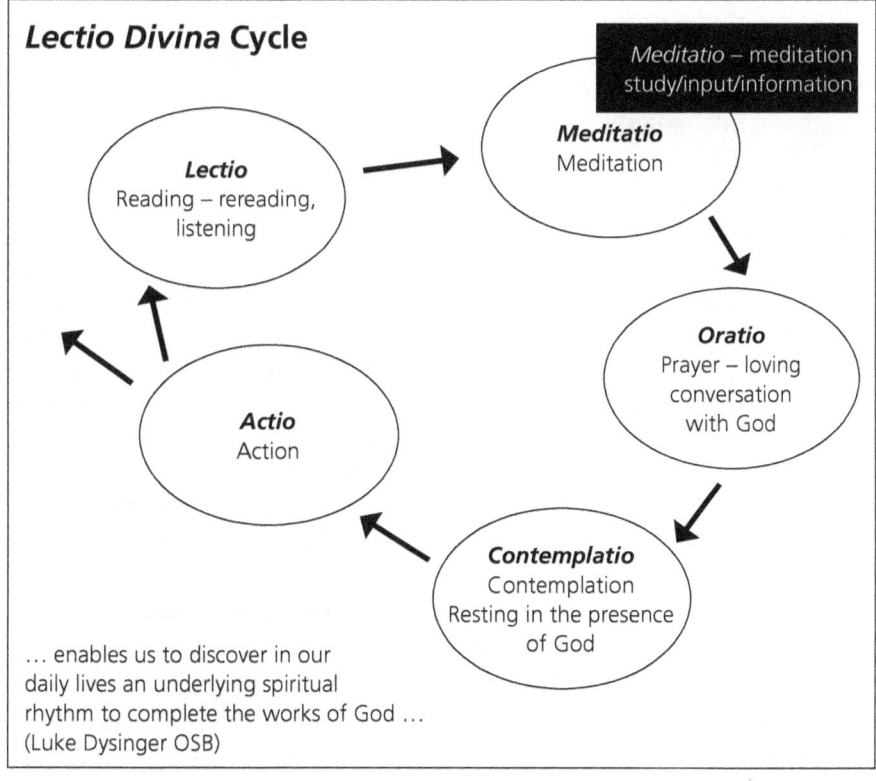

My reflections on the readings from John proclaimed in the lectionaries follow this cycle:

- *Lectio*/Reading. A question or statement is offered as a guide for the reader to hear *both the cry of the earth and the cry of the marginalized* as the text is read and reread.
- *Meditatio*/Meditation. This book is offered as a resource to provide information on the history *behind* the text and the theology *in* the text.
- *Oratio*/Prayer, *Contemplatio*/Contemplation, *Actio*/Action. '[S]pirituality is *called forth by* the text as it engages the reader.'[18] I approach these combined sections in two ways, with the aim of offering possible ways to enable us to move with Jesus towards transformation. One way is to offer questions because questions are a remarkable feature of John. Not only does Jesus ask questions but the first disciples are portrayed as asking questions. The reader is encouraged to ask questions of Jesus, of characters and situations, and in particular to ask questions concerning the implications of a text for today. The other way is to offer reflections of varying lengths. Our hope is that prayer and contemplation will flow into action, taking small steps to complete the works of God by responding *to the cry of the earth and the marginalized* in an evolving unfinished universe. *Lectio divina* emerged from monks who lived in touch with the garden of earth through the oscillating rhythm of 'pray and labour' (Latin *ora et labora*). This way of living is associated with the Rule of Saint Benedict who viewed prayer and work as partners and believed in combining contemplation with action.

Toward reading John's Gospel for social and ecological justice

My love of John's Gospel began in the 1960s when my parents gave me a Missal on the occasion of my going to boarding school. Among the Prayers after Holy Communion were long passages from the farewell discourses. Their beauty and mystery became etched on my young heart. During my early social justice years, John took a back seat as I was led to believe, along with most, that it was the Synoptic Gospels where Jesus and justice were to be found. Then, in the search for a doctoral topic that would inspire passion for the hard yards ahead, I returned to John – not specifically on Jesus and social justice.

The question was always there and was extended to include ecological justice. My research on reading the cosmology of the prologue in the light of twenty-first-century cosmology and evolutionary biology began during my time as a Cardinal Hume Scholar at Margaret Beaufort Institute of Theology, Cambridge, UK in 2011. I discovered that ancient and biblical cosmologies as well as biblical promises for a better future (later known as eschatology) both have an ethical dimension related to right relationship with God, the land and people. Linking this with Jesus who speaks 'openly' or 'frankly', as does Wisdom, led me to look anew at Jesus in John. My work extended when I discovered the overlooked studies on social justice by Robert J. Karris, Richard J. Cassidy, Stephen Motyer, Samuel Rayan, José Miranda and José Comblin.[19] On the Roman background I have drawn on David Rensberger and Warren Carter.[20] The only ecological reading of John to date is Margaret Daly-Denton's 2017 volume in the Earth Bible Commentary Series, in which she invites readers to identity with Mary, who believes Jesus is the gardener and that, given the symbolism of this Gospel, he is earth's gardener restoring humanity to the vision of life as it was intended to be in the Garden of Eden.[21] On a personal note, although now living at opposite ends of the world, Ireland-based New Zealander Margaret and I were at school together in Timaru. Decades later we are working in our diverse ways to complete the works of God through earth-conscious readings of John.

While often there are new, original aspects in the reading of John I offer, I draw on representative and highly regarded commentaries, books and articles, especially by Raymond Brown, Francis Moloney, B. F. Westcott, Sandra Schneiders, Gail O'Day, Jerome Neyrey, Brendan Byrne and R. Alan Culpepper.[22] Fine commentaries exist on preaching John. I draw attention to Ronald J. Allen and Clark M. Williamson's significant *Preaching the Gospels without Blaming the Jews*.[23] To my knowledge, my book is the first to address both lectionaries and the first to attempt to address both ecological and social justice in John's Gospel from an evolutionary perspective.

Reading this book

When variations in verses of a Gospel reading occur, or if a particular reading is found in only one lectionary, this will be noted by the insertion of RL for Roman Lectionary or RCL for the Revised Common Lectionary. The different terms for, or ways of naming, the seasons of the liturgical year are also acknowledged. The sequence of the Gospel, chapter by chapter, is followed so that a reader may easily locate and place a reading in context of the gospel story. Throughout we shall move and oscillate among three contexts or worlds. I shall refer often to the framework of the prologue, which is explained in the section on John 1.1–5, 9–18. The reader is encouraged to consult the Notes section for further explanations and references. Often meanings of significant Greek words are highlighted. In the main, the English transliterations of these words will be found in the Notes on the relevant Gospel passage and/or in the Key Words List. Reflections vary in length as some chapters of the Gospel are proclaimed in full (e.g. John 1 and 6) while from other chapters only a few verses are included in a lectionary (e.g. 5.1–9; 7.37–39).

Unless otherwise stated, biblical quotations are from the NRSV Bible. (On versions of the Bible, see the Glossary, p. 217.) This book addresses both the Roman Lectionary, which may use different versions of the Bible in different countries (see p. 211), and the Revised Common Lectionary, which uses the NRSV. To address this situation, I refer sometimes to other translations, in order to guide a reader who may be using a different version. This is illustrated, for example, in my discussion of the saying of Jesus, 'Amen, amen I say to you', which is expressed in the JB as 'I tell you, most solemnly' (p. 124).

I acknowledge any literal translation of my own, or quote that of a biblical scholar, who is likewise acknowledged. In a book that seeks social justice, I do give attention to gender. For example, in John 9.24, 'we know this person (*anthrōpos*) is a sinner' (p. 99): the Greek here means a human being, a person, as opposed to *anēr*, man; that is, a male.

The next chapter will explain some key understandings of the Fourth Gospel that alert the reader *to hear both the cry of the earth and the cry of the marginalized*. The structure of this Gospel and the concerns of Johannine biblical scholarship are referred to, often in detail, in the *Meditatio*/Meditation sections to highlight aspects embedded in the text, and most likely recognized by the earliest readers/listeners but obscured for present-day readers. In *Lectio*/Reading sections and the *Oratio*/Prayer, *Contemplatio*/Contemplation, *Actio*/Action sections, the reader is encouraged to ponder the implications of the Gospel passage explored in the *Meditatio*/Meditation section so as to respond to *hearing both the cry of the earth and the cry of the marginalized*.

Notes

1 Pope Francis, 2015, *Laudato Si': An Encyclical Letter on Ecology and Climate Change*, Strathfield NSW: St Paul's Publications, §49. Further references to this encyclical letter will use the abbreviation *LS* and the relevant paragraph, for example, *LS* §49. Also see Leonardo Boff, 1997, *Cry of the Earth, Cry of the Poor*, Maryknoll NY: Orbis.

2 Mary Robinson, 2018, *Climate Justice: Hope, Resilience and the Fight for a Sustainable Future*, London: Bloomsbury, pp. 1–13.

3 Rogate R. Mshana and Athena Peralta (eds), 2015, *Economy of Life: Linking Poverty, Wealth and Ecology*, Geneva: WCC Publications, pp. vii, ix–x.

4 Denis Edwards, 2017, 'Celebrating Eucharist in a Time of Global Climate

Change', first published 2006, in Denis Edwards, *The Natural World and God: Theological Explorations*, Scholars Collection, Hindmarsh SA: ATF Press, p. 157.

5 It is important to acknowledge that the Churches understand and use the lectionary pattern in different ways. The detail of this is beyond the scope of this book. The differences arise especially because of views from differing positions on the continuum of the communal memory and the written memory of the Church. That is, from the balance between the memory of the Church to interpret the Bible and the Bible to structure the memory of the Church. For a helpful discussion of this hermeneutical difference, see Fitz West, 1997, *Scripture and Memory: The Ecumenical Hermeneutic of the Three-Year Lectionaries*, Collegeville MN: Liturgical Press.

6 Walter Kasper, 2007, *A Handbook of Spiritual Ecumenism*, New York: New City Press, p. 10.

7 Kasper, *A Handbook of Spiritual Ecumenism*; Rowan Williams, 2003, 'Keynote Address', in *May They All Be One ... But How?: Proceedings of the Conference Held in St Albans Cathedral on 17 May 2003*, St Albans: St Albans Centre for Christian Studies; Paul D. Murray (ed.), 2008, *Receptive Ecumenism and the Call to Catholic Learning: Exploring a Way for Contemporary Ecumenism*, Oxford: Oxford University Press.

8 Ecology comes from Greek *oikos* ('household') and *logos* ('word'). The term ecology comes into English through German from *oekologie*.

9 Sandra M. Schneiders, 1999, 'The Community of Eternal Life (John 11:1–53)', in *Written that You May Believe: Encountering Jesus in the Fourth Gospel*, New York: Crossroad, p. 151 (italics hers).

10 On contemplation, see Dean Brackley, 2004, *The Call to Discernment in Troubled Times: New Perspectives on the Transformative Wisdom of Ignatius of Loyola*, New York: Crossroad, pp. 22–3.

11 Brackley, *Call to Discernment*, p. 22.

12 Brendan Byrne SJ, 2016, *Freedom in the Spirit: An Ignatian Retreat with Saint Paul*, Mahwah NJ: Paulist Press, p. 50.

13 Brackley, *Call to Discernment*, p. 225.

14 Karen Armstrong, 2019, *The Lost Art of Scripture: Rescuing the Sacred Texts*, London: The Bodley Head, see pp. 402–30, especially pp. 405–6, for her insightful discussion.

15 Schneiders, 'Community of Eternal Life', p. 151 (italics hers).

16 Luke Dysinger OSB, 1989, 'Accepting the Embrace of God: The Ancient Art of Lectio Divina', pp. 1, 3. For a downloadable copy, see www.valyermo.com/ld-art.html.

17 Richard Rohr OFM, 2017, 'An Interview with Richard Rohr, OFM: Living with Paradox, Uncertainty and Mystery', in Annmarie Sanders IHM (ed.), *The Occasional Papers: Leadership Conference of Women Religious* 46.2, p. 11.

18 Schneiders, 'Community of Eternal Life', p. 151 (italics hers).

19 Robert J. Karris, 1990, *Jesus and the Marginalized in John's Gospel*, Collegeville MN: Liturgical Press; Richard J. Cassidy, 2015, *John's Gospel in New Perspective: Christology and the Realities of Roman Power, With the New Essay, 'Johannine Footwashing and Roman Slavery'*, first published 1992, Eugene OR: Wipf & Stock; Stephen Motyer, 1995, 'Jesus and the Marginalized in the Fourth Gospel', in Antony Billington, Tony Lane and Max Turner (eds), *Mission and Meaning: Essays Presented to Peter Cotterell*, Carlisle: Paternoster Press, pp. 70–89; Samuel Rayan, 1993, 'Jesus and the Poor in the Fourth Gospel', in Rasiah S. Sugirtharajah and Cecil Hargreaves (eds), *Readings in Indian Christian Theology*

Vol. 1, London: SPCK, pp. 213–28; José Porfirio Miranda, 1997, *Being and the Messiah: The Message of St. John*, John Eagleson (trans.), Maryknoll NY: Orbis; and José Comblin, 1979, *Sent from the Father: Meditations on the Fourth Gospel*, Carl Kabat (trans.), Dublin: Gill & MacMillan.

20 David Rensberger, 1998, *Johannine Faith and Liberating Community*, Philadelphia PA: Westminster, and Warren Carter, 2008, *John and Empire: Initial Explorations*, New York: T&T Clark.

21 Margaret Daly-Denton, 2017, *John: An Earth Bible Commentary: Supposing Him to be the Gardener*, London: Bloomsbury T&T Clark.

22 Raymond E. Brown, 1966–1970, *The Gospel According to John*, 2 vols, The Anchor Bible 29–29A, Garden City NY: Doubleday; Francis J. Moloney, 1998, *The Gospel of John*, Sacra Pagina Series 4, Collegeville MN: Liturgical Press; B. F. Westcott, 1903, *The Gospel According to St. John*, London: John Murray; Sandra M. Schneiders, 1999, *Written that You May Believe: Encountering Jesus in the Fourth Gospel*, New York: Crossroad; Gail O'Day, 1995, 'The Gospel of John', in *The New Interpreters Bible*, Vol. 9, Nashville TN: Abingdon, pp. 493–865; Jerome H. Neyrey SJ, 2007, *The Gospel of John*, New York: Cambridge University Press; Brendan Byrne SJ, 2014, *Life Abounding: A Reading of John's Gospel*, Collegeville MN: Liturgical Press; R. Alan Culpepper, 1998, *The Gospel and Letters of John*, Nashville TN: Abingdon Press, especially his chapter, 'The Gospel of John as a Document of Faith', pp. 287–305.

23 David Fleer and Dave Bland (eds), 2008, *Preaching John's Gospel: The World It Imagines*, St Louis MO: Chalice; Gail R. O'Day, 2002, *The Word Disclosed: Preaching the Gospel of John*, St Louis MO: Chalice Press; Lamar Williamson Jr, 2004, *Preaching the Gospel of John: Proclaiming the Living Word*, Louisville KY: Westminster John Knox Press; Ronald J. Allen and Clark M. Williamson, 2015 (2004), *Preaching the Gospels without Blaming the Jews: A Lectionary Commentary*, Louisville KY: Westminster John Knox Press. This is a commentary on Years A, B and C of the RCL. See their very helpful introduction, pp. xv–xxvi.

Overview of the Gospel of John

The written 'Gospel' is a way of writing (genre) with two interrelated concerns. It is both an interpretative narrative of the life and death-resurrection of Jesus and, at the same time, an invitation to the hearers/readers to embrace and understand the significance of that story for their way of being in the world.[1] The Gospel of John was told by believers for believers in particular situations. The Gospel is not only informative, it is performative – it not only tells us about things that can be known but makes things happen. It is life-changing. This overview outlines features that will be developed to enable Christians today to participate in finishing the works of God by hearing *both the cry of the earth and the cry of the marginalized* in an evolving universe. Other features that cannot be touched upon here may be found in books in the bibliography.

In placing a reading within the wider gospel story, we oscillate backwards and forwards among three contexts or worlds, which are described in this overview. The ancient context (world *behind* the text) is the time of Jesus and the later time of the Evangelist. The gospel story creates a symbolic world of images and symbols (world *of* the text). Awareness of interaction between the ancient world and the symbolic world open up the transformation Jesus calls us to live today (world *in front of* the text). We recall Schneiders' summary referred to in the Introduction, 'While history lies *behind* the text and theology is expressed *in* the text, spirituality is *called forth by* the text as it engages the reader.'[2] The interface between history, theology and spirituality calls us to hear and to respond to *both the cry of the earth and the cry of the marginalized*.

The world behind the text

After the fall of Jerusalem and the destruction of the temple by the Romans in 70 CE, the crisis for late first-century Jews was more widespread than poverty, loss of property and displacement. Religion and identity, especially for Palestinian Jews, had been bound closely to the temple and its cult. There were religious and political tensions as groups vied for leadership and sought conflicting solutions. Biblical traditions were reinterpreted in the light of their new situation. For some, Wisdom was found in the Torah, for others in Jesus and in their long-held hope for a Messiah. Some felt their situation was worse because their hated neighbours, the Samaritans, were perceived to have collaborated with the Romans.

The social context of the Mediterranean world in which believers were to join with Jesus in finishing the works of God (John 4.34; 5.36; 17.4; 19.28, 30) was, therefore, more complex than merely Jewish–Christian tensions. Believers were subjects of the Roman Empire, which was undergirded by slavery.[3] All religious, social and economic life was lived under imperial domination that lay heavily upon the people and the land (e.g. taxation, exploitation). Titles attributed to Jesus were also titles of the emperor (e.g. 'Saviour of the World' in 4.42). The Roman trial and the death of Jesus by the crucifixion proceeded under Roman authority. In washing the feet of his disciples, Jesus engaged in slaves' work. The commonly held view is that John was written in Ephesus in the prosperous Roman province of Asia Minor (modern Turkey) and the 'hub' of Roman slavery. Slaves were brought from Asia Minor and Syria to the *statarion*, the slave market of Ephesus, where they were auctioned and transported to places of demand, especially Rome.[4] This overview of the Roman Empire prepares us to be aware of how its pervasive influence impinged on this Gospel's community. Sejf van Tilborg reminds us that the earliest 'readers of the Johannine story enter into a dangerous world, when they finish their reading and are going to confront their daily city life', where they sought to retain Jewish-Christian values within a multicultural and cosmopolitan world.[5]

In the devastation that followed the public execution of Jesus by the Roman authorities in collusion with the local religious leaders, this Gospel was written in light of his ministry and death-resurrection. John extends historical details of time, place and event to include a deeper sense of the historical, which, as Samuel Rayan explains, 'is what concerns the life of the people, what relates to the sorrows, hopes, struggles and movements of the oft-oppressed masses'. He continues: 'the mysticism of the Fourth Gospel is historical mysticism ... its contemplation fixes on the glory of God as revealed in Jesus's love for and service of the people.'[6] Our brief overview of the ancient world (the world *behind* the text) identified aspects that shaped the theology the Evangelist expressed *in* the world of the text, where a 'genuinely subversive consciousness' can be identified in the radical Jesus of this gospel story[7] and in the actions, words, images and symbols that create the symbolic world of the text.

The world of the text

Among the ways the Evangelist tells an old story in a new evolving way is to begin with a prologue that not only gives a summary of the Gospel but is a framework containing vital clues for reading the story that follows (see the section on John 1.1–18). The prologue speaks of the enduring story of the ever-unfolding interconnection of God, the cosmos, flesh and 'all things' that continues in the gospel story. Throughout this book, I shall refer to the prologue, which evokes both biblical and ancient cosmologies that centre on the relationship of the divine, the human and creation. Jesus is inserted into God's 'community of creation', where human beings are interconnected with all God's creatures and true reconciliation with God involves the entire creation.[8]

Jesus is a person on the move. This is highlighted in the table of Contents of this book, which is arranged around the place where Jesus was at the time. He moves in a first-century Palestinian Jewish setting under the rule of the Roman Empire and within the traditions of the Scriptures. The Evangelist recalls memories and interpretation of the life of Jesus as he moves up, down and across the lands of his ancestors – Galilee, Judea and Samaria – to finish the works of God. As you reread this Gospel you might notice how many verbs of movement are there. Time and place give meaning to Jesus' words and actions. The materiality of John's symbolic world is embodied in the incarnation and in the materiality of the Word who 'became flesh and lived among us' (1.14). Scriptural stories and images centre on the land, its landscapes, flora and fauna. Imagery teems with creation and ordinary rural life in ways that challenge accepted views – harvest, a wedding, wine, wheat, water, vines, pruning, sheep, shepherd, bread, barley loaves (food of the poor), going fishing and breakfast on the shore. 'I am the true vine', for example, which is embedded in cultural and rural life, caused shudders in the religious establishment. Jesus' claim 'I am' took to himself the Holy Name of God. He declared himself to be 'the true vine' that was applied to Israel. Connection with eco- and biosphere, expressing the interconnected relationship with God, the land and the people, would have been Jesus' inherited tradition.[9] His words and actions cause a shift in that tradition and context.

'Search the Scriptures' (John 5.39)

God, in the evolving creation, in the events of history and in the Torah, has now extended Godself in Jesus of Nazareth. The Evangelist continues the Jewish tradition of reinterpreting Scripture to bring hope in a new challenging situation. This Gospel emerges out of the Scriptures in its call for justice in two main ways. First, Jesus is imaged as the biblical figure of Wisdom who was with God at the beginning. Both Jesus and Wisdom have the relational quality suggested by the recurring word 'abide'. Both cry out for justice in public places and are rejected. Second, the Spirit is prominent in John. The biblical prophets tell of a future outpouring of the Spirit on the people of Israel that will bring about hope for a better future. When this outpouring occurs, the people will be transformed. This Gospel follows this tradition. The Spirit is 'the Breath of God who always accompanies the Word'. God creates with two hands, that of the Word and that of the Spirit in ongoing creation, in the incarnation and death-resurrection of Jesus.[10] Both Word and Spirit are essential for hearing *the cry of the earth and the cry of the marginalized* in this Gospel. The same God is at work, through the Word, through Wisdom, through the Spirit and through Jesus. There is continuity and discontinuity.

Jesus is not called 'friend' explicitly, but friendship and the language of friendship are found at significant moments of John's Gospel and 'is one of the ways in which the revelation of God in Jesus is extended beyond the work of Jesus to the work of the disciples'.[11] His life is the incarnation of a quality of an ancient ideal of friendship concerning love and death, described by writers such as Plato and Aristotle as the love that leads one to lay down one's life for friends. The disciples are to imitate Jesus by carrying his love commandment even to the point of laying down their lives for others as Jesus does (15.13; 10.11).

Jesus embodies a second characteristic of ancient friendship whereby a friend was to speak or act 'openly' or 'frankly'. Here, as elsewhere, the Evangelist integrates both cultural and biblical characteristics in the portrayal of Jesus. The prologue prepares us to discover Jesus imaged as Wisdom-Sophia in the gospel story. Like Wisdom-Sophia, Jesus makes people 'friends of God and prophets' (Wisd. 7.27), cries out at street corners (Prov. 8), shows boldness of speech and action by speaking 'openly' in public places, especially in the temple surroundings. In John 1—11, his healings and actions usually take place in public when the political risk is apparent. At the beginning of his ministry in the temple, Jesus announces, in both word and deed, the truth that shaped his work in the world (2.13–22). This act sets the tone for what is to follow and demonstrates the truth of Jesus' statement in 18.20, 'I have spoken openly to the world.' His trial before Pilate embodies open speech because Jesus does not hesitate to speak the truth to this figure of authority (18.33–38).

Finishing the works of God

God's work into which Jesus is inserted in the prologue continues in Jesus' ministry, passion and death-resurrection. John tells us repeatedly that the works of God are to be finished by Jesus. As his death approaches, 'Jesus knew that all was *finished*' (19.28). His last words are, 'It is *finished*' (19.30). Earlier, Jesus has explained that his food is to *finish/complete* the works of God (4.34). God gave him works to *finish/complete* (5.36; on 'works' and finish/complete, see work/working in Appendix 2, Key Words in the Gospel of John). The question of the crowd is our question: 'What must we do to work the works of God?' (6.28, literal translation). Jesus speaks of God doing works through him (14.10) and those who believe in Jesus 'will do the works that I do and, in fact, greater works than I do' (14.12). 'Those born of God who believe' (1.13) do 'good works' or 'evil works' (5.18–21; 7.1–9). The shadow of rejection begins in the prologue (1.11). Judgement takes place in this life – in the historical life of Jesus and in relation to him (3.18–21). The criterion is 'good works' and 'evil works'. These are not general expressions but 'a precise technical term referring to helping those in need' in their particular context.[12]

In John 1—11, Jesus is presented as being profoundly concerned about social reconciliation. In his barrier-crossing ministry of reconciliation, he moves between groups in conflict with each other over the way forward after the disaster of the Roman War and destruction of the temple to create a new community.[13] The word 'messiah', the Christ, raised contemporary understandings that Jesus rejected – he seeks a mind shift. Jesus leads the people of his time into a new era that came to be named after him. However, he does that 'by exposing, questioning and challenging the criteria of judgment, the determining values he found among his contemporaries'.[14] Jesus calls the nationalist Nathanael, the 'true Israelite' who was searching for a new King of Israel (1.47). Jesus moves to the Pharisee, Nicodemus (3.1–21), the woman of Samaria (4.7–26), the official of Herod who collaborated (4.43–54), the marginalized lame man (5.1–18), the woman accused by the religious leaders (8.1–11) and the beggar born blind (9.1–41). Each one is representative of groups or communities and characterizes a type of faith-or-lack-of-faith response to Jesus who is the Christ and Son of God. Jesus, too, is surrounded by scenes of communal relationships – people in the temple (2.14–22), secret Christian Jews (2.23–25), followers of John (3.22–36), Samaritans (4.39–42) and Greeks (12.20).

We are called to participate in finishing the works of God by hearing *both the cry of the earth and the cry of the marginalized*. These works of God are not just good works, they are the work of a Messiah who ministers to the marginalized and who becomes marginalized himself. This

Gospel 'has much to contribute to any discussion of Jesus' ministry to those who are on the fringes of society and religion'.[15] Rather than speak of Jesus and the poor (only mentioned in 12.5, 6, 8 and 13.29), it is more accurate to speak of the marginalized, who are presented in narrative form: by ignorance of the Torah (7.49); physically (the poor man by the pool (5.1–18); the beggar born blind (9.1–41)); and geographically and culturally (the official (4.43–54); the woman of Samaria (4.4–42)). Like many in Jesus' time, we can hold the marginalized in place by our stereotypes. The reader is called to be 'on the move' with Jesus. Awareness of the 'p' codes within a text – power, privilege, property, poverty and persecution – move us from a quest for biblical interpretation that is objective and detached to a quest for an ethics of interpretation to hear *both the cry of the earth and the cry of the marginalized*, which is based on the highest ideals of the Scriptures and the Christian tradition.[16] We are concerned with the ways the text undermines prevailing power relationships: male–female, master–slave, rich–poor, patron–client, citizen–alien.

The particular concerns of John are found in several words used frequently in the world *of* the text. In a sense, the theology *in* the text revolves around those words (see Appendix 2). The words and discourses of Jesus focus on all the possible connections among these words. Particularly significant for the aims of this book are the three meanings of the complex term, 'the world' (see section on John 1.9–10). Sandra Schneiders sums it up by suggesting that 'the "world" with which we are concerned ... [is] the *good world* to which we are missioned, the *evil world* which we confront, and the *alternative* world' we are called into with Jesus in the ongoing re-creation of finishing the works of God.[17]

An important guide when 'you search the scriptures' (5.39) to discover social and ecological justice is to 'let John be John'.[18] When reading a Gospel, it is easy to blend the four Gospels together. This obscures what a particular Gospel has to say in its own right. Robert Karris calls for this awareness because when reading John, more often than not, 'the tape of harmonization that sounds in our mind's ear is that of the Synoptics'.[19] Consequently, what is particular to John is overlooked. Look at this Gospel with new eyes rather than seek there for what is found in the Synoptics. John's Gospel, as we shall see, tells an old story in a bold new way.

World in front of the text

In the Introduction, I suggested that this book may be a resource when the study of a Gospel passage is desirable at the second movement of meditation (*meditatio*) of the sacred reading (*lectio divina*) cycle. Such information is found in the history that lies *behind* the text (the ancient world) and theology is expressed *in* the text (world of the text). We come now to the 'spirituality ... *called forth by* the text as it engages the reader'.[20] We come not simply to 'What does the text say?' but, 'What is the meaning of the text for the believing community?' This dialogue with John's Gospel is grounded in faith. Engaging with a Gospel passage moves the reader into a possible alternative reality. The reader is challenged to enter into the world opened up by the text – the world in front of the text – to be transformed and to be on the move with Jesus into a new way of being to finish the works of God for social and ecological justice. For believers, the text is revelatory – revealing – for this Gospel is *both* an interpretative narrative of the life and death-resurrection of Jesus *and* about the significance of that story of Jesus for the hearer/reader. It is highly likely that what opens up leads to the third movement of prayer (*oratio*), which is loving dialogue with God who speaks in and through the sacred text. We allow the Word to touch and change us so our horizon expands in solidarity to include the earth and the poor. This leads to contemplation (*contemplatio*). We sit with what has touched our heart, taking time to allow and adjust to good news and new reality. In the same way, we appropriate the reality of injustice and the complexity of life as did Jesus and the earliest Christians. What is the equivalent of the Empire of Rome today? How do Christians in power relate to the powerless today? What small consistent steps (*actio*) can be taken to finish the work of God by working for social and ecological justice to hear *both the cry of the earth and the cry of the marginalized*?

Of course, twenty-first-century readers face issues never faced in the first century and are influenced, knowingly or unknowingly, by their own cultural, social, geographical and political environment. New questions are raised by new understandings of cosmology, evolutionary science, ecological and social justice. The influences we bring to reading this Gospel comprise the lens or filters through which we read or hear. Readers are encouraged to identify what they carry in their invisible backpack as they interpret this Gospel. I am a Pākehā (European heritage) woman of Aotearoa New Zealand, a nation of the Pacific Ocean shaped by the signing of Te Tiriti o Waitangi (Treaty of Waitangi) between Māori and the British Crown in 1840. My Irish and English forebears arrived here in the 1860s–70s. A hill country farm upbringing enriches my understanding of creation. My experience of the evolving universe throughout the 2010–12 earthquakes and aftershocks in my Otautahi Christchurch region was life-changing. I am influenced by belonging to a particular Christian tradition, the Catholic Church, and my academic theological education. The danger is that if we are unaware of our particular context, we denude Jesus of his context. We spiritualize the materiality and particularity of the earthed, incarnated Jesus who walked in sandals (1.27) on the earth in a particular time and place, as well as the context in which John's Gospel was written and first circulated several decades later.

Notes

1 I hyphenate death-resurrection to stress the interdependence of the two terms. The four Gospels present Jesus' death in close conjunction with his resurrection. However, the Christian tradition has emphasized his death and suffering. This obscures that it is the risen One who is present in communities from which the Gospels arose, and also has led to overemphasis on the death and suffering of Jesus. For an overview of the history of this unity and its subsequent separate emphasis, see Kathleen P. Rushton, 2011, *The Parable of the Woman in Childbirth of John 16:21: A Metaphor for the Death and Glorification of Jesus*, Lewiston: The Edwin Mellen Press, p. 6.

2 Sandra M. Schneiders, 1999, 'The Community of Eternal Life (John 11:1–53)', in *Written that You May Believe: Encountering Jesus in the Fourth Gospel*, New York: Crossroad, p. 151 (italics hers).

3 For an accessible overview of slavery at this time, see Richard J. Cassidy, 2015, *John's Gospel in New Perspective: Christology and the Realities of Roman Power, With the New Essay, 'Johannine Footwashing and Roman Slavery'*, first published 1992, Eugene OR: Wipf & Stock, pp. 119–23.

4 W. V. Harris, 1999, 'Demography, Geography and the Source of Roman Slaves', *Journal of Roman Studies* 89, p. 74.

5 Sjef van Tilborg, 1996, *Reading John in Ephesus*, Supplements to Novum Testamentum Series, Leiden: Brill, p. 219.

6 Samuel Rayan, 1993, 'Jesus and the Poor in the Fourth Gospel', in Rasiah S. Sugirtharajah and Cecil Hargreaves (eds), *Readings in Indian Christian Theology Vol 1*, London: SPCK, p. 214.

7 David Rensberger, 1998, *Johannine Faith and Liberating Community*, Philadelphia PA: Westminster, p. 129.

8 Richard Bauckham, 2010, *The Bible and Ecology: Rediscovering the Community of Creation*, Waco TX: Baylor University Press, pp. 87–92.

9 Sean Freyne, 2004, *Jesus, A Jewish Galilean: A New Reading of the Jesus-Story*, London: T&T Clark International, p. 25.

10 Denis Edwards, 2004, *Breath of Life: A Theology of the Creator Spirit*, Maryknoll NY: Orbis, pp. 26, 40, 46.

11 Gail R. O'Day, 2004, 'Jesus as Friend in the Gospel of John', *Interpretation: A Journal of Bible and Theology* 58.2, p. 148. See her reference to Aristotle, *Nicomachean Ethics* (*Eth. Nic.* 9.8.9) [LCL translation], p. 146; Plato, *Symposium* (*Symp.*179B).

12 Rensberger, *Johannine Faith*, pp. 126–7. On 'good works' and 'evil works', see José Porfirio Miranda, 1997, *Being and the Messiah: The Message of St. John*, John Eagleson (trans.), Maryknoll NY: Orbis, pp. 96–100, especially p. 97, and Rensberger, *Johannine Faith*, pp. 126–7.

13 Stephen Motyer, 1995, 'Jesus and the Marginalised in the Fourth Gospel', in *Mission and Meaning Essays Presented to Peter Cotterell*, Antony Billington, Tony Lane and Max Turner (eds), Carlisle: Paternoster Press, pp. 70–89.

14 Frank O'Loughlin, 2012, *This Time of the Church*, Mulgrave, Vic: Garratt, p. 58.

15 Robert Karris, 1990, *Jesus and the Marginalized in John's Gospel*, Collegeville MN: Liturgical Press, p. 12.

16 R. Alan Culpepper, 1998, *The Gospel and Letters of John*, Nashville TN: Abingdon Press, p. 297.

17 Sandra M. Schneiders, 2013, *Buying the Field: Catholic Religious Life in the Mission to the World*, Mahwah NJ: Paulist Press, p. 37.

18 James D. G. Dunn, 1983, 'Let John Be John: A Gospel for Its Time', in Peter Stuhlmacher (ed.), *Das Evangelium und die Evangelien*, WUNT 28, Tübingen: Mohr Siebeck, pp. 309–39.

19 Karris, 1990, *Jesus and the Marginalized in John's Gospel*, p. 19.

20 Schneiders, 'Community of Eternal Life', p. 151 (italics hers).

PART I

The Prologue

From the Beginning to Word Made Flesh
The Prologue (John 1.1–5, 9–18)

'In the beginning' (John 1.1)

Christmas: Mass during the Day of Years ABC (RL)
John 1.1–18
Second Sunday after Christmas of Years ABC
John 1.1–18
Nativity of the Lord of Years ABC (RCL)
John 1.1–14

Lectio/Reading of John 1.1–18

In reading and rereading John 1.1–18, be aware of how the One revealed to be Jesus is introduced. What biblical images are evoked? How can the horizon of the prologue and the horizon of a present-day reader informed by twenty-first-century cosmologies and evolutionary biology meet in order to inspire a transforming spirituality that sustains ethical action to complete the works of God by *hearing both for the cry of the earth and the cry of the marginalized*?

Meditatio/Meditation

The prologue of John 1.1–18 is proclaimed at Christmas time. We shall explore the prologue by considering the cosmic story of the Word who was with God (1.1–5) and the coming of the Word made flesh in the world (1.9–18). Then John 1.6–8 and 15 will be discussed along with other passages (1.19–51) about the one 'sent from God whose name was John' (1.6).

Genre of prologue

Among the ways the Evangelist tells an old story in a new way is to begin with a prologue. 'Prologue' comes from the Greek *pro* (before) and *logos* (word). A prologue is an introduction to a work of literature which calls attention to the theme, enhances the plot, introduces characters, gives background information, indicates the wider context, sets the tone, language and style of the story that follows. The wider context often includes an earlier story from the past that ties into the story that follows yet is out of time sequence with the rest of that story and does not follow its time flow. The aim is to grab attention and frame the story that follows to craft an atmosphere of historical reality. It is rather like a short story without the ending. There is a tendency, unfortunately, to skip a prologue in order to get into the story that follows. Consequently, vital clues in the prologue and implanted in the story that follows remain obscure or missed entirely. John's prologue is like a pair of tinted glasses through which we read the Gospel that follows.

The cosmological framework of the prologue

Scenes and images from the infancy narratives of the Gospels of Matthew and Luke tell of the wonder, humanity and vulnerability of the newborn Child which has inspired cribs, cards, midnight and dawn liturgies, and the hearts of millions of young and old. The Christmas Day reading from the prologue expands this horizon: 'In the beginning was the Word ... All things come into being through him ... the true light ... was coming into the world ... And the Word became flesh and lived among us' (John 1.1–3, 9, 14). English translations capture the poetry of this ancient hymn yet obscure what it would have meant for first-century hearers. For them, as we shall explore, the prologue was not human centred (anthropomorphic). Certain words evoke biblical and ancient Hellenistic cosmologies and hopes for the future.[1] To put it simply, the prologue plunges Jesus into God's interconnected cosmic story and is about its significance for the reader/hearer today. Integral to ancient cosmologies are three interconnected relationships – with the divine, with human persons and with all creation.

The French philosopher Rémi Brague explains how ancient cosmologies – understandings of the world or world views – link cosmology and the human person.[2] Those cosmologies are linked to a wisdom in this world which leads to contemplation that leads to ethical action. This wisdom and ethical dimension are also found in what was believed about biblical 'promises concerning a better future'. In the interplay between the sense of radical wrongness and the radical changes needed are three types of hope for the future that I understand form the background to John's Gospel: hope for transformation of human society, the transformation of human persons and the transformation of nature.[3]

The ethical, cosmological framework of the prologue of John 1.1–18 places the story of Jesus of Nazareth, a historical human person (1.9–10, 14), in a wider context by drawing in information from the vastly different time of 'In the beginning' (Gen. 1.1) and of his being with God (John 1.1–5). In other words, the prologue inserts Jesus into the unfolding drama of God's never-ending story of ongoing creation. Later, I shall draw on Stephen Motyer, who describes Jesus' ministry to the marginalized as 'barrier-crossing' as he forms his new interrelated community.[4] It would seem Jesus is 'barrier-crossing' in that the divine assumes flesh and enters into ongoing creation (1.14). Creation and incarnation are interrelated. Margaret Daly-Denton emphasizes that Jesus is the gardener 'totally aligned with the Creator's intentions for the flourishing of creation'.[5] Interestingly, the biblical creation account of the 'garden' entrusted by God to humankind to frame the relationship between humanity and the earth is not found in *Laudato Si'*.[6] Pope Francis uses the image of a 'common home', which is the original meaning of the Greek word *oikos* from which is deprived the concepts of economy, ecology and ecumenism. Maybe the notion of a common home is more inclusive in that it is broader than the environment and suggests a relationship between creation and society. In addition, creation tends to be closely linked to Christianity.

In the prologue, a reader finds not only a summary of this Gospel but also a framework providing vital clues for understanding the story that follows. Symbols, too, are at the very core of the prologue and are expanded in the Gospel that follows. As readers, we are drawn in *this* world into an evolving new future as the plot and characters are introduced. Read in this way, the prologue speaks of a long, enduring love story of the ever-unfolding interconnection of God, the cosmos and human persons. The wonder and beauty of this both affirms and challenges the present-day reader, who has the perspective of twenty-first-century cosmology and evolutionary biology, to live with a wisdom that cares for our cosmic home on the earth and all people in a complex, evolving, beautiful, suffering and global world.

We shall explore how the cosmological framework for reading the Gospel that follows introduces characters, the wider context and background information. Words and images create new theological nuances: 'In the beginning', the Word, the Spirit, Wisdom-Sophia, all things, light and darkness, the world, rejection, flesh, and 'believe *into*'.[7] These nuances evoke both biblical cosmologies of Genesis and Wisdom literature, and also contemporary Hellenistic (Greek) cosmologies. Integral to biblical and ancient cosmologies are three interconnected relationships – with the divine, human persons and all creation.

'In the beginning' (John 1.1)

In John's Gospel, many strands of creation, re-creation and creation's renewal[8] are evoked to tell the story of the incarnation and death-resurrection of Jesus. Creation and re-creation interweave. 'In the beginning' (John 1.1) evokes the Genesis creation account where the Spirit hovers over the waters and creation is presented as the Garden of God.[9] God is the Gardener. John's Gospel ends with: 'Now there was a garden in the place where he was crucified, and in the garden there was a new tomb ...' (19.41). Here incarnation and death-resurrection are linked with ongoing creation. 'Deep incarnation' is the phrase used by the Danish theologian Niels Gregerson for the 'the radical divine outreach in Christ through human flesh all the way down into the living web of organic life with its growth and decay, amid the wider process of evolving nature that beget and sustains life'.[10]

The opening lines of the creation account of Genesis 1.1—2.4 have been described as a 'geography of the cosmos'. In the first five verses of the prologue, other motifs are evoked: light, life, darkness and darkness against light and life. For the Evangelist's earliest readers/hearers, 'in the beginning' also held a multiplicity of Hellenistic (Greek) notions. For philosophers, it was what was there before anything else existed, thereby providing an explanation for the world and its phenomena. It does not have to be explained. It is a 'beginning' although it does not have a beginning itself and has a continued existence. It also surrounds and steers all that is holding the whole and, in some way, is responsible for and explaining its direction. It is the basic 'stuff' of the world.

'In the beginning was the Word' (John 1.1)

The term for the Word (*logos*) also expresses many Hellenistic ideas. *Logos* cannot be confined to the meaning 'word'. It is the main principle for the reason underlying all reality. This term enabled the Evangelist to express the central truth of the life and death-resurrection of Jesus in the context of an understanding that saw the world's wonders as living and moving images of the eternal. The Jewish writer Philo of Alexandria (*c*.20 BCE–*c*.50 CE), uncovered the principle of creation and gave this a Greek name that evokes a thousand resonances: *logos*. For him, *logos*, which contained the world of ideas, is the instrument of creation and the principle that held the cosmos together.

Calling Jesus 'the Word' recalls the dynamic energy and power of the word and deed of the biblical 'Word of God'. Word and deed go together. In the creation account, speaking the word 'God said' is repeated ten times as God creates (Gen. 1.3–26). In the prophetic tradition, 'the word of God came to Joel' (e.g. Joel 1.1), challenging and propelling action (Hos. 1.1). The Word of God is a life-giving factor (Deut. 32.46–47); has the power to heal (Ps. 107.20); is a light for the people (Ps. 119.105); and has a creative function (Ps. 33.6). Many times, the Word of God is shown to have a seeming existence of its own carrying out an independent personal function (Isa. 55.11).

More often than not, the Word is emphasized and the Spirit is overlooked. The recalling of the biblical creation story in John 1.1 evokes the Wind (Spirit) from God hovering over the waters (Gen. 1.2). In the Gospel that follows, we shall be aware of the Spirit as 'the *Breath of God who always accompanies the Word*' and that God creates '*with two hands*', that of the Word and that of the Spirit holding together the Word and the Spirit in creation (Ps. 33.6), in the incarnation and death-resurrection of Jesus.[11] Word and Spirit are essential for hearing *both the cry of the earth and the cry of the poor* in this Gospel. A strong strand in biblical 'promises concerning a better future' is the future outpouring of the Spirit. The prophets tell of a future outpouring of the Spirit on the people of Israel which foresees that, when this occurs, they will be transformed (Isa. 32.14–15; 44.3; Ezek. 11.17–19; 36.26–27; 39.29; Joel 2.28–29). This Gospel follows this biblical tradition because, as we shall discover, the Spirit is also prominent in John.

'Before the beginning of the earth' (Prov. 8.23)

The Word theology outlined above would be familiar to first-century hearers of the prologue. In contrast, they would have been surprised by John's particular telling of the story of Jesus because the male *logos* (the Word) is being spoken about in the way the Wisdom books speak of the female figure, Wisdom-Sophia. The one declared to be with God from the beginning (John 1.1), pre-existent with God and through whom 'all things' came to be, is named not as the female Wisdom-Sophia (Prov. 8.22–25) but as the male *logos*. Instead of Sophia (Wisd. 8.13, 16), the *logos* is the source of life and light (John 1.4, 5, 9). It is important to remember that the term Word/*logos* is not found beyond the prologue. By the end of the prologue, however, it is firmly established that the male Word/*logos* is Jesus who is imaged as the female biblical figure of Wisdom. This continues as the Gospel unfolds.

'*All things came into being through him*' (John 1.3)

By Plato's time (c.428–347 BCE), the word 'all things' was one of several ways of naming the universe. In the Wisdom traditions, this refers to the wider-than-human creation (Wisd. 7.15–22). The narrator addresses God, you 'have made all things by your word,/ And by your wisdom have formed humankind' (Wisd. 9.1–2). Thus, the word and wisdom, along with humankind and 'all things', are linked. Wisdom 'pervades and penetrates all things' (7.24) and 'can do all things' and 'renews all things' (7.27). Wisdom, reaching from one end of the earth to the other, 'orders all things well' (8.1). Because 'she is an initiate in the knowledge of God', Wisdom is 'the active cause of all things' (8.4–5). This biblical use of the phrase 'all things' to convey a sense of the cosmos matches a similar phrase, 'holds all things together', found in ancient Stoic philosophy to express a concept for a divine bond that unified the world. In summary, in the divine Wisdom, the Hellenistic intellectual tradition of a unified cosmos is expressed in biblical terms.

'*The light shines in the darkness*' (John 1.5)

Christmas is about what people most need, the 'light [that] shines in darkness … The Word … The true light, which enlightens everyone, was coming into the world' (1.5, 9). Theological reflection on light, which we find in the prologue, depends on our being aware of the natural phenomenon of light. We become aware of light, of the mystery of the universe where light surrounds us in constant, unobserved patterns which were known often in ancient times and are waiting to be recovered and extended by our knowledge of science today. Later in the gospel story, Jesus declares, 'I am the light of the world' (8.12). He reminds us that those walking in light do not stumble. The image of light in the story of the woman at the well who comes to Jesus at noon, the brightest time of the day, draws us to bring the Light to our own people as she does (4.6, 39). We participate in the Light. We spread the Light – little by little, like lighting a candle, which radiates light even in the furthest dark corners.

'*Coming into the world*' (John 1.9)

When the term 'the world' is used in conversation, can we assume we are talking about the same thing? How does our understanding of world sit with our understanding of church? Are worldly and secular the same? Scripture is the soul of theology and an essential starting point for theological reflection on the world because from the New Testament arises much of the ambiguity that Christians have for the world. Interpretations of John, where 'the world' occurs 78 times, have influenced and blurred this understanding. 'The world' (*kosmos*) has several rich meanings, which depend usually on its context.

'The world' appears for the first time in John 1.9–10, where it is repeated four times and has two meanings:

> The true light which enlightens very human being was coming *into the world*. It was *in the world* and through it the *world* came to be, and the *world* did not know him. He came to his own and his own did not receive him.[12]

According to some interpreters, these sentences are about the Word (the true light) in creation. For others, they are about the coming of Jesus, the incarnate Word in the human story as the Light of the World. Both these views centre on the first meaning of 'the world', which is not just planet Earth but the entire universe, which for ancient people included the three-storeyed creation of the heavens of the divine being or beings, the earth and the underworld of the dead. This first meaning of world is basically positive. This is the natural universe that God, at creation, found to be 'good', indeed 'very good', and where the revelation of God unfolds in creation and in history.

A second meaning, referring to the universe as related to the human race, is hinted at in the last part of 1.10 and expanded in 1.11. In this sense, 'the world' suggests a creation that is able to respond. 'The world' finds expression in humankind created in the image and likeness of God and in relationship to God and to each other. It seems this biblical sense is what Teilhard de Chardin evokes when he speaks of evolution coming to consciousness in the human person.[13] He understands the human person to be the arrow of evolution; the direction evolution will take because of human creativity and knowledge. Yet there is choice, for the human race as a whole 'appears morally poised between recognition and nonrecognition of the Creator'.[14] A world exists that rejects Jesus who came to 'his own' (1.11). The most striking examples of this second meaning will be discussed in the section on John 3.16–17.

The third meaning of 'the world' is not a place or a race or a religious identity. It is a choice about how reality is seen to be for God or against God, or for the Evil One or against the Evil One. Evil is made flesh in the world by individual and collective human actions in the political, economic, social and religious systems that organize both natural and human reality. Ongoing re-creation and renewal are needed. Through his life and death-resurrection, Jesus completes the works of God by defeating the

Ruler of this World. Jesus' victory over the evil world has been achieved in principle, 'In the world you face persecution. But take courage; I have overcome the world' (16.33 RSV). The world in John is a way of making meaning of our rich and multi-layered experience. Sandra Schneiders sums up by suggesting that 'the "world" with which we are concerned ... [is] the *good world* to which we are missioned, the *evil world* which we confront, and the *alternative* world' we are called into with Jesus in the ongoing creation of completing the works of God.[15]

'His own received him not' (John 1.11)

The shadow of rejection is there from the beginning, for Jesus came to 'his own and his own received him not' (1.11; cf. Wisdom in Prov. 1.20–23; Bar. 3.9—4.4). It is not simply rejection. In the second half of John, opposition and hostility accompany the use of 'the world'. We face rejection and opposition in our work of completing the works of God. John Paul II wrote about 'sin' and 'structures of sin' seldom being applied to the situation of the contemporary world. He names 'the collective behaviour of certain social groups, big or small, even whole nations or blocs of nations' where 'cases of *social sins* are the result of the accumulation and concentration of many *personal sins*'. These personal sins cause or support or exploit evil. Those in a position to avoid, eliminate or at least limit social evils fail to do so out of laziness, fear, silence, complicity, indifference or take refuge in the supposed impossibility of changing the world or sidestep the effort or sacrifice needed. Thus, individuals comprise and support the structures of sin.[16]

The coming of Jesus, the light, made a decisive difference between the past and the present, for darkness had been the prevailing atmosphere (John 1.5). Each person, and consequently society or humankind, that is 'the world' in the sense of those who are able to choose, makes a response to choose light or darkness, to believe or not to believe. Faith and action are connected. There is no list of 'dos' and 'don'ts'. In the present, in 'the world', human persons judge themselves in the now by choosing light or darkness (3.19–21). That there is no description of Jesus' return in future or of the heavens opening or Jesus coming down on the cloud of heaven in judgement is striking. Instead, the language is relational, 'I ... will take you to *myself*' (14.3). This promise centres on a person, on relationship rather than place.

'The Word became flesh' (John 1.14)

The coming of Jesus is not expressed as a birth. He did not become 'a man' in the sense of a male person, or even 'a human person'. Instead, 'the Word became flesh and lived among us' (literally, 'pitched a tent in us'). Wisdom pitched her tent (Ecclus. 24.8) and 'appeared on earth and lived with humankind' (Bar. 3.37) but never becomes flesh as Jesus does. 'Flesh' refers to human persons such as when 'flesh' is circumcised (Gen. 17.11, 14), and man and woman are 'one flesh' (Gen. 2.24–25). The 'Word become flesh' blurs boundaries and moves beyond the anthropomorphic because in classical and biblical writings, 'flesh' has a range of other meanings, among which is a strand that links human persons with other living creatures. Often the word 'all' is inserted. God's continuing relationship with ongoing creation is with 'all flesh' not just human persons. In the flood, the focus is on 'all flesh' (Gen. 6.13–22; 7.15–16,) and later the covenant is made with 'all flesh' (Gen. 9.8–11). God sustains 'all flesh' (Ps. 136.25) and 'all flesh' praises God (Ps. 145.21). So, significantly, flesh signals the interconnection of the incarnation of Jesus with not only human persons but with all living creatures, because in both ancient and biblical Greek it is applied to the wider-than-human. This deep incarnation means Jesus as a creature of earth was a complex living unit of fluids and minerals, part of the carbon, oxygen and nitrogen cycles. The genetic structure of the cells of his body were akin 'to the whole community of that descended from common ancestors in the ancient seas'.[17]

'Believe into his name' (John 1.12)

Two small words, 'in' and 'into', have deep and subtle meanings. We read, 'to all who received [the Word], believed *in* his name, he gave power to become children of God' (John 1.12). What Bibles translate as 'believed *in*' means 'believed *into*'. This is one of the Fourth Evangelist's favourite phrases. It is repeated 34 times. Let us tune into the Evangelist's wavelength. Today, 'believe *in*' may suggest an intellectual faith or belief. Faith and belief permeate John's Gospel, yet those nouns are not there. In the Middle Eastern world, these words, along with fidelity and faithfulness, bound one person to another. These sentiments come from the heart, the centre of a person's being, and are the external expression of social and emotionally rooted values of solidarity, commitment and loyalty.[18] All this underpins 'believing *into*'. This Evangelist prefers verbs – doing words and action. 'Believing *into*' is dynamic and denotes an active commitment. The expression 'believing *into*' is unique to John. Raymond Brown describes it as 'an active commitment to a person and in particular to Jesus ... it involves much more than trust in Jesus or confidence in him; it is an acceptance of Jesus and of what he claims to be and a dedication of one's life to him'.[19] This means a willingness to respond to God's demands as they are presented in and by Jesus.

'We have seen his glory' (John 1.14)

The glory of God is a central theme in Scripture – the greatness, majesty and beauty of God's presence and activity in creation and with God's people. In John's Gospel, we find that 'the Word became flesh and lived among us, and we have seen his glory ... full of grace and truth' (1.14). In the biblical tradition, 'glory' is associated with the glory of the unseen presence of God in the saving event of the Exodus. 'Glory' and its related terms of 'glorify' and 'glorification' are used to portray Jesus as the abundant, visible human presence of the unseen God. In 'the first of his signs' Jesus 'revealed his glory' (2.11). Jesus tells of the glory of his death-resurrection to 'his own' (13.1) who are his friends (15.14), and for whom he will lay down this life because of his great love (15.13). 'When Jesus was glorified' – a way of speaking of his death-resurrection – they remembered what had been written about him (12.16).

In summary, this Gospel begins with a cosmological framework that inserts Jesus into God's ongoing and ever-evolving creation by drawing on understandings from biblical and Hellenistic cosmologies. Characters are introduced: God, the Spirit, the Word imaged as Wisdom becomes flesh, and children of God, who are those who 'believe *into*' him. Words and images create new theological nuances: 'all things', flesh, the world, light and darkness and glory. Integral to the framework of the cosmological prologue are three interconnected relationships with the divine, with human persons and with all creation – which guide our reading of the gospel story that follows. One way of plunging into this evolving story in new unfolding ways is to be attuned to the prologue, which tells an old story in a new way and gives vital clues for reading the Gospel that follows.

Oratio (Prayer) → *Contemplatio* (Contemplation) → *Actio* (Action) →

- Let us return to ponder the question: how can the cosmological horizon of the prologue and that of a present-day reader informed by twenty-first-century cosmologies and evolutionary biology meet in order to inspire a transforming spirituality that sustains ethical action to complete the works of God by responding to *both the cry of the earth and the cry of the marginalized*? The Evangelist presumed that early Christian communities knew their Scriptures and also that they knew about contemporary understandings of science. Both are evoked in the cosmological framework of the prologue through which the Gospel that follows is to be read to draw readers to the significance of Jesus and to ethical action in their new evolving situation. And what of our evolving situation? The World Council of Churches (WCC) points out, 'Our world has never been more prosperous, and, at the same time, more inequitable than it is today' (§12), and continues, 'We discern the fatal intertwining of the global financial, socio-economic, climate and ecological crises accompanied ... by the suffering of the people and their struggle for life' (§10).[20] Ann Braudis understands that ecology presupposes evolution and sees that evolutionary biology is woven into Pope Francis' encyclical *Laudato Si'* (e.g. §18, §81). For her, 'the value of this document lies in its harmony with evolutionary consciousness',[21] which refers to the capacity of human beings to be conscious participants in the evolution of their cultures and human society in order to 'contribute, both as one human family and each one in our own modest way, to the ongoing creation of a now-awaking universe'.[22] Braudis identifies four ways in which this is so.[23] First, *Laudato Si'* is informed not only by Scripture and other spiritual insights but by the results of scientific research (e.g. §62, §201). Second, it is inclusive in character: 'I would like to enter into dialogue with all people about our common home' (§3). Third, it has awareness of a shifting world view. Pope Francis refers explicitly to 'a strategy for real change' that requires 'rethinking processes in their entirety, for it is not enough to include a few superficial ecological considerations while failing to question the logic which underlies present-day culture' (§197). Fourth, the keyword 'integral' is often found: 'What is needed is a politics, which is far-sighted and capable of a new, integral and interdisciplinary approach to handling different aspects of the [environmental] crisis' (§197). Finally, there is understanding of the qualities of truth, beauty and goodness as 'expressions of the longings of the human heart, where the human spirit and consciousness are ceaselessly touched by and yearn for the Infinite and from which cultural change flows'. How does 'believing *into* Jesus' enable us to plunge into this story in new unfolding ways to *hear both for the cry of the earth and the cry of the marginalized*?

Notes

1 This section draws on my two articles: Kathleen P. Rushton, 2013, 'The Cosmology of John 1.1–14 and Its Implications for Ethical Action in this Ecological Age', *Colloquium* 45.2, pp. 137–53; and 2015, 'The Implications of the Cosmology of the Prologue for Johannine Eschatology', *Interface Theology* 1.1, pp. 37–54.

2 Rémi Brague, 2003, *The Wisdom of the World: The Human Experience of the Universe in Western Thought*, Teresa Lavender Fagan (trans.), Chicago IL: University of Chicago Press, pp. 4–5, speaks of the experienced cosmology of pre-modern humanity which (1) makes clear a link between cosmology and the human person; (2) considers 'the world' as the resting place for humanity; (3) links cosmology to wisdom; and (4) leads to contemplation (*theōria*) as the precursor to ethical action. This view of cosmology underpinned what Israel believed about 'the world' as found in their creation accounts and, in turn, what the writer of the Fourth Gospel believed. This worldly wisdom and ethical dimension are also found in what was believed about biblical 'promises concerning a better future', which later came to be known as eschatology.

3 Donald E. Gown, 2000, *Eschatology in the Old Testament*, 2nd edn, Edinburgh: T&T Clark, pp. 1–2.

4 Stephen Motyer, 1995, 'Jesus and the Marginalised in the Fourth Gospel', in *Mission and Meaning: Essays Presented to Peter Cotterell*, Antony Billington, Tony Lane and Max Turner (eds), Carlisle: Paternoster Press, pp. 70–89.

5 Margaret Daly-Denton, 2017, *John: An Earth Bible Commentary: Supposing Him to be the Gardener*, London: Bloomsbury T&T Clark, p. 14.

6 Pasquale Ferrara, 2019, 'Sustainable International Relations: Pope Francis' Encyclical *Laudato Si*' and the Planetary Implications of "Integral Ecology"', *Religions* 10.466, p. 10, www.mdpi.com/2077-1444/10/8/466/htm (accessed 10.10.19).

7 The Greek of some key words in the prologue are: *en archē* (in the beginning); *logos* (word); *sarx* (flesh), which translates meanings of Hebrew *basar*; *kosmos* (world); *panta* (all things); *sarx* (flesh); *phōs* (light); *doxa* (glory); and *pisteuein eis* (believe *into*).

8 I use the terms 'creation's renewal' and 're-creation' to convey creation as John appears to view it. In no place does this Gospel conceive of a dichotomy between original creation and a kind of replacement for it. See Jeannine K. Brown, 2010, 'Creation's Renewal in the Gospel of John', *Catholic Biblical Quarterly* 72.2, p. 276.

9 From an ecological perspective, see Daly-Denton, *John*, pp. 27–41, who sets out extensively the biblical echoes related to the garden of God evoked in the prologue.

10 Elizabeth Johnson, 2018, *Creation and the Cross: The Mercy of God for a Planet in Peril*, Maryknoll NY: Orbis, pp. 184–5.

11 Denis Edwards, 2004, *Breath of Life: A Theology of the Creator Spirit*, Maryknoll NY: Orbis, pp. 26, 40 (italics his).

12 Sandra Schneiders, 2013, *Buying the Field: Catholic Religious Life in the Mission to the World*, Mahwah NJ: Paulist Press, pp. 26–7 (translations and emphases hers). José Porfirio Miranda, 1997, *Being and the Messiah: The Message of St. John*, John Eagleson (trans.), Maryknoll NY: Orbis, pp. 100–2, treats 'world' in a similar way.

13 Louis M. Savary, 2010, *The New Spiritual Exercises: In the Spirit of Pierre Teilhard de Chardin*, Mahwah NJ: Paulist Press, pp. 13–20.

14 Schneiders, *Buying the Field*, p. 27.

15 Schneiders, *Buying the Field*, p. 37 (italics hers).

16 John Paul II, 1988, *Encyclical Letter Sollicitudo Rei Socialis (On Social Concerns)*, Homebush NSW: St Paul Publications, §36 (italics his).

17 Johnson, *Creation and the Cross*, pp. 185–6.

18 On faith in John, see John J. Pilch, 1996, *The Cultural World of Jesus: Sunday by Sunday. Cycle B*, Collegeville MN: Liturgical Press, pp. 118–20.

19 On 'believing *into*' (*pisteuein eis*), see Raymond E. Brown, 1966–1970, *The Gospel According to John*, 2 vols, The Anchor Bible 29–29A, Garden City NY: Doubleday, pp. 512–13.

20 WCC, 'Economy of Life', §12 and §10, in Rogate R. Mshana and Athena Peralta (eds), 2015, *Economy of Life: Linking Poverty, Wealth and Ecology*, Geneva: WCC Publications. The Bogor Statement, 'Economy of Life, Justice and Peace for All: A Call to Action', presented at the 10th WCC Assembly in Busan in 2013, summarizes the outcomes of a several-year process addressing economic and ecological injustices launched by the previous WCC Assembly in Porto Alegre in 2006. I have accessed this document in Mshana and Peralta, pp. 1–26. When I refer to the document, I do so as: 'Economy of Life' and give the paragraph.

21 Ann Braudis, 2016, '*Laudato Si*' and Evolutionary Consciousness', in *Maryknoll Office for Global Concerns NewsNotes*, May–June, p. 3, https://maryknollogc.org/sites/default/files/newsnotes/attachments/MayJune2016_NewsNotes.pdf (accessed 10.10.19).

22 John E. Haugh, 2015, *Resting on the Future: Catholic Theology for an Unfinished Universe*, New York: Bloomsbury Academic, p. 113.

23 Braudis, '*Laudato Si*' and Evolutionary Consciousness', p. 3.

PART 2

The Ministry of Jesus (1.19—12.50)

Bethany Across the Jordan
A Man Whose Name was John
– John 1.6–8, 15, 19–34

'A burning and shining lamp' (John 5.35)

Third Sunday of Advent of Year B
John 1.6–8, 19–28

'What are you looking for?' (John 1.38)

Second Sunday in Ordinary Time of Year A (RL)
John 1.29–34
Second Sunday in Ordinary Time of Year B (RL)
John 1.35–42
Second Sunday after Epiphany of Year A (RCL)
John 1.29–42
Second Sunday after Epiphany of Year B (RCL)
John 1.43–51

Having considered the cosmic story of the Word who was with God (1.1–5) and the coming of the Word made flesh in the world (1.9–14), we now turn to John 1.6–8 and other passages about the one 'sent from God whose name was John' (1.6).

Lectio/Reading of John 1.6–8 and 1.19–28

In John 1.6–8 and 1.19–28 the cosmic story becomes earthed. In your sacred reading imagine the location and imagery of these passages: light, wilderness and the waters of the Jordan where John is baptizing.

Meditatio/Meditation

No character is more associated with Advent, the coming of Jesus or the *adven*ture a disciple undertakes by following the way of life set out by Jesus than John, who is known as the Baptist or the Baptizer. The Evangelist may well have assumed that those who first heard this Gospel proclaimed already knew about John. No mention is made of John's clothing, of his denouncing people, of his baptizing Jesus, of his imprisonment or death. He is a witness, one who gives testimony, and is never called the Baptist or the Baptizer. He is quite a different character in John's Gospel (1.6–8, 15, 19–37; 3.22–36; 5.31–47; 10.41) from the Baptizer of the Synoptic Gospels. Using an analogy, John sums up his relationship with Jesus by calling himself 'the friend of the bridegroom, who stands and hears him, rejoices greatly at the bridegroom's voice' (3.29).

'A man sent from God' (John 1.6)

A move occurs from the cosmic (1.1–5) to earth. Events happen in time and place, 'There was a man sent from God.' In this Gospel's textual world, the only other character described as 'sent from God' is Jesus (1.14, 6.46; 7.29; 9.33; 16.27; 17.18). The prologue states that the Word 'was life, and the life was the light of all people' (1.4) and that John 'came as a witness to the light, so that all might believe through him' (1.7). John 'was not the light'. In the words of Jesus, John 'was a lamp that was kindled and shining' (5.35). The stage is set for John's role of bearing witness to Jesus (1.7, 15, 32, 34; 3.32; 5.33). His cry of witness rings out through this Gospel's early scenes. The other Gospels tell us, 'a voice came from heaven, "This/You are my beloved son with whom I am well pleased"' (e.g. Mark 1.11), while in the Fourth Gospel, John testifies, 'I myself have seen and have testified that this is the Son of God' (John 1.34). He is the first in a line of witnesses: the woman of Samaria (4.39), the Father (5.32, 37; 8.18), the works of Jesus (5.36; 10.25); the Scriptures (5.39), the crowd (12.17); the Advocate (15.26) and the followers of Jesus (15.27).

A distinctive feature of Jesus in the Gospel of John is that he set out a way of living. The reign of God or of the heavens does not feature as it does in the Synoptics. Instead, Jesus is presented as having people seek him out, to believe *into* him (see discussion on 1.12), to become disciples. Disciples are followers of a teacher from whom they learn a way of living. Jesus the teacher sets out a way of living that is centred on attachment to him. John's role is that of 'a witness' who testifies to Jesus so that 'all might believe through him' (1.7). This links with the purpose of this Gospel, 'these things are written so that you may [the reader/hearer] come to believe that Jesus is the Messiah, the Son of God' (20.31). Believing *into* and knowing Jesus is a process of unfolding discovery, a lifelong pilgrimage.

First concern

John's social status and honour come from his father, Zechariah, a faithful rural priest (see Luke 1.5–8). Concern arises in Jerusalem. John is behaving like a prophet, which is not in keeping with his priestly heritage.[1] The traditional tension between priests and prophets lingers. So the Judeans and the Pharisees send priests and Levites to John (John 1.19, 24) with two concerns. The first leads to three questions around the identity of Jesus: 'Who are you?' John denies being the Messiah, Elijah or 'the prophet'. Then, adapting the words of Isaiah who says 'a voice cries out' (40.3), John declares he is that voice: 'I am the voice of one crying out in the wilderness, "Make straight the way of the Lord"' (John 1.23).

Why the Jordan? Why in the wilderness? The location where John is baptizing is full of meaning for his questioners. He is not preaching or baptizing in villages or cities but in the wilderness. Two Hebrew terms, one for the desert in a strict sense and one for a wilderness where there is little or no human habitation, are translated in the Greek Bible by one word (*erēmos*). Either landscape evokes the wanderings of the people of Israel. God was close in the wilderness. The wilderness was a place that enabled deeper encounter with the self and discovery of new purpose when one was freed from what filled life lived in 'the real world'. The wilderness was the place near where they most likely once crossed the Jordan to enter a new land, the Promised Land. John is preaching to Israel. A new Exodus and a new coming into the Promised Land is near. Hosts of associations are evoked. The River Jordan is found as a proper name in over eighty contexts in the Old Testament. Crossing of the Jordan is a recurring motif. Time and again, mention is made of its strong flow. Crossing into that green, fertile land is not easy.

Second concern

Since John is not one of the expected figures, a second concern emerges: 'Why are you baptizing?' Baptism was common in the ancient world both within and beyond Judaism. The rite derived meaning from a particular tradition or context and was regarded as symbolic. John's questioners, therefore, want to know what his baptism means. In Mark and Luke, it is 'a baptism for the forgiveness of sins'. Not so in John's Gospel. John, who baptizes with water, says one is coming whom his questioners do not know. He continues, 'the one who is coming after me; I am not worthy to untie the thong of his sandal' (1.26–27). Maybe the immersion into water suggests that humanity is restored to the state enjoyed with God when they were doing the work God gave them in the garden.[2] Implied in John's testimony and later is that the One who would come would bring a deeper, more radical purification. Clearly, he points to Jesus' divine identity. The role of John is subordinated to that of Jesus as suggested in the untying of sandals, which was the work of slave (1.27).

Bethany-beyond-the-Jordan

John is not described specifically as baptizing people 'in the River Jordan' but in Bethany across the Jordan (1.28), a site in the Hashemite Kingdom of Jordan known today as Al Maghtas. While the exact location is unknown, John is placed in the powerful mythic landscape of the River Jordan, which most Jews and Christians throughout history, and today, have never visited. Knowledge of the symbolism of the purifying water of this region comes through biblical texts and cultural traditions. A huge gap exists between rich biblical symbolism and material reality today.

The River Jordan is in an area of the planet most threatened by a decline in water supply. Generations of intense conflict are easily inflamed by water shortage. Most pilgrims who visit the three possible baptismal sites, and those who hear this Gospel proclaimed, are unaware these sacred waters are both an intently watched international border and polluted. The moral theologian Christiana Peppard describes this river as 'a limp toxic strip of water. A warning sign conveys the hazard posed by coming into contact with this water.' There is little Christian ethical engagement with the waters of the Jordan. She continues: 'The material and symbolic status of the river needs to be drawn together more tightly if ecology is indeed a vital part of faith.'[3] Such ethical engagement permeates the remarkable documentary film *Seven Rivers Walking – Haere Mārire*.[4] This film depicts the journey made by walkers, rafters, farmers and fishers along seven polluted or threatened Canterbury rivers in the South Island of Aotearoa New Zealand. These walks began on Ash Wednesday 2017 and continued weekly throughout Lent as an act of repentance for polluting and reducing the flow of water. Participants explored above and below the surfaces of the rivers to uncover possible ways through the freshwater crisis in their local region.

Oratio (Prayer) → *Contemplatio* (Contemplation) →
Actio (Action) →

- In making right relationship happen with God, the earth and the people as we 'complete the works of God', we could ponder some ways to walk creatively during Advent in the footsteps of our ancestors. In the liturgical year, we find that they expressed the relationship of John and Jesus, who in sandals walked the earth (1.27), in the rhythms of the universe. The birth of John is celebrated on 24 June (midsummer in the northern hemisphere), when the sun begins to decrease. The birth of Jesus is celebrated on 25 December at the time of the midwinter solstice, when light begins to increase.

Lectio/Reading of John 1.29–34

In a sacred reading of John 1.29–23, note what John tells us about the Spirit who enters the narrative explicitly for the first time.

Meditatio/Meditation

John admits twice that he did not know his kinsman Jesus and maybe even had difficulty recognizing him (1.30, 33). Nevertheless, John previously (1.15, 19), and now, continues to proclaim himself 'witness' to Jesus (1.29, 32, 34). Later, Jesus affirms that John 'testified to the truth' (5.33). The day that begins in John 1.29 is dominated by John. The only other character in this scene is Jesus, who has no active role. He is only 'coming towards' John who declares, 'Behold the Lamb of God who takes away the sin of the world' (1.29). 'The lamb' may evoke the paschal lamb (Exod. 12) and other biblical traditions. There is also a possibility the title 'lamb of God' had cosmic connotations as found in the mapping of the 12-lunar-month year by the signs of the zodiac.[5] Whatever was meant by 'the lamb' must not overshadow the fact that Jesus is 'of God'. While in the past the lamb was used in sacrificial rituals for communion and reconciliation, Jesus the lamb is not a cultic victim or offering. Jesus is 'of God'. God enters the human story through Jesus. An old symbol is used in new ways.[6]

'He on whom you see the Spirit descend and remain' (John 1.33)

John not only has his origins with God (1.6) but also with the Spirit who descends from the skies as a dove. This is the first of the other-than-community of earth to enter the narrative, and biblical associations are evoked (Gen. 8.11). The Spirit who will 'abide'/'remain' with the disciples and continue the works of God enters the human story through his testimony (1.32). The central point here is that not only humans like John testify to Jesus but God's own Spirit also testifies to his identity. Jesus is the one who baptizes with the Holy Spirit (1.33). This Gospel speaks of God's Spirit often and has several names for the Spirit. Significantly, there is a 'Holy Spirit' frame, which begins here (1.33), where the Spirit is introduced first as the one descending on and remaining with Jesus. In the middle of the Gospel, the continuity between the revelation of Jesus and that of the Holy Spirit is emphasized (14.26). The final frame is found when Jesus sends the Holy Spirit (20.22).

A key word found some 40 times in John's Gospel is first heard on the lips of John and translated variously in Bibles as remain, stay, continue, endure, live, dwell or abide (see Appendix 2). John testifies to the relationship between Jesus and the Spirit by describing the Spirit descending 'from heaven like a dove, and it *abided/remained* on him' (1.32). This word characterizes the relationship between God and Jesus, the Spirit and Jesus, and Jesus and his disciples. It describes what being a disciple is all about – abiding in Jesus. Abiding describes the Spirit's presence with Jesus here and again in 14.17. The Spirit and the Father abide with Jesus (14.10, 17). The relationship of disciples with both Jesus and the Spirit is described in terms of *abiding/remaining* and being one (1.38–39; 14.20, 23; 15.4–5; 17.23, 26).

Much emphasis is given in writings and preaching to God and the Word, even to the point of excluding the Spirit. John's testimony reminds us of the vital connection between Jesus the Word and the Spirit. In exploring the prologue, we saw how the Word evokes the biblical figure of Wisdom. John's testimony to the Spirit 'abiding/remaining' on Jesus connects the Spirit also with Wisdom who, 'while abiding/remaining (*menō*) in herself, she renews all things; in every generation she passes into holy souls and makes them friends of God' (Wisd. 7.27). The theologian Denis Edwards, who develops biblical, patristic and contemporary insights into a theology of the Creator Spirit, highlights the insights of two early Church writers, Basil (d. 379) and Irenaeus (c.130–200). Basil has a favourite image for the Spirit. He sees the Spirit as the *Breath of God who always accompanies the Word*.[7] The Breath of God gives life – both in the sense of biological life and in the sense of resurrection life (20.22). Edwards observes: 'While most of the Christian tradition identified Wisdom with the Word of God,

Irenaeus equates Wisdom with the Holy Spirit. He liked to speak of God creating *with two hands*, that of the Word and that of the Spirit.'[8] Further, Edwards points out that the ancient patristic tradition kept Word and Spirit (or Breath) together. Irenaeus, Athanasius, Basil and Ambrose gave a central place to the words of Psalm 33.6: 'By the word of the Lord the heavens were made, and all their host [sun, moon and stars] by the breath of [God's] mouth' (LXX).[9]

Oratio (Prayer) → *Contemplatio* (Contemplation) → *Actio* (Action) →

- John is the first person in this Gospel to see Jesus, who became flesh to complete the works of God. John sees Jesus 'coming towards him' (1.29) and testifies to the relationship between Jesus and the Spirit by describing the Spirit descending 'from heaven like a dove, and it *abided/ remained* on him' (1.32). How might the vital connection between Jesus the Word and the Spirit *abide/remain* with disciples today to empower them to complete the works of God by responding to *both the cry of the earth and the cry of the marginalized*?

Notes

1 On the two concerns that John the Baptizer was not behaving like a priest and the meaning of his baptism, see John J. Pilch, 1996, *The Cultural World of Jesus: Sunday by Sunday, Cycle B*, Collegeville MN: Liturgical Press, pp. 7–9.

2 Margaret Daly-Denton, 2017, *John: An Earth Bible Commentary: Supposing Him to be the Gardener*, London: Bloomsbury T&T Clark, p. 46.

3 For an overview of the religious symbolism of the River Jordan and its environmental state today, see the chapter, 'The Jordan River', in Christiana Z. Peppard, 2013, *Just Water: Theology, Ethics, and the Global Water Crisis*, Maryknoll NY: Orbis, pp. 96–114.

4 On the documentary, *Seven Rivers Walking – Haere Mārire*, see http://sevenrivers.nz/ (accessed 16.07.19).

5 Daly-Denton, *John*, pp. 50–1.

6 On the 'Lamb of God', see Francis J. Moloney, 1998, *The Gospel of John*, Sacra Pagina Series 4, Collegeville MN: Liturgical Press, p. 59.

7 Denis Edwards, *Breath of Life: A Theology of the Creator Spirit*, Maryknoll NY: Orbis, p. 26 (italics his).

8 Edwards, *Breath of Life*, p. 40 (italics his).

9 Edwards, *Breath of Life*, pp. 29–43.

Bethany Across the Jordan
The First Disciples of Jesus – John 1.35–51

Lectio/Reading of John 1.35–51

One of the challenges of focusing only on passages in John that are proclaimed in the lectionaries is that parts that are integral to the flow of the narrative are omitted. This is the case with John 1.35–51, which divides into three scenes. In Scene 1, two unnamed disciples come to Jesus (1.35–39), while in Scene 2, Andrew and Simon approach him (1.40–42). We shall include in our sacred reading Scene 3 (1.43–51), which is not in the Roman Lectionary. You might read and reread John 1.35–51, attentive to Jesus as he walks from near the River Jordan to Galilee seeking disciples to work with him as he moves across social barriers creating a new community to complete the works of God by responding *to both the cry of the earth and the cry of the marginalized.* Imagine you are walking with him. What do you see, hear, touch and smell?

Meditatio/Meditation

The first called disciples enter this gospel story in three scenes, which climax with the self-revelation of Jesus (John 1.51) and in the context of the testimony given by John (1.19–34). An overview has been given above of references to John, the first character in the Johannine story, who essentially does nothing but testify to Jesus. It becomes clear in this Gospel that one becomes a disciple through another person who witnesses to Jesus.

'That you may come to believe' (John 20.31)

John's Gospel shows a recurring pattern of Jesus' self-revelation to disciples so 'that you [the reader/hearer] may come to believe that Jesus is the Messiah, the Son of God, and that through believing you may have life in his name' (20.31). A feature that differs from the Synoptic Gospels is that Jesus is often portrayed as speaking at length to individual characters. The stories of these characters are shaped to enkindle faith in Jesus. Some point about faith or the lack of it is shown to teach the Evangelist's readers something about faith in Jesus which is life-giving. Each person represents a type of faith-or-lack-of-faith response to Jesus who is the Christ and Son of God. Such individuals are John, Nathanael, the mother of Jesus, Nicodemus, the woman of Samaria, the royal official, the man who is lame, Philip, the beggar born blind, Lazarus, Judas, Mary Magdalene, Thomas, Peter and the Beloved Disciple. The communal aspect of Christian faith is paramount. The characters are not just individuals but are representative of groups or communities.[1] This aspect is woven into the language and symbolism found in the stories about these representative characters.

Readers who interpret this Gospel through vital clues provided in the framework of the prologue will recognize strands that are embedded in some of the language of 1.35–51. The words and actions of Jesus evoke Wisdom-Sophia, who

> is radiant and unfading, and she is easily discerned by those who love her and *found* by those who *seek* her. She has hastened to make herself known by those who desire her ... because she goes about *seeking* those worthy of her, and she graciously appears to them in their paths. (Wisd. 6.12–13, 16)

Jesus *found* Philip, Philip *found* Nathanael and declared, 'We have *found* him' (1.43–45; cf. 1.41). Wisdom cries out in the streets inviting people to come to her. Some refuse this call. They looked for her and did not find her (Prov. 1.20–28). Those who find Wisdom find life (8.3–5). Likewise, the disciples later announce to others what they have heard (John 1.41, 45).

'What are you looking for?' (John 1.38)

We turn now to the first disciples whom Jesus calls in John 1.35–42, which may be divided into Scene 1 – two unnamed disciples (1.35–39) – and Scene 2 – Andrew and Simon (1.40–42). These scenes introduce the reader to six significant features of John's Gospel: Jesus takes the initiative; questions are asked; the reader enters the story at two levels (narrative and symbolic); four key words are introduced: 'to follow', 'to seek', 'to stay/abide' and 'to see'; the way people come to Jesus through another person; and the portrayal of Peter.

In the beginning of the process of discipleship, Jesus is the one who takes the initiative as he affirms later, 'You did not choose me but I chose you' (15.16). Jesus turns. Then in his very first words spoken in this Gospel, he asks, 'What are you looking for (seeking)?' (1.38). Questions are a remarkable feature of John. Not only does Jesus ask questions but the first disciples are portrayed as asking questions (1.38, 48). The verb 'to seek' in Jesus' question in 1.38 is echoed again after his resurrection (20.15). This significant word is found 34 times throughout this Gospel (see Appendix 2). That this sense is obscured in English translations is illustrated by the following renderings of three commonly used versions of the Bible. 'What *are* you *looking for?*' (NRSV); 'What *do* you *want?*' (NJB); and 'What *do* you *seek?*' (RSV) (1.38).

Raymond Collins suggests readers can enter into the stories in John's Gospel at two levels. The first is the level of *narrative or story*.[2] These are simple incidents about the first disciples (1.35–39) and Andrew and Simon (1.40–42). No details are given about them, such as their being fishers. The narrative level is a backdrop for the second level, the *symbolic* level, which unfolds around key words: 'to follow', 'to seek', 'to abide/stay' and 'to see'. While at the level of story, these words report that the disciples meet Jesus and abide/stay with him, they function in the world *of* the text, to tell the story of the Johannine community with its faith and its struggles. Symbolic language enables the readers to glimpse faith convictions and the real-life struggles that those convictions throw up.

Those four verbs function in these incidents, and elsewhere, as special or technical words for discipleship. We the readers are invited to enter into the gospel story 'to follow', 'to seek', 'to abide/stay' and 'to see' as disciples. Often the translations of English Bibles do not use the same English word, so it is important to search for a word similar in meaning (synonym). For example, the word 'to follow' is used at the symbolic level: between Jesus and his disciples (1.37, 38, 40, 43); in sayings on discipleship (8.12; 12.26); the shepherd and the sheep (10.4–5, 27); and Peter (21.19, 20, 22). The verb 'abide/stay' is found in the question of the disciples (1.38). It is used to describe the relationship of Jesus and the Spirit (1.32, 33); the relationship of Jesus and God (14.10); the many dwelling places (as a noun) in God's house (14.2); the relationship of the vine and branches, Jesus and his disciples (15.1–17 (15x)); 6.56; 8.31). In 1.39 is found the verb 'to see', which has the sense of perceiving, seeing with real comprehension.

John exclaims, 'Look, here is the Lamb of God' (1.36) to the two unnamed disciples. They follow Jesus. This introduces another pattern found throughout this Gospel. One comes to Jesus through another. Later, we learn one of those two unnamed disciples is Andrew (1.40) who finds his brother Simon and says, 'We have found the Messiah' (1.41). John's particular portrayal of Peter also begins here. Unlike the other Gospels

(Mark 8.29), it is Andrew who confesses Jesus as Messiah, not Simon, whose name is nevertheless changed to Peter. These called disciples share their enthusiasm about Jesus, evangelizing another person by using a title of Jesus – 'Lamb of God' (1.36), 'the Messiah' (1.41) and now 'him about whom Moses in the law and also the prophets wrote' (1.45).

'That they may be one' (John 17.21)

We turn now to Scene 3 (1.43–51), which is not proclaimed in the Roman Lectionary but is integral to the flowing of the narrative. The emphasis on Galilee may suggest that those for whom this Gospel was written may have been Galileans who moved to Asia Minor. On the other hand, the emphasis may be on how Galilee as a more 'peripheral "frontier"' welcomed Jesus while 'his own' in Judea would prove hostile (1.11; 4.43–44; 7.1, 9).[3] Jesus is always on the move. We see him and for the first time hear his voice, in the flesh, somewhere near the River Jordan where John is baptizing. He is probably staying somewhere in the neighbourhood (1.29–39).

Later, he decides to go to Galilee (1.43), where he meets Philip from Bethsaida (1.44; 12.20), which was also the city of Andrew and Simon. Situated north-east of the Sea of Galilee, this city is close to the border of the Decapolis, a Gentile region of Greek cities. This may explain why those three Jews have Greek names. It is to Philip and Andrew that the Greeks will come later (12.20–22). The contrast between wilderness and Galilee landscapes may be why Jesus took on a different ministry from the Baptist. The Nazareth range and the valleys of the Shephelah are of a type of rock that produces soil-cover and has springs. Unlike other craggy ranges in lower Galilee, the Nazareth ridge had villages near the summit because the fertile land was cultivated. Jesus' shift in the natural environment recalls the contrast expressed in Deuteronomy. Perhaps in an Exodus experience, he moved from an arid landscape to one 'with flowing streams, with springs and underground waters welling up in hills and valleys, a land of wheat and barley, of vines and fig trees' (Deut. 8.6–10). His inherited belief in the gift of the land is the backdrop to his role in God's call. In his experience of contrast, suggests Sean Freyne, the *potential blessedness* of life in the land moved Jesus to see the present as a graced moment which influenced the direction of his ministry.[4]

Nathanael, although Galilean himself from Cana (21.2; 1.46), seems to have taken offence that Jesus came from Nazareth – 'Can anything good come out of Nazareth?' (1.46). He objects to that specific Galilean town, while the chief priests and Pharisees dismiss that whole region, for 'no prophet is to arise from Galilee' (7.52). According to custom, Jesus, son of Joseph from Nazareth, is identified by his place of origin. This points to his humble origin and his humanity. Nazareth was a comparatively small village among other villages and small towns in a region where the only cities in the Hellenistic sense were Tiberias and Sepphoris. Like all people in the region, they would have been subjected to the Roman rule of Galilee. Halvor Moxnes highlights the importance of three dimensions of place for the mission of Jesus and the changing face of Galilee: the experience of place, which means how it is managed and controlled; the legitimation of place, meaning the ideological underpinning of the dominant controlling view; and the imagination of place, or the way in which an alternative vision of place can be developed as well as strategies to implement the new vision.[5]

What was the experience of place during Roman rule? Recent excavations suggest Nazareth was a farming settlement with watchtowers, terraces, grape presses and field irrigation. This would be typical of nearby villages where small-scale peasant landowners worked the land intensively, producing wheat, maize, olives, figs and grapes. Life was precarious, depending on the weather and factors such as demands from passing armies and absent rulers. In the legitimation of place, native elites, such as the ruler Herod Antipas, and Rome required taxes to be paid. The rebuilding of nearby prosperous Sepphoris, where the carpenters Joseph and Jesus may or may not have worked, exerted pressure on peasant life. A sophisticated water system comprising aqueducts and a huge underground reservoir have been uncovered. This example of human manipulation of the environment by elites was undertaken presumably without consideration of the impact on the water supply of nearby villages. The third dimension of imagined place raises biblical ideals. As lived in the land in the present, the original vision was distorted. Jesus raised awareness of an alternative. He had heard 'A voice of one crying out in the wilderness' (1.23). His imagery shows an imagination grounded deeply in the natural world and the human struggle with it.

In the late first century, following the disaster of the Roman War and the destruction of the temple, various groups of Jews sought different solutions in this situation. In the first half of John, it is possible to see Jesus moving between representatives of these groups who are in conflict with each other. In action, he seeks to bring into practice what he will pray later, 'that they may be one' (17.21). His barrier-crossing ministry of reconciliation across social barriers creates a new community.[6] The first representative of such a group is Nathanael, of whom Jesus says, 'Here is truly an Israelite in whom there is no deceit' (1.47). The Israelite Nathanael recognized Jesus as 'the King of Israel' (1.49). In using the term 'Israelite', Jesus implies that Nathanael belongs to those Jews who seek a nationalist and political liberator to free them from Roman domination.[7] Jesus identifies him as championing Israel's cause in the spirit, and possibly in the action, of the Zealots. In confessing Jesus to be 'the King of Israel', Nathanael sees Jesus as fulfilling that longed-for role. 'No deceit' is an allusion to Jacob who was also known as Israel (Gen. 32.28–29), who supplanted his twin brother deceitfully to receive his father's blessing (Gen. 27.35). In the Son of Humanity saying of John 1.51, Jesus corrects Nathanael's confession. This is reflected in the triumphal entry of Jesus into Jerusalem when only in John 12.13 is found the title 'King of Israel'. This national political title is undercut in two ways. First, Jesus is sitting on a donkey evoking the 'humble' one of Zechariah 9.9. Second, the disciples failed to understand then but 'when Jesus was glorified' – a way of speaking of his death-resurrection – they remembered what had been written about him (12.16).

Oratio (Prayer) → *Contemplatio* (Contemplation) → *Actio* (Action) →

- What are the implications for today of Jesus' barrier-crossing ministry of reconciliation as he moves across social barriers creating a new community to work with him in completing the works of God?
- The importance of the three dimensions of place for the mission of Jesus and the changing face of Galilee was outlined. What difference does this make to our understanding of place today, as with Jesus we complete the works of God by responding *to the cry of the earth and the cry of the marginalized*? What is your *experience* of place (how it is managed and controlled)? In what ways do some of the 'p' codes (power, privilege, property, poverty and persecution – see the Introduction) operate in the legitimation of place (the ideological underpinning of the dominant controlling view) in your local area and country? The mission of Jesus may be said to be about the imagination of place or the way in which an alternative vision of place can be developed as well as strategies to implement the new vision. What little steps can you be part of taking towards implicating an alternative vision of place?

Notes

1 On representative characters in John, see Raymond F. Collins, 1990, 'Representative Figures', in *These Things Have Been Written: Studies on the Fourth Gospel*, Louvain Theological and Pastoral Monographs 2, Louvain: Peeters, pp. 1–43.

2 On narrative and symbolic levels, see Raymond F. Collins, 1990, 'Discipleship in John's Gospel', in *These Things Have Been Written*, pp. 46–55, especially pp. 49–50.

3 Craig S. Keener, 2003, *The Gospel of John: A Commentary*, 2 vols, Peabody MA: Hendrickson Publishers, pp. 482, 480.

4 Sean Freyne, 2004, *Jesus, A Jewish Galilean: A New Reading of the Jesus-Story*, London: T&T Clark International, p. 42.

5 Halvor Moxnes, 2003, *Putting Jesus in His Place: A Radical Vision of Household and Kingdom*, Louisville KY: Westminster John Knox Press, pp. 1–21.

6 On Jesus' boundary-crossing ministry of reconciliation, see Stephen Motyer, 1995, 'Jesus and the Marginalised in the Fourth Gospel', in *Mission and Meaning: Essays Presented to Peter Cotterell*, Antony Billington, Tony Lane and Max Turner (eds), Carlisle: Paternoster Press, pp. 70–89.

7 On Nathanael as a nationalist, see John Painter, 1977, 'Christ and Church in John 1, 45–51', in M. De Jonge (ed.), *L'Evangile de Jeanources, Redaction, Theologie, BETL* 44, Leuven: Leuven University Press, pp. 359–63.

Cana
A Wedding – John 2.1–12

'They filled them up to the brim' (John 2.7)

Second Sunday in Ordinary Time of Year C (RL)
Second Sunday after Epiphany of Year C (RCL)
John 2.1–11

Lectio/Reading of John 2.1–12

Become aware of the ways in which Jesus, his mother and his new community of disciples are earthed in a particular place where the cultural practices and gifts of earth come together in the joyful wedding festivities of local people. Imagine you are there. What do you see, hear, touch and smell?

Meditatio/Meditation

'Wine to gladden the human heart' (Ps. 104.15)

Bread, olive oil and wine comprised the three main food groups of the Ancient Near East and Palestine.[1] From these cultures emerged the Jewish-Christian world, where wine was important culturally and economically. It was a common drink, as well as being used for medicinal purposes and in religious ceremonies.

After the Flood, God repeats the earlier command to be fruitful, multiply and fill the earth, which is then given to Noah, who is described as 'a man of the soil'. Significantly, he does not begin by planting grain as his ancestors did (Gen. 3.18–19). Noah plants a vineyard and produces wine (Gen. 9.20). Later, we are told that wine gladdens the human heart and comforts in times of distress (Ps. 104.15; Prov. 31.6–7). Farming grain provides the necessities of life, whereas the vintner produces the highly esteemed beverage of wine, which may bring joy, delight and comfort.

The vine and its fruit are also a sign of the blessed life in the messianic age (Micah 4.4). The banquet is a metaphor for joy. From the time of Noah onwards, vines, vineyards and wine feature often in the biblical narrative.

'A community of creation'

Although we have touched briefly on their complexity and significance in the Scriptures, it is crucial to move beyond seeing wine and vines as just being mentioned incidentally here and there. The Bible unfolds the deeply interconnected story of God's creation and redemption, which are not separate categories but are intertwined. The imagery of wine invites us to a view of Christian life that sees human life in profound relationship with God and in deep relationship with God's creation. Redemption encompasses all of creation, including the land and its fruitfulness.

In his re-evaluation of the biblical tradition of 'dominion', Richard Bauckham discovers a tradition of a 'community of creation' in which human beings are interconnected with all God's creatures and true reconciliation with God involves the entire creation.[2] The biblical tradition begins with God creating the heavens and the earth. All living beings are seen as an interconnected community that is fundamentally good. Psalm 104 encourages gratitude for creation and rejoicing in it. The psalmist proclaims creation to be a gift from God and sees wine as a gift that gladdens the human heart (Ps. 104.15). The wedding at Cana, and the images portraying God as the vine grower, along with Jesus and his disciples as a vine and its branches (John 15), build on this background of Old Testament images. In addition to this rich biblical background, it is enlightening to consider the possible context and impact of this story in the first-century social and cultural world of the writer and the community.

Social and cultural context of wedding festivities (John 2.2–3)

The first sign of Jesus at a village wedding would evoke for John's first hearers and readers three social and cultural factors that were linked inextricably to their experience of Jewish weddings festivities: a division of labour and space according to male and female roles; relations between mother and son; and honour.[3]

In Mediterranean cultures, there tended to be a division of labour and space according to male and female roles. Space was often divided into 'the outside' of the public space of the male, which was the world of the market, the law courts and of all that comprised the public sphere. The female world was the 'inside', the private domestic space of the home and certain outdoor places like wells and communal ovens. This division was seen even in the way special family events such as weddings were organized when the house was opened to the wider community and this inside private space functioned like a public space.

So the wedding was a public event rather than a private family celebration. It formalized the union not of two individuals but of two households and their honour. Accompanied by music, dancing and applause, the bride processed from her father's house through the main street(s) of the village to the home of her husband. Wedding festivities were hosted by the groom or his father inside his house, which was opened to the invited public. Those occasions of joyful celebration ideally lasted seven days and included music, dancing and wine drinking.[4] Family, friends, neighbours and associates of the groom, the bride and their families shared their joy. As in the public space, women were present throughout but they dined and celebrated apart from the men.

Because a father's proper place was the public space, he spent very little time at home. The care and raising of the children were the sphere of the mother. Consequently, the most important person in a son's life was his mother. The bond and relations between mother and son were the closest of Mediterranean affective relationships. This mother–son relationship was a source of power that a mother could use. An 'honourable' son was expected to obey his mother. Nevertheless, it was not improper nor out of the ordinary for a son to talk down to his mother.

In our discussion above, the word honour recurs. Honour, which can be defined as a socially acknowledged claim to worth, indicated a person's social standing within a community and its associated rights and obligations. All social interactions happening outside of the house or beyond one's closest circle were viewed as a competition for honour. Honour is maintained through working on informal mutual alliance with both peers and those of higher status. Village men, for example, would agree to help each other with money and other resources to make sure family weddings were celebrated in an honourable way. When informal means could not meet their needs, men would seek the assistance of a well-to-do patron in a patron–client relationship.

In summary, four factors – male and female roles, the relations between a mother and a son, the deep concern for honour, and the rich biblical background of wine and celebration – help us reconstruct the context of John 2.1–11.

'The mother of Jesus was there' (John 2.1)

The events of John 2.1–11 occur at a wedding in the village of Cana in Galilee where at least one of the disciples, Nathanael, lived (21.2). The festivities are being hosted by the bridegroom in his home (2.9). Among the guests are Jesus and his mother. As Cana was about a 14-kilometre walk south of Nazareth, they may not have necessarily been close relatives. Their presence at a local wedding highlights that they are embedded in a local community in a particular area. The mother of Jesus appears only twice in this Gospel, yet she is not marginal to the story – she ushers in his first sign, in public, at a wedding in Cana (2.1–11) and is near the cross (19.25–27). Her presence frames the public ministry of Jesus. She takes her place among the women found at key points of the narrative. Such prominence needs to be considered as 'reflecting part of the continuum of first-century Jewish practice'.[5] In John, Jesus does not disassociate himself from her. The rift is between himself and his brothers (7.1–9). He places her not in their care but in that of the Beloved Disciple at the cross (20.26–27). Unlike the other Gospels, John does not name Jesus' mother. On the other hand, Joseph is named (6.42).

The setting of a village wedding

The household seems to have been large. Servants are present (2.5, 9) and six pots of water (2.6) are a very large amount even for the bride's purification ritual and the ritual hand-washing. The bridegroom and his chief steward appear not to know that the wine is running out. To be short of wine or food during these festive days would reflect badly on the bridegroom's honour, his reputation and place in the community. The presence of Jesus and his mother at this wedding suggests there is an ongoing relationship between the two families. Maybe a female member of the household asks the mother of Jesus for help. In the context of this relationship of mutuality/reciprocity, when she learns of the impending crisis, she approaches Jesus, the head of her household, certainly not in the public male space of the wedding but maybe in a space near a door or entrance close to where the water jars were stored.[6]

'They have no wine' (2.3), his mother informs Jesus. Implicit in this statement is her unrelenting faith that he would do something. In the gospel story, Jesus has been off doing his own thing. He has met with John at the Jordan, and many were following him (1.29–42) and have continued to do so (1.43–51). His mother uses her privileged access to her son, the head of her household, to remind him of their family obligations.

THE MINISTRY OF JESUS

'They filled them up to the brim' (John 2.7)

Jesus directs the servants to the six stone jars, which were used for the Jewish rites of purification. They are to fill them 'to the brim' with water. Each jar literally held 'two or three measures', probably 75–115 litres or 16–24 gallons. Six times these measures is a lot of wine! The language and imagery of fullness weaves through this Gospel in different ways – with food (6.12–13, 26); with joy (3.34; 15.11; 16.24; 17.13), and with grace and truth (1.14, 16). Jesus is the one who 'gives the Spirit without measure' (3.29). An abundance of fine wine flows. This sign of abundant choice wine shows that Jesus provides materially as well as spiritually (10.10). The first meal presented in this Gospel shows interdependence and interconnection between the gifts of the earth and people in an experience of eating and drinking. We are invited to approach this scene in a new way. Jesus does not intervene in the processes of nature. He comes to share and to increase the joy of ordinary people. Wine is a gift of creation. This raises awareness of the role of the senses and of joyous feasting for Christian spirituality.

The glory of God is a central theme in Scripture – the greatness, majesty and beauty of God's presence and activity in creation and with God's people. In John's Gospel, we find that 'the Word became flesh and lived among us, and we have seen his glory ... full of grace and truth' (1.14). In the biblical tradition, 'glory' is associated with the glory of the unseen presence of God in the saving event of the Exodus. 'Glory' and its related terms of 'glorify' and 'glorification' are used to portray Jesus as the abundant, visible human presence of the unseen God.

'And your joy may be complete' (John 15.11)

The adjective translated as 'good' wine in John 2.10 has the meaning of 'beautiful' and 'choice'. Wine evokes joy, delight and pleasure. This Gospel stresses the gift of joy: 'I have said these things to you so that my joy may be in you, and your joy may be complete' (15.11; also 16.24). John, cast as a witness in this Gospel and known as the Baptizer, witnesses to this joy: 'The friend of the bridegroom, who stands and hears him, rejoices greatly at the bridegroom's voice. For this reason, my joy has been fulfilled' (3.29–30).

The good, beautiful, choice wine kept until last is a symbol of Jesus who is the climax of God's revelation. Christian feasting promotes celebration and gratitude as God's presence and gifts are remembered. In the biblical tradition, wine 'plays an important role in helping us live into this posture of thanksgiving and joyful celebration, and it anchors our lives in God's generosity'.[7] In contrast, the beautiful and complex liquid of wine can be associated by some Christians with a false, joyless sense of asceticism and a source of temptation rather than with a Christian spirituality of joy, delight, celebration and pleasure as found in the motifs of vine, viticulture (the cultivation of grapes and vines) and viniculture (the making of wine) that are found frequently in the Bible. Indeed, there is a Jewish saying, 'Without wine there is no joy.' The revelation of God's glory is not just about living ethically by loving one's neighbour but about beauty, festival and playing before God.[8]

'And his disciples believed into him' (John 2.11)

The incident at Cana ends with the narrator commenting, 'Jesus did this, the first of his signs, in Cana of Galilee, and revealed his glory; and his disciples believed *into* him' (2.11). In this typical, densely packed Johannine theological sentence are three key words: sign, glory and 'believe *into*'. For the first time we find the term 'sign' (*sēmeia*) that names what the Synoptic Gospels call 'mighty deeds' of Jesus. Interestingly, the term 'miracle' is never used in this Gospel or in the Synoptics. While the seven signs that Jesus performs are mentioned in John (2.11, 18, 23; 3.2; 4.54; 6.2, 14, 26; 9.16; 11.47; 12.18), we are told, 'Now Jesus did many other signs in the presence of his disciples, which are not written in this book' (20.30). The prologue (1.1–18) has prepared us for two other aspects of John 2.11. There we were told that the Word became flesh and pitched his tent among us and 'we have seen his glory as a father's only son' (1.14). Although the water is changed into wine in public, those present do not know of this action, which is 'the first of his signs' through which Jesus 'revealed his glory' (2.11). This is the first mention of 'his glory' in this gospel story. Second, the prologue also prepared us to be aware of another Johannine expression, 'believed *into*'. We are told that those who received the Word, 'who believed *into* his name', will be given power to become children of God (1.12). This Evangelist prefers action words. 'Believing *into*' is dynamic and requires an active commitment (see Appendix 2). When Jesus reveals his glory, the disciples are enabled to 'believe *into*' him so that with him they may complete the work of God. 'To believe *into*' is characteristic of his mother, his brothers and his disciples who go down from Cana to Capernaum and remain (abide) with him.

First sign in public space

In public places and outdoors, Jesus gathers the first disciples. In the public space of a wedding, Jesus 'revealed his glory' in this first of his signs. This sets a pattern because in the first 11 chapters of John, the healings and actions of Jesus usually take place in public. The first sign of Jesus is not a healing of a sick person, or is it? Those who hear this story today are led into the profound healing of the communal delight, celebration, joy and merry-making of God's abundance. We are led to rediscover the biblical tradition of the community of creation where redemption and creation are intertwined. The availability of the abundance of choice wine during the festivities of this wedding evokes the biblical messianic banquet that we are called to anticipate in our Christian lives today. The biblical tradition of the revelation of God's glory continues with Jesus revealing his glory to his disciples who 'believe *into* him' as we are called to 'believe *into* him' in the ongoing pilgrimage of our communal lives to complete the work of God by responding to *both the cry of the earth and the cry of the marginalized.*

Oratio (Prayer) → *Contemplatio* (Contemplation) → *Actio* (Action) →

- Those who hear this story today are led into the profound healing of the communal delight, celebration, joy and merry-making of God's abundance made flesh in Jesus who 'came that may they have life, and have it more abundantly' (10.10). In other words, we are to experience beauty, festival and playing before God. Christian spirituality 'incorporates the value of relaxation and festivity' (*LS* §237). One expression of an attitude of gratitude is to stop and give thanks to God before and after meals in a moment of gratitude. This 'beautiful and meaningful custom' unites us with ever so many others, reminds us 'of our dependence on God for life; strengthens our feeling of gratitude for the gifts of creation; it acknowledges those who by their labours provide us with these gifts; and reaffirms our solidarity with those in greatest need' (*LS* §227). Joy as an expression of gratitude to God is at the heart of the Christian understanding of the spiritual life. This leads us to ask why, if this is so, is there so little joy in life and particularly in the life of the Church? Joyful feasting has traditionally been part of how Christians have 'believed *into*', lived into and nourished a life of gratitude and joy. In the meals in John, Jesus is with friends. Eucharist is derived from *eucharistia*, meaning thanksgiving. We need to recover 'a decidedly Christian understanding of festive play before God, and wine can play an important role in that'.⁹ The *Earth Charter* highlights joy in our pilgrimage of life:

> As never before in history, common destiny beckons us to seek a new beginning ... Let ours be a time remembered for the awakening of a new reverence for life, the firm resolve to achieve sustainability, the quickening of the struggle for justice and peace, and the joyful celebration of life.¹⁰

Notes

1 Gisela H. Kreglinger, 2016, *The Spirituality of Wine*, Grand Rapids MI: Eerdmans, p. 12.

2 Richard Bauckham, 2010, *The Bible and Ecology: Rediscovering the Community of Creation*, Waco TX: Baylor University Press, p. 64.

3 Ritva H. Williams, 1997, 'The Mother of Jesus at Cana: A Social-Science Interpretation of John 2:1–12', *Catholic Biblical Quarterly* 59.4, pp. 680–3. Gendered Space: the gendered categories of labour and space are helpful to give a background to biblical stories but, as with any insight or tool that helps with understanding the far distant ancient past, it must be used carefully and with the realization that such categories may not have been the general rule and that there were probably many exceptions depending on social status.

4 Craig S. Keener, 2003, *The Gospel of John: A Commentary*, 2 vols, Peabody MA: Hendrickson Publishers; for an overview of Jewish wedding celebrations, see p. 499.

5 Judith Plaskow, 1993, 'Anti-Judaism in Christian Feminist Interpretation', in Elisabeth Schüssler Fiorenza (ed.), *Searching the Scriptures. Volume One: A Feminist Introduction*, New York: Crossroad, p. 126.

6 Williams, 'The Mother of Jesus', pp. 685–6.

7 Kreglinger, *Spirituality of Wine*, p. 88.

8 Jürgen Moltmann, 1973, *Theology and Joy*, London: SCM Press, p. 33.

9 Kreglinger, *Spirituality of Wine*, p. 5.

10 *Earth Charter*, The Hague, 29 June 2000, quoted in *Laudato Si'*, §207.

Jerusalem
Jesus in the Temple – John 2.13–25

'Jesus went up to Jerusalem' (John 2.13)

Third Sunday of Lent of Year B (RL)
Third Sunday in Lent of Year B (RCL)
John 2.13–22

Lectio/Reading of John 2.13–25

To prepare to read and reread John 2.13–25, reflect on your experience of pilgrimage or what you know about being a pilgrim in order to become aware of Jesus, a pilgrim among pilgrims in Jerusalem. How does the concept of pilgrimage enhance our understanding of Jesus' behaviour in the temple?

Meditatio/Meditation

> The restless heart is the starting point of pilgrimage. Everyone harbours a longing that impels him or her to leave behind the indifference of everyday life and the narrowness of habitual surroundings … All the paths … point to the fact that life is a path, a way of pilgrimage towards God.[1]

These words of St Augustine ushered me into the world of pilgrimage when I walked the Camino Francés to Santiago de Compostela in 2011. My understanding of John's so-called 'cleansing of the temple' story expanded. It is also about a pilgrimage. Jesus is a pilgrim. Philo and Josephus, who went on pilgrimage to Jerusalem in the first century CE, describe exhilarating experiences when pilgrims left the demands and constrains of everyday life imposed by social structures and concerns to enter another world.[2] Pilgrims mixed together, shared experiences, often wore the same pilgrim clothing, walked lightly on earth and emerged at the sacred site for the common purpose of festival worship.

'Jesus went up to Jerusalem' (John 2.13)

'The Passover ... was near and Jesus went up to Jerusalem' (2.13). This festival inaugurates the ministry of Jesus in Jerusalem and is the first of three at key points of his public life – the second is the backdrop to the Bread of Life (6.4–14) and the third is the context of his arrest, trial and execution (11.55—19.14). He goes to Jerusalem for the week-long spring festival celebrating the Exodus from Egypt (Exod. 12.1–18). Passover is associated with liberation and with God's salvation past and future. Jesus, like all Israelite males, is commanded to go on pilgrimage to Jerusalem three times a year, 'at the festival of unleavened bread, at the festival of weeks, and at the festival of booths'; that is, Passover, Pentecost and Sukkoth (Deut. 16.16). Passover at the time of Jesus was seen as a celebration of the renewal of creation.[3] In the spring, summer and autumn, pilgrims travel to Jerusalem. The focus is the temple, which is God's dwelling place and the place of worship, reconciliation and covenant renewal. These festivals are also the background to John 5—10.

The temple – the order of creation

The temple in Jerusalem was invested with meaning from both within Israel and within the Middle Eastern culture. Temples were constructed according to a divinely revealed plan to be a worthy dwelling place for God/the god(s) who visited and dwelt in the sky immediately above the temple.[4] The understanding was that God/the god(s) above did not actually come to earth but could be accessed by people in the temple, which was usually built on a hill. A temple replicated a palace. A temple existed for God/gods as the palace for the king. Like surrounding temples, the pattern of the Jerusalem temple's personnel, interactions and activities followed that of the palace. God was accessible in the temple as the king was in the palace. God too had a household ordered according to rank – high priest, priests, Levities, an army with officers and soldiers, slaves, household staff.

The temple was a cosmic centre, a navel of the world, a place where heaven and earth met, replicating in physical space the holy order of creation. In this focal religious place for all Israel, social relationships were mapped in the concentric circles that moved out from the Holy of Holies to the sanctuary, to the Court of Israelites, to the Court of the Women and to the Court of the Gentiles. Cosmic, social and religious significance interconnected with the temple's political and economic aspects. As a king collected taxes so too did the deity. According to Bruce Malina and Richard Rohrbaugh, 'it would be hard to overestimate the import of the temple as the center of a redistributive political economy'. Within its precincts were large treasuries and storehouses in which were deposited a great amount of money and goods 'extracted from the surplus product of the peasant economy'.[5] As only a few priests had access to most of the temple precincts, what was stored there was secure and inaccessible.

In addition, the Jerusalem elites (2.18, 20) held power by being allied with Rome and under Roman supervision. The Roman governor appointed the chief priest and controlled the use of the priestly garments, which were kept in the adjoining Antonia palace. This alliance between the elites and the Romans is threatened by Jesus' actions.

Jesus in the temple

In what looks like a cleansing of the temple, John gives more detail. There is more force. Jesus is more radical.[6] The animals are named as 'cattle' and 'sheep' and there are doves. Jesus made a whip to drive the animals out. He 'poured out' the coins of the money-changers and overturned their tables. Caged doves cannot be driven out so Jesus orders the sellers to 'Take these things out of here' and adds, 'Stop making my Father's house a marketplace!' The disciples 'remembered' words from the Scriptures, 'Zeal for your house will consume me.' What Jesus does in effect is to shut down the temple as a place of worship.[7] The animals required for sacrifice are driven out – cattle and sheep, as well as doves (the offering of the poor). The necessary exchange of foreign currencies for the official temple tax half-shekel (Exod. 30.11–16) becomes unavailable. The purpose of the temple as a place of reconciliation and covenant renewal between God and Israel is over. What Jesus does is to shut down the temple as a place of worship. Where is God's dwelling place now?

God's dwelling place

In the prologue, we learn God's dwelling place, in the midst of humanity, is in the humanity of Jesus: 'the Word became flesh and lived/dwelt among us' (John 1.14). Jesus' words draw out the meaning of his actions. A shift of term occurs. Jesus 'drove all of them out of the temple' (*hieron*, 2.15). The term *hieron* refers to the whole area of the temple and is used for pagan shrines. John uses another term, *naos*, which refers to the whole area of the temple: 'Destroy this temple (*naos*)', and, 'But he spoke of the temple (*naos*) of his body' (2.19, 21). The Evangelist, however, makes a distinction and associates the term *naos* with the temple of Jesus' risen human body, now the dwelling place of God, the place of reconciliation and covenant renewal. Earlier, John the Baptizer pointed to Jesus' role in reconciliation when he saw him and declares, 'Here is the Lamb of God who takes away the sins of the world' (1.29). Soon, Jesus will inform the woman of Samaria about the shift that is taking place, for 'the hour is coming when you will worship the Father neither on this mountain nor in Jerusalem' (4.21).

So the Evangelist, probably writing from Ephesus, interprets an event of 60 years before, in the early 30s, in the now non-existent temple destroyed in 70 CE. Perhaps some of the community have been drawn into the activities of the local Roman temple of Artemis. Others may have longed for the Jerusalem temple. The disciples 'remembered' words from the Scriptures and also words of Jesus about his body (2.17, 22). While Mark, Matthew and Luke place this incident in the last week of his life, this Gospel begins Jesus' public ministry by focusing on his now ever-present raised humanity as the dwelling place of God, the place of reconciliation and covenant renewal.

Oratio (Prayer) → *Contemplatio* (Contemplation) → *Actio* (Action) →

- How might Lent, a time of preparing for deeper participation in the paschal mystery of Jesus who is the dwelling place of God, become a pilgrimage towards God and a time of 'completing the works of God' by responding *to the cry of the earth and the cry of the marginalized*?
- What little steps can be taken in Lent to make right relationship happen with God, the land and people?
- How does the experience of being a pilgrim evoke a way of being on earth?
- Reflect on what may need to be 'shut down' in our lives and in the life of our Christian community in order to respond *to the cry of the earth and the cry of the marginalized*.

Notes

1 Augustine, quoted in Peter Müller and Angel Fernández de Aránguiz Sca, 2010, *Every Pilgrim's Guide to Walking to Santiago de Compostela*, Laurie Dennett (trans.), Norwich: Canterbury Press, p. ix.

2 On pilgrimage and the temple, see Bruce J. Malina and Richard L. Rohrbaugh, 1998, *Social-Science Commentary on the Gospel of John*, Minneapolis MN: Augsburg Fortress Press, pp. 75–9.

3 Margaret Daly-Denton, 2017, *John: An Earth Bible Commentary: Supposing Him to be the Gardener*, London: Bloomsbury T&T Clark, p. 71.

4 Malina and Rohrbaugh, *Social-Science Commentary*, pp. 77–9.
5 Malina and Rohrbaugh, *Social-Science Commentary*, pp. 77–9.
6 Brendan Byrne SJ, 2014, *Life Abounding: A Reading of John's Gospel*, Collegeville MN: Liturgical Press, pp. 58–63. See also Mary L. Coloe, 2001, *God Dwells with Us: Temple Symbolism in the Fourth Gospel*, Collegeville MN: Liturgical Press, pp. 65–84, especially p. 84, and Craig S. Keener, 2003, *The Gospel of John: A Commentary*, 2 vols, Peabody MA: Hendrickson Publishers, pp. 518–32.
7 Byrne SJ, *Life Abounding*, p. 60.

Jerusalem
A Pharisee Named Nicodemus
– John 3.1–21

Nicodemus 'came to Jesus by night' (John 3.2)

Second Sunday in Lent of Year A (RCL Alternative)
Trinity Sunday of Year B (RCL)
John 3.1–17

'God so loved the world' (John 3.16)

Fourth Sunday of Lent of Year B (RL)
Fourth Sunday of Lent of Year B (RCL)
John 3.14–21
Sunday after Pentecost: Holy Trinity of Year A (RL)
John 3.16–18

Lectio/Reading of John 3.1–15

In reading and rereading John 3.1–15, a way to enter into the implications of this story is to be aware of Nicodemus' first words, 'Rabbi, we know'. His tone suggests a certainty of knowing or knowledge that obscures what Jesus is revealing to him through the images of 'water and spirit/wind'.

Meditatio/Meditation

'That they may be one' (John 17.11)

We have seen Jesus in his barrier-crossing ministry of reconciliation move across social barriers or frontiers to create a new community when he called the nationalist Nathanael, the 'true Israelite' who was searching for a new king of Israel (1.47). Jesus moves, now, to the Pharisee, Nicodemus (3.1–21) and then to the woman of Samaria (4.7–26), surrounded by scenes of communal relationships – people in the temple (2.14–22), secret Christian Jews (2.23–25), followers of John (3.22–36) and Samaritans (4.1–42). Before discussing Nicodemus and the woman of Samaria, we shall look at the implications of their stories being placed side by side in the barrier-crossing ministry of Jesus.

After the fall of Jerusalem and the destruction of the temple in 70 CE, the crisis experienced by late first-century Jews was more widespread than poverty, loss of property and displacement. Their religion and identity, especially for Palestinian Jews, had been closely bound to the now destroyed temple and its cult. Another factor was the division between Judea and Samaria that had raged for centuries. Tensions increased because many believed that Samaritans were complicit with the Roman invasion of Judea. In this context, the followers of Jesus, in dialogue with the Scriptures and in relation to their own situations, reinterpreted Scripture with their Jesus-glasses to express their understandings and experiences of God in Jesus. Behind the placing of the stories of Nicodemus and the woman of Samaria side by side, and aspects of John 3.1–15, is Ezekiel 37.15–23, which looks forward to the coming together again of the northern and southern kingdoms, which at the time of Jesus were known as Samaria and Judea.[1] God, whom they need to discover in Jesus, 'will gather them from every quarter ... make them one nation ... one king ... they shall be my people, and I will be their God' (Ezek. 37.21–23). As people gather and unite around Jesus in his new community, the hateful divisions of the past will fall away and the people of God will be rebuilt.

Nicodemus 'came to Jesus by night' (John 3.2)

The actions and words of Jesus take place usually in public. Nicodemus, a Pharisee, a 'ruler of the Jews' and 'the teacher of Israel', however, comes to him 'by night' (3.2). Jesus engages with him alone. What is going on here? Earlier, we discussed how individual characters in this Gospel represent a type of faith-or-lack-of-faith response to Jesus. A character speaking alone with Jesus is not just an individual but is representative of groups or communities. Woven into each of the stories of these representative characters are the language and symbolism of this Gospel. So Nicodemus appears in a sequence of people who come to Jesus.[2] He could be representative of the Jewish leaders and people, who believe in Jesus because of the signs he works, yet were secret believers lacking courage to leave the synagogue or fearing to be cast out of it (9.21–22; 12.42; 16.2).

That Nicodemus is part of a group is clear. He speaks to Jesus in the plural and Jesus speaks to him in the plural. When he first addresses Jesus, he does not say 'I know' but with certainty asserts, 'We know you are a teacher from God' (3.2). His 'we know' suggests a certainty of knowing or knowledge that obscures what Jesus is revealing to him through the images of the 'water and spirit/wind', which are drawn from creation. Later Jesus tells him, '*You* (plural) must be born from above' (3.7). Then Jesus applies the plural to himself and Nicodemus: '*We* speak of what *we* know and testify to what *we* have seen; yet *you* (plural) do not receive our testimony.' Jesus continues speaking to him – '*you*' (plural) – about the earthly and heavenly things that '*you*' (plural) do not believe (3.11–12). From our perspective of being conscious of the earth, the Greek word for 'earthly things' or 'on-Earth-things' is a thought-provoking word because it is made up of two words 'upon' and 'earth' as distinct from 'heavenly things' ('upon' and the 'heaven or sky').[3] Jesus speaks to Nicodemus of 'on-Earth-things': water, the human body and the wind. While he appears not to understand, he is portrayed sympathetically and sensitively. Nicodemus is a sincere seeker after truth who comes to one whom he recognizes as 'a teacher from God'. He receives what he is seeking. However, this teaching means he has to renounce his status as 'a teacher of Israel' and all else that is required to receive the new birth promised (Ezek. 37.15–23 and 37.1–14).

'*The wind blows where it chooses*' (John 3.8)

In his conversation, Jesus said he would bring a renewing and regenerating Spirit. This is not about returning to the womb of one's human mother but about being born of the wild and uncontrollable Spirit. The word translated as Spirit can mean wind, breath or spirit – each is unpredictable, unable to be seen or grasped but essential for life and able to express great power. 'People born from above' (John 3.7) enter into the mystery of the 'reign (*basileia*) of God' (3.3, 5), like the wind that blows where it wills.[4] These 'born from above' are to become a mystery to the world as Jesus is because people do not know from where or to where he comes and goes (7.27–29; 8.14; 9.29; 19.9). Nicodemus is invited to enter into the mystery of the Son of Humanity who must be lifted up so that whoever believes *into* him may have this new and eternal life (3.15).[5]

Birth 'from above' is not an invisible event. It alters a person's place in the world and stance towards the world by aligning him or her with others who are, also, out of step with the world.[6] This birth is from both *water* and spirit. To translate the Greek word expressed as 'born from above' or as 'born again' loses the ambiguity of the original word, for it has both meanings.[7] These words are associated with being from God (3.31; 19.11) and have links with being 'born of the Spirit' (3.6, 8). This recalls the prologue, where those who receive the Word and believe *into*

God's name are born as children of God (1.12–13). Further, being 'born from above' means belonging to a community, as we have seen above in the plural verbs and pronouns used in John 3.1–12. To be 'born from above' requires a decision, a change of stance, an action that has a social dimension as one enters and becomes part of a community of believers.[8] It requires a break with the past – an open crossing of the border in the public act of being born of and immersed in water. While being 'born from above' is a spiritual event, it also requires a change of communal affiliation. It is both a spiritual and a social event.

While Jesus is the human face of God made flesh in our midst, the Spirit is revealed mysteriously as the Breath of God breathing through all creation and through human persons. Jesus is the One on whom the Spirit descends and remains/rests (1.32–33). Jesus gives the Spirit 'without measure' (3.34). Usually the Spirit is described not in human terms (anthropomorphic) but in images taken from the natural world – as breath, wind, water – which preserve 'the otherness' of the Spirit as 'the wind that blows where it wills' (3.8). This resists human tendencies to domesticate the Spirit, who is experienced in the depths of human relationships and in the wilderness and beauty of the natural world. We see yet again 'the Spirit as the *Breath of God who always accompanies the Word*' and 'God creating *with two hands*, that of the Word and that of the Spirit',[9] inviting us to hear *both the cry of the earth and the cry of the marginalized.*

'One of them' (John 7.50)

Nicodemus reappears again in the trial scene when Jesus, his message and ministry are under scrutiny by the chief priests and Pharisees, whose own officers, sent out to arrest him, are overawed by him (7.45–52). Those described as being for Jesus are the crowd. Described as 'one of them', Nicodemus may have been among those religious leaders who regard the crowd as ignorant of the law and cursed (7.49) and who marginalize 'the people of the land'.[10] They are marginalized because of ignorance of the law. Nicodemus speaks up for Jesus by referring to 'our law'. In John, 'the law' is always the law of the Jews or of Moses but never that of Jesus or his disciples. Nicodemus speaks within confines of 'our law' as a 'teacher of Israel' who cannot bring himself completely to Jesus. He is presented as being representative of a group. The struggle with the synagogue permeates, too, for 'secret' Christians like the upper-class Nicodemus (3.2), who have allegiance to Jesus yet who seek accommodation with the synagogue, contrast with the poor beggar born blind who declares his allegiance openly (9.30–33). Our attention is drawn to the community aspect of the Christian faith through Nicodemus, a communal symbolic figure – 'many, even of the authorities, believed *into* him. But because of the Pharisees they did not confess it, for fear they would be put out of the synagogue ... loved human glory more than the glory that comes from God' (12.42–43). The Pharisees are not a monolithic block (9.16). Nicodemus appears yet again in 19.38–42.

'They shall be my people, and I shall be their God' (Ezekiel 37.23)

Against the background of Ezekiel 37.15–23, which looked forward to the coming together again of the northern and southern kingdoms, we have considered Nicodemus, a Pharisee, who as 'ruler of the Jews' and 'the teacher of Israel' is required to give up his status (3.1, 10) in order to meet God in Jesus' barrier-crossing ministry.[11] On the other side of this bitter barrier is the woman of Samaria who meets the long-awaited Messiah and is required to give up her people's distinctive claim to the Samaritan temple and religion (4.7–26). In contrast to Nicodemus, she is not only female but an unnamed outcast without status, a member of a despised people and a poor water-carrier who comes to Jesus at a very different time of the day and engages in a spirited dialogue. A reader must also consider how a representative character's type of faith-or-lack-of-faith response contrasts with another character's response. A significant similarity is the imagery of water in each story.

Oratio (Prayer) → *Contemplatio* (Contemplation) → *Actio* (Action)

- The Spirit, the breath of God, is imaged as 'the wind that blows where it chooses' (John 3.8). Imagine how we who are born of the wild and uncontrollable Spirit are invited and enabled to pray and respond to *both the cry of the earth and the cry of the marginalized*.
- As we move with Jesus on his barrier-crossing ministry, Nicodemus' sense of certainty ('we know') invites us to enter into our knowledge of power, privilege, property and poverty (see Overview for 'p' codes), which might obscure both our hearing and responding to *both the cry of the earth and the cry of the marginalized*.

Lectio/Reading of John 3.16–21

In reading and rereading John 3.16–21, be aware that perceptions of 'the world' may be shaped by a sense of dualism that is often associated with 'the world' in John. A commonly held view is also that 'the world' is restricted to the human world. Likewise, the word 'judgement' conjures up perceptions that may cloud out the theology of self-judgement found in the words of Jesus.

Meditatio/Meditation

John presents 3.16–21 as Jesus' own words to Nicodemus.[12] Some remarkable information is given. Here reflection is offered on two interrelated aspects. The first concerns 3.16 and the second 3.17–21.

'God so loved the world' (John 3.16)

Of his time on the surface of the moon during the Apollo 14 mission in February 1971, Alan Shepard said if before the flight someone had said, '"Are you going to get carried away looking at the Earth from the Moon"? I would have said, "No, no way". But yet when I first looked back at the Earth, standing on the Moon I cried.'[13] It was similar for Apollo 8 and 11 astronaut Jim Lovell: 'We learnt a lot about the Moon, but what we really learnt about was the Earth.'[14] The first person to travel in space in 1961, Yuri Gagarin, exclaimed, 'What beauty. I saw clouds and their shadow on the distant dear Earth ... The water looked like darkish, slightly gleaming spots ... the rich colour spectrum. It is surrounded by a light blue aureole that gradually darkens ...'[15] According to the Apollo 14 astronaut Edgar Mitchell,

> We went to moon as technicians; we returned as humanitarians ... you develop an instant global consciousness, a people orientation, an intense dissatisfaction with the state of the world, and a compulsion to do something about it. From out there on the Moon ... You want to grab a politician by the scruff of the neck and draw him [/her] a quarter of a million miles out and say 'Look at that ...'[16]

Two strands emerge from the experience of these astronauts. One is their surprise at learning about the beauty and mystery of the earth. The other is how they were changed and came to understand the state of the world from a new perspective. According to Neil Armstrong, the first person to walk on the Moon in July 1969, 'Mystery creates wonder and wonder is the basis of [humanity's] desire to understand.'[17] This desire to understand the paradox of the beauty of earth and the state of the world as caused by human persons is a helpful way to deepen our understanding of the 'the world' in the Gospel of John.

In Old Testament Hebrew, what we would call 'the universe' is described as 'heaven and earth', which was created by God's word. Later, the 'world' (*kosmos*) expressed the Greek appreciation of the order of the universe. The 'world' is the reality God so loved that God gave the Son (3.16). The expression 'comes into the world' highlights the physical universe and is associated with Jesus, the light who has 'come into the world' (1.9; 3.19; 12.46). Another take on 'coming into the world' relates to Jesus as the Messiah (6.14; 9.39; 11.27; 16.28). It is like a technical term for the work of Jesus. 'To be sent into the world' is used of Jesus (3.17; 10.36). The disciples and Christians today are drawn into these works of God when at the supper Jesus prays, 'As you have sent me into the world, so I have sent them into the world' (17.18). The 'world' (*kosmos*) can mean more than the physical universe. It may refer to that universe as related to humankind. In this sense, 'the world' suggests a creation that is able to respond (see section on John 1.10–11).

Being with Jesus is about enduring relationships of abiding (14.10; 15.4–10). In the outpouring of the Holy Spirit, who 'abides with you and will be in you' (14.17), and the work of his disciples, the risen Jesus continues to abide with us in the world that God loved. This is what the Trinity is about – relationship. The Eastern Church has a word for this: *perichoresis* (*peri*, around; *chorea*, dance), which suggests a being-in-one-another, a continuous dynamic interaction between persons mutually permeating each other, interdependence, the divine dance, the mystery of the one communion of all persons in diversity, divine as well as human. For Catherine Lacugna, the doctrine of the Trinity is not 'a teaching about "God" but a teaching about *God's life with us and our life with each other*'.[18] Further, uniquely, John's Gospel tells of eternal life being experienced *now* in the world God so loved. In relationship to the world in all its senses, humankind has the potential to respond with awe and wonder. Such a response to beauty changes the ones who see the *now* in a new perspective, and fires the human imagination to abide in, care for and protect the earth and the whole earth community.

'Their works have been done in God' (John 3.21)

God did not send Jesus to judge the world but to save it (3.17; cf. 8.15; 12.47). 'To judge' (*krinein*) and 'judgement' (*krisis*) are two expressions that appear here for the first time in the narrative (3.17–19). A theology of self-judgement is one of John's contributions to Christian thought.[19] Rather than wait for the Son of Humanity who will return in final judgement at the end of time as in Matthew 25.31–46 (traditional eschatology), human persons judge themselves, in the present, by accepting or refusing the ongoing revelation of God made flesh in Jesus Christ and by the 'works [that] have been done in God' (3.21) or bad works (3.19) that flow from this decision.

There is a tendency for us to connect those people who 'are judged already' (3.18) because their works are evil with behaviour that western morality would see as bad. This is not the case. In the cultural context of this time, there is frequent, clear biblical evidence and evidence elsewhere that 'good works' and 'evil works' were technical terms 'with precise and limited meanings'. Walter Grundmann tells us: 'Good works are actions of mercy on behalf of all those in need of them, and they are works of peacemaking that eliminate discord among people.'[20] This is shown not only in Matthew 25.31–46 and 5.38–48 but also in the Old Testament (Isa. 58.6–7; Micah 6.8) and in the New Testament (Mark 3.4; 1 Tim. 5.10, 25; 6.18). In the only description of the Last Judgement in the New Testament (Matt. 25.31–46), the only criterion is good or evil works. The God of the Old Testament is certainly not neutral towards the poor and needy. In John, the works of Jesus are not merely related to good works, they consist in good works. The unbelief of the world towards Jesus is expressed by 'its denial of food to the hungry and drink to the thirsty'.[21] It is timely to recall Sandra Schneiders' suggestion when we discussed John 1.9–10 'that the "world" with which we are concerned ... [is] the *good world* to which we are missioned, the *evil world* which we confront, and the *alternative* world'.[22] With Jesus, we are called into an alternative world of God's ongoing re-creation to play our part in finishing the works of God by hearing *both the cry of the earth and the cry of the marginalized*, as we shall further explore in this Gospel.

Oratio (Prayer) → *Contemplatio* (Contemplation) → *Actio* (Action)

- John's Gospel tells of eternal life being experienced *now* in the world God so loved. In the experience of beauty, humankind has the potential to respond with awe, wonder and respect. In contrast, Pope Francis points out that 'The earth, our home, is beginning to look more and more like an immense pile of filth' (*LS* §66). What changes can be made in my life to make a difference?
- Human persons judge themselves, in the present, by accepting or refusing the ongoing revelation of God made flesh in Jesus Christ and by the 'works [that] have been done in God' (3.21) or evil works (3.19) that flow from this decision. Maybe look back over your last week and bring to prayer your self-judgement of how you have responded to the *both the cry of the earth and the cry of the marginalized*.

Notes

1 On Ezekiel 37.15–23, for the parallel between Nicodemus and the woman of Samaria, see Stephen Motyer, 1995, 'Jesus and the Marginalised in the Fourth Gospel', in *Mission and Meaning: Essays Presented to Peter Cotterell*, Antony Billington, Tony Lane and Max Turner (eds), Carlisle: Paternoster Press, pp. 77–8. See also Linda Belleville, 1980, 'Born of Water and the Spirit: John 3:5', *Trinity Journal* 1.2, pp. 125–40.

2 For an overview of how 'Nicodemus the Marginalizer Becomes a Disciple', see the chapter in Robert J. Karris, 1990, *Jesus and the Marginalized in John's Gospel*, Collegeville: Liturgical Press, pp. 96–101.

3 The Greek word (*epigeia*) for 'earthly things' or 'on-Earth-things' comes from 'upon' (*epi*) and 'earth' (*gē*), as distinct from 'heavenly things' (*epi* 'upon' and *ouranos* 'heaven' or 'sky'); see Margaret Daly-Denton, 2017, *John: An Earth Bible Commentary: Supposing Him to be the Gardener*, London: Bloomsbury T&T Clark, p. 75.

4 The 'Reign (or kingdom) of God' which is central to the message of Jesus in the Synoptic Gospels occurs only twice in this Gospel (John 3.3, 5).

5 In the title of Jesus, 'Son of Man', the word translated as 'man' is not *anēr* (man), which means man in contrast to woman, but *anthrōpos*, which means the human person as a living being, or humanity. Therefore, I shall translate this title as 'Son of Humanity'.

6 David Rensberger, 1998, *Johannine Faith and Liberating Community*, Philadelphia PA: Westminster, p. 70. On Nicodemus, see pp. 37–41, 52–63, 66–70, and Motyer, 'Jesus and the Marginalised', p. 77.

7 Brendan Byrne SJ, 2014, *Life Abounding: A Reading of John's Gospel*, Collegeville MN: Liturgical Press, pp. 64–71. The Greek word *anōthen* means both 'born from above' and 'born again'. For this reason, Byrne (p. 65) leaves 'the word qualifying "born" in transliteration because once it is translated its ambiguity in the original is lost'.

8 Rensberger, *Johannine Faith*, pp. 68–9.

9 Dennis Edwards, 2004, *Breath of Life: A Theology of the Creator Spirit*, Maryknoll NY: Orbis, pp. 26, 40 (italics his).

10 Karris, *Jesus and the Marginalized*, p. 97.

11 Motyer, 'Jesus and the Marginalised', p. 77.

12 English translations of John 3.16–17 insert the pronoun 'his' where the Greek has the definite article, 'the' to describe the relationship between God/Father and son; see Kathleen P. Rushton, 2011, *The Parable of the Woman in Childbirth of John 16:21: A Metaphor for the Death and Glorification of Jesus*, Lewiston NY: The Edwin Mellen Press, p. 226.

13 Alan Shepard, quoted in www.nmspacemuseum.org/halloffame/detail.php?id=55 (accessed 18.07.19).

14 Jim Lovell, quoted in Patricia Lund, 2011, *Massively Networked: How the Convergence of Social Media and Technology is Changing Your Life*, San Francisco CA: PLI Media, p. 138.

15 Yuri Gagarin, quoted in www.nmspacemuseum.org/halloffame/detail.php?id=8 (accessed 18.07.19).

16 Edgar Mitchell, quoted in www.nmspacemuseum.org/halloffame/detail.php?id=45 (accessed 18.07.19).

17 Neil Armstrong, quoted in www.azquotes.com/quote/10823 (accessed 18.07.19).

18 Catherine Mowry Lacugna, 1992, *God for Us: The Trinity and Christian Life*, New York: HarperCollins, p. 35 (italics hers).

19 On John's sense of self-judgement as translated by 'condemn' (*krinein* and *krisis*), see Francis J. Moloney, 1998, *The Gospel of John*, Sacra Pagina Series 4, Collegeville MN: Liturgical Press, p. 102.

20 On 'good works' and 'evil works', see José Porfirio Miranda, 1997, *Being and the Messiah: The Message of St. John*, John Eagleson (trans.), Maryknoll NY: Orbis, pp. 96–100. He quotes Walter Grundmann on p. 97.

21 Miranda, *Being and the Messiah*, p. 99.

22 Sandra M. Schneiders, 2013, *Buying the Field: Catholic Religious Life in the Mission to the World*, Mahwah NJ: Paulist Press, p. 37.

Samaria
Living Water – John 4.5–42

'Living water' (John 4.11)

Third Sunday of Lent of Years ABC (RL)
Third Sunday in Lent of Years A (RCL)
John 4.5–42

Lectio/Reading of John 4.5–42

'Look around you and see', declares Jesus (4.34). In reading and rereading John 4.5–42, see the interplay between the 'on-Earth-things' (3.12) and the marginalized woman whom Jesus meets as he moves on his barrier-crossing ministry into Samaria. Those who read his story today live in a world where 785 million people do not have access to safe water.[1]

Meditatio/Meditation

Jesus, in his barrier-crossing ministry of reconciliation, moves across social barriers to create a new community when he calls the nationalist Nathanael, the 'true Israelite' who is searching for a new king of Israel (John 1.47), and the Pharisee Nicodemus (3.1–21), a named Jewish man of status, who comes to Jesus by night. Nicodemus is representative of those who believe in secret. Jesus, now, moves from Jerusalem to Samaria, where he meets a woman who is marginalized religiously and by poverty (4.7–26). Along with the other characters with whom Jesus engages alone, she represents a type of faith-or-lack-of-faith response to him. For the implications of the stories of John 3—4 being placed side by side, see the beginning of the discussion of John 3 above.

While the motif of water in John is less consistent than that of light and darkness, like a 'stream on a hillside, it maintains a general direction of movement while conforming to the contours of the narrative through which it flows'.[2] Water's significance is usually connected to washing or drinking. Water is poured in baptism, fills the jars in Cana, is used of rebirth by Jesus when speaking to Nicodemus, collected in a well, flowing in spring water, found in the pools of Bethzatha and Siloam, crossed in the Sea of Galilee, washes feet and flows from Jesus' side.

Living water from an overflowing well – John 4.4–42

Creation and revelation are intimately linked for the universe is a treasure trove of symbols revealing God. In the symbol of living water, Jesus invites us into the mystery of creation to enter into the mystery of the Word who became flesh, the flesh of all living creatures.[3] He explains, 'I came that they may have life, and have it abundantly' (10.10). Living water is universal. It is necessary for all forms of life and for the search for life. Its multiple meanings come from many contexts, which include cosmic and local contexts.

The cosmic story of water began 13.8 billion years ago with hydrogen emerging in the first moments after the Big Bang.[4] Millions of years later, oxygen emerged. When hydrogen and oxygen met finally, water enabled new possibilities of creativity. Water assisted the forming of earth, cooled and enveloped earth with a fluid blanket, which permitted creativity to flourish. As vapour, water permeates the atmosphere. As liquid, water forms the clouds of the atmosphere, falls as rain and covers most of earth's surface with oceans. In its solid state, frozen water falls as sleet and snow, covers mountains and forms the polar caps.

Human persons, like other mammals, are about 70 per cent water.[5] Vital systems function because of water. Water maintains interconnections within each living cell and by the intercellular fluids between the cells of a whole organism. Water keeps essential ingredients in suspension until it is needed by a cell. Water's capacity to dissolve diffuses waste from the cell. The same life force maintained by water is replicated in every living being, as Linda Gibler summarizes: 'Creation is water-drenched. All living beings on Earth are born of water – in oceans or ponds, within eggs, seeds or wombs.'[6]

Each person lives in a local context. Mine is Canterbury, Aotearoa New Zealand, which has, or had, exceptionally pure water flowing from the mountains in interconnected spaces across the plains and out to sea. Some water surfaces as springs and rivulets, which flow into streams and rivers. The rest remains buried as groundwater and moves eastwards on its way towards the sea, which takes a century or more. The groundwater in these aquifers are the habitat of some 500 different species of minute invertebrate animals that filter the groundwater. As irrigation for cropping and dairying expands, so does the pressure on the rivers and groundwater aquifers. Living water is contested. In the Canterbury region, and elsewhere, there is conflict over water.

'But he had to go through Samaria' (John 4.4)

Samaria, through which Jesus 'had to go', has been a region of conflict.[7] The ancient town of Sychar, 'near the plot of ground that Jacob had given to his son Joseph' (4.5), was called Shechem. This name comes from the Hebrew: 'I now give to you one portion (*shekim*) more than your brothers' (Gen. 48.22). Some traditions tell of Jacob's peaceful coming to Shechem.[8] Others tell of livestock, property and trade leading to breakdowns in the relationships between his clan and the clan from whom he purchased the land.

The unnamed Samaritan woman, whom I shall call Photini – as she is known in the Eastern Church – comes at noon, the brightest time of the day.[9] Over and over again, we hear commentators and preachers tell us that she is a sinner. She goes at that time to avoid the other women, they tell us. John tells of light and darkness, which in this Gospel are symbolic of believing and not believing. In the beginning, the Word came to be 'the light of all people' and 'the light shines in the darkness, and the darkness did not overcome it' (1.4–5). Jesus tells us: 'I am the light of the world. Whoever follows me will never walk in darkness but will have the light of life' (John 8.12). Those of the light understand the purpose of this gospel, 'that you may come to believe that Jesus is the Messiah, the Son of God, and that through believing you may have life in his name' (20.31). Interpreters of this story get caught up with speculation about Photini's husbands. Overlooked totally is her plight as a poor woman attending to the task of carrying water over a great distance for the benefit of others.[10] In her female role of water carrier, she is caught in a system that demands hard physical work. This is the lot of poor women and girls today.[11]

Photini engages in a robust theological dialogue with Jesus on Samaritan traditions. He is seen by the woman within the tradition of the prophets who speak of Israel's relationship with God in terms of spousal imagery. If the woman is representative of her people, as is likely, the five husbands may well symbolize the worship of the gods of the five foreign tribes (2 Kings 17.13–34) and Samaria's departure from the law. Jesus infers that Photini's present husband 'is not your husband' (John 4.18). The words of Jesus evoke classic prophetic denunciations (e.g. Hosea 2.2). Interestingly, in encounters involving other biblical women at wells, such as Rachel's midday meeting with Jacob (Gen. 29.7), there are no references to their immorality. Sexual literalism does not take seriously the symbolic significance of the woman's story, which is woven into the very fabric of this Gospel.

'Living water' (John 4.14)

Samaria is dotted with natural aquifers deep under the earth, which surfaced in springs and met the needs of nomads.[12] Jacob may have dug a well or bought a field with a well or spring. At some stage he asserts his rights over this water source in a way that excludes others; in other words, what is practised in today's privatization of water. A significant subtlety highlights two understandings of water. When the woman describes the well (*phrear*), the word means 'still water' (John 4.11–12). This had been separated from its source by being collected and stored in a cistern or pool. 'Living water' is wild water from a river or spring. 'Spring' (*pēgē*) is used twice (4.6) to refer to Jacob's well: when Jesus is sitting by this well and again when he speaks of 'living water' (4.14).

When requested to give Jesus a drink, Photini replied, 'How is it that you, a Jew, ask a drink of me, a woman of Samaria?' (4.9). Behind her words are centuries of hostile separation between their peoples. The spring-fed well of their common ancestor is to provide 'living water' for all. Yet, over centuries, land made valuable because of this water was held in private ownership by succeeding generations. Is the living water of our physical environment polluted because we are drying up spiritually? Do we drink deeply of 'a spring of water welling up to eternal life' to enable transformation and change?

Releasing living water

The encounter between the Jew and the Samaritan released water for the thirsty. Restrictions imposed on the water are released.[13] The water is freed from economic and legal ownership restrictions. In response to Jesus' presence and request, Photini responds. Where thirst is concerned, proprietary rights and separation must give way. Photini transcends the privatization of water.

Excavations of what may be Jacob's well show that it was very deep in order to reach a hidden spring. Jewish legends tell of Jacob's well *flowing* to offer life to all. One legend tells of its water overflowing when Jacob removed its stone covering. According to another, so much water was flowing from this well that it flowed into the wilderness, thus keeping the people and their animals alive in their wandering. Early Christians must have known of these traditions, for in the scene from the Roman

Catacomb of St Callistus, Photini is bucketing water from an *overflowing* well and standing in its *flowing* waters.[14]

'I thirst' (John 19.28)

Reading from the perspective of thirst, Jesus the fountain/spring of 'living water' cries out just before his death, 'I thirst' (19.28). The time of his meeting with Photini is 'at the sixth hour' (usually translated as 'noon') and seems to be linked with the time of his crucifixion at 'the sixth hour' (4.6; 19.14). This link is further supported when later Jesus speaks of 'the hour' (4.23). In this Gospel, 'the hour' is an image for Jesus' death at which he 'handed over the Spirit', and later the Church is created when the blood and the water flow from his side (19.30, 34).[15]

Living water is a gift (4.10), a gift of earth, a wonder and a necessity nurturing all interconnected life, yet today it is privatized, bottled and endangered. Jesus' cry, 'I thirst', echoes through time. His sisters and brothers cry out, 'I thirst'. Let us recall the depiction of Photini standing in *flowing* waters from an *overflowing* well. Her encounter with Jesus frees and releases for all. This woman drank from 'the water I will give' that becomes in her 'a spring of water welling up to eternal life'. She is a called disciple, the only one in this Gospel to leave tools of trade. She leaves her water jar behind (4.28), as Matthew leaves his tax table (Matt. 9.9) and Peter and others leave their boats (Mark 1.18). The woman is a fine example of mission because, in John, people are led to Jesus by another. She leads her own people to Jesus. She tells them of her experience.[16] They then come to believe themselves: 'we believe, for we have heard for ourselves' (John 4.42). To what extent is this pattern of leading people to Jesus in our lives?

Jesus' mission is to 'complete the works of God'. These words are found within Photini's story (4.34), in the ministry of Jesus (5.36), in his prayer (17.4), on the cross and in his last words (19.28, 30). How are these words found in the gospel of our lives? Like John (known as the Baptizer), the woman precedes the disciples as a witness, which is a key word in John. Later, after the Last Supper, Jesus prays 'on behalf of those who will *believe in me through their word*' (17.20). This echoes the words about the missionary activity of Photini in 4.39, where 'many Samaritans ... believed in him through the words of the woman bearing witness' (literal translation of the Greek). How do we action this prayer of Jesus for us – for those who believe in him through the words of our bearing witness?

'The Saviour of the world' (4.42)

In Photini's witnessing to Jesus among her townsfolk, there is movement in how he is seen. She recognizes Jesus as a human person and as the Messiah (4.29). Through her words of witness and from the action of Jesus ('he stayed [abided] there for two days' (4.40)), her people come to know that Jesus is 'the Saviour of the world' (4.42). We have learnt already that Jesus' work is that 'the world might be saved through him' (3.17). The title 'saviour' (*sōtēr*) was widely used in the ancient world.[17] God is the one who saved the people during the Babylonian exile (Isa. 43.3, 11; 45.15, 21–22). 'Saviour' was used for gods such as Zeus and, in feminine form, for the goddess Artemis. It was used of high officials who benefitted the people. There was widespread use of 'saviour' throughout the Roman Empire for the emperor. Such diverse use means caution is needed to link 'the Saviour of the world' (4.42) only with the Roman emperor. That said, this text attributes to Jesus a title of the emperor and does so in a scene with many layers of meaning – especially in relation to five significant factors, as we shall explore below.[18]

First, when 'Saviour' is used for God it appears in situations with political and anti-imperial associations. God is intervening to save the people from imperial powers, as when freeing exiles from the power of the Babylonians (Isa. 45.15, 21). Second, the scene of the Samaritans going out of Sychar to meet Jesus, welcoming him into their town and calling him 'Saviour of the World', was similar to ancient descriptions of welcoming rulers (cf. Jesus' entry into Jerusalem in John 12.12–19). Third, in seeking to reconcile Jews and Samaritans, both Jesus and Photini are not just individuals but are representatives of their peoples – they discuss worship, which is an issue of national identity and power (4.19–22). The plural is used of the Samaritans in John 4.20 when Photini speaks of '*our* ancestors [who] worshipped on this mountain' and 'you' (plural) refers to the Jewish people. This 'our'/'you' (plural) language continues in 4.20–22. Jesus calls Photini and her people into God's inclusive new community. Fourth, referred to above were the 'five husbands' (4.18), who recall the five nations or empires that had colonized Samaria (2 Kings 17.24). The sixth husband ('the one you have now') is the Roman Empire, with which Samaria experienced serious ongoing conflict. Fifth, we have seen how 'the world' can suggest those who oppose God's purposes (see section on John 1.10–11). The title 'Saviour of the world' recognizes that Jesus is the one who shows God's sovereignty over the nations. According this title to Jesus contests the right of the emperor to it.

Photini may be representative of Samaritan Christians, whom Jewish Christians had to struggle to accept because of the long enmity between them. In the Gospel itself, the seven named male disciples, along with

Mary, Martha and Lazarus of Bethany and all other characters, are presumably Jews. This Gospel is embodied in people struggling with the religious and political tensions of the late first century. Likewise, we who read it today are immersed in those same tensions in our own time and place. Jesus in his barrier-crossing ministry of reconciliation calls the Samaritans into his new community.[19] Warren Carter sees the Samaritans' confession that Jesus is 'the Saviour of the world' as an example for the believers in Ephesus to follow.[20] Once again, we see where a 'genuinely subversive consciousness' can be found in the radical Jesus of this gospel story.[21] All who ponder this story are invited into the mystery, the intimacy, the mission and transformation of relationship with Jesus, so that 'The water I will give will become in them a spring of water welling up to eternal life' (4.14).

Oratio (Prayer) → *Contemplatio* (Contemplation) → *Actio* (Action) →

- Readers are invited to apply the words of Jesus, 'If you knew the gift of God' (4.10), to the consumption and sustainability of clean water in their local area, and maybe to do some research on this. Living water is a gift of the earth, a wonder and a necessity nurturing all interconnected life, yet today it is privatized, bottled and endangered. Every person needs a sustainable supply of clean water for drinking, washing, cooking and cleaning. It is a basic human right.[22]
- In *contemplatio*/contemplation, sit with the reality that today we read this story in a world where 785 million people do not have access to safe water. In the Introduction, contemplation and action were discussed. Contemplation enables us to sit with what we may resist and to appropriate the reality of injustice, absorbing its impact. Feelings and thoughts arise by 'sitting with' it. The experience reshapes us. Working with it leads us out of ourselves and often moves our hands and feet to act. For Dean Brackley, 'Sitting with reality, allowing it to work on us, working through the feelings and the thoughts it stirs is what we mean by *contemplation*.'[23]

Notes

1 WHO/UNICEF Joint Monitoring Programme (JMP) Report 2019, www.wateraid.org/facts-and-statistics (accessed 10.10.19).

2 Craig K. Koester, 2003, *Symbolism in the Fourth Gospel: Meaning, Mystery, Community*, 2nd edn, Minneapolis MN: Augsburg Fortress, p. 176.

3 On John 4.5–42 I draw on my article, Kathleen P. Rushton, 2018, 'Waterlings from Water: Exploring a Cosmological Reading of "Living Water" in John 4.4–42 amidst the Braided Rivers of Canterbury, Aotearoa New Zealand', in Nicola Hoggard Creegan and Andrew Shepherd (eds), *Creation and Hope: Reflections on Ecological Anticipation and Action from Aotearoa New Zealand*, Eugene OR: Pickwick Publications, pp. 90–108.

4 On the early universe and origins of water, see Philip Ball, 2001, *Life's Matrix: A Biography of Water*, Berkeley CA: University of California Press. For an overview, see Linda Gibler, 2010, *From the Beginning to Baptism: Scientific and Sacred Stories of Water, Oil, and Fire*, Collegeville MN: Liturgical Press, pp. 3–11.

5 Gibler, *From the Beginning*, p. 10.

6 Gibler, *From the Beginning*, p. 2.

7 Joseph Fitzmyer, 1981, *The Gospel According to Luke (I–IX)*, Anchor Bible 28, Garden City NY: Doubleday, p. 629.

8 Jerome H. Neyrey, 1979, 'Jacob Traditions and the Interpretation of John 4:10–26', *Catholic Biblical Quarterly* 41.3, pp. 419–37.

9 In the Orthodox Liturgy, the Feast of St Photini and St Phota is on 26 February. See Satoko Yamaguchi, 2002, *Mary and Martha: Women in the World of Jesus*, Maryknoll NY: Orbis, pp. 32–3. B. F. Westcott, 1903, *The Gospel According to St. John*, London: John Murray, p. 68, states that in later legends she was called Photina.

10 I have found only three interpreters who refer to Photini being a poor water-carrier: Luise Schottroff, 1998, 'The Samaritan Woman and the Notions of Sexuality in the Fourth Gospel', in F. F. Segovia (ed.), *'What is John?' Volume II: Literary and Social Readings of the Fourth Gospel*, Atlanta GA: Scholars Press, pp. 157–81; Alan Cadwallader, 2011, '"Give the Girl a Drink": Reading John 4 from a Dry, Parched Land', in *Water: A Matter of Life and Death*, Norman Habel and Peter Trudinger (eds), *Interface* 14.1, pp. 97–100; and Christiana Z. Peppard, 2014, *Just Water: Theology, Ethics, and the Global Water Crisis*, Maryknoll NY: Orbis, pp. 179–80. The only commentary I have found that mentions she is poor because she draws water is Westcott, *Gospel According to St. John*, p. 68.

11 Water shortage most affects women and girls; see Wateraid, www.wateraid.org/us/what-we-do-gender-equality (accessed 10.10.19).

12 Jerome Murphy-O'Connor, 1998, *The Holy Land: An Oxford Archaeological Guide from Earliest Times to 1700*, 4th edn, Oxford: Oxford University Press, pp. 372–3.

13 Cadwallader, '"Give the Girl a Drink"', pp. 107–10.

14 For a coloured photograph of the third-century image of Jesus and the woman at the well in the Chapel of the Sacraments in the Roman Catacomb of St Callistus, see Pierre du Bourguet, 1971, *Early Christian Art*, Thomas Burton (trans.), New York: William Morrow and Company, p. 31.

15 On translating John 19.30 as he 'handed over the Spirit' rather than 'gave up his spirit', see the section on John 19.30 in this book.

16 In Photini's invitation to her townsfolk, 'Come and see a man ...', the word

translated as 'man' is not *anēr* (man), which means man in contrast to woman, but *anthrōpos*, which means the human person as a living being, or humanity.

17 On the significance of the 'Saviour (*sōtēr*) of the World' in the context of the Roman Empire, see Warren Carter, 2008, *John and Empire: Initial Explorations*, New York: T&T Clark, p. 188. On Pilate and the role of Roman Governor, see pp. 188–91.

18 Carter, *John and Empire*, pp. 188–91.

19 Stephen Motyer, 1995, 'Jesus and the Marginalised in the Fourth Gospel', in *Mission and Meaning: Essays Presented to Peter Cotterell*, Antony Billington, Tony Lane and Max Turner (eds), Carlisle: Paternoster Press, p. 76.

20 Carter, *John and Empire*, p. 191.

21 David Rensberger, 1998, *Johannine Faith and Liberating Community*, Philadelphia PA: Westminster, p. 129.

22 WHO/UNICEF, JMP, www.wateraid.org/facts-and-statistics.

23 Dean Brackley, 2004, *The Call to Discernment in Troubled Times: New Perspectives on the Transformative Wisdom of Ignatius of Loyola*, New York: Crossroad, p. 22 (emphasis his).

Jerusalem
Cry of the Marginalized – John 5.1–47

'My father is still working and I also am working' (John 5.17)

Sixth Sunday of Easter of Year C (RCL)
John 5.1–9
(John 5.19–47 – Discourses)

Lectio/Reading of John 5.1–18

In reading and reading the story of the man at the pool of Bethesda (5.1–18), we may notice that this story begins by telling us that Jesus the pilgrim 'went up to Jerusalem' to continue his barrier-crossing ministry – be aware of the barriers he is crossing.

Meditatio/Meditation

By the end of John 1—4, Jesus has moved across social barriers to Nathanael, Nicodemus and the woman of Samaria – all characters from conflicting groups.[1] Jesus, the One who gives new life, attracts a variety of faith responses. This is further developed in John 5—12, which is set in the context of Jewish festivals that follow the seasons of the year – an unnamed festival (5.1), Passover (6.4), Booths (7.2), Dedication (10.22) and Passover (12.1) – and against the background of increasing hostility to Jesus. It is significant that this section contains stories of two people marginalized by chronic illness (5.1–18; 9.1–41). John 5 comprises three units: the healing of the man at the pool of Bethesda on the Sabbath (5.1–18); a discourse in two parts: Life and Judgement – Jesus' Authority (5.19–30); and Witness and Accusation (5.31–47). Although only John 5.1–9 is proclaimed from the RCL, this passage will be considered within the wider context of John 5 to enable *the cry of the earth and the cry of the marginalized* to be heard. After an overview of evidence from the Scriptures for the marginalization of those with physical afflictions, we shall look at how John describes this man's illness and then at the man's response to Jesus.

'My strength is diminished in my poverty' (Ps. 31.10)

The Scriptures speak often of those with chronic illnesses and afflictions.[2] The lament psalms link physical affliction and incapacity with poverty, as shown in a literal translation of Psalm 31.10: 'My strength is diminished in my poverty and my bones waste away.' The poetry of Job 29.12–17 links the poor with sickness and incapacity. Again and again, the condition of the poor is seen side by side with illness, affliction, loneliness and approaching death. Restrictions apply to those who may offer worship. They must be without bodily defects. No one may offer sacrifice who is blemished, blind, lame, has a mutilated face; has 'a limb too long' or a broken foot or hand; is a hunchback or a dwarf; has blemished eyes, an itching disease, scabs or crushed testicles (Lev. 22.17–23). Nevertheless, despite such prescriptions, God sides consistently with the oppressed, the poor, marginalized and outcast. They receive God's special care and attention. In our times, as in ancient times, those afflicted by chronic illness are pushed aside to the margins of society and religion by the healthy and by those who control access to the centres of public life and religion.

At an unnamed festival, Jesus goes up to Jerusalem as a pilgrim, as he will do several times in the narrative. Water features again in the narrative. Near the Sheep Gate, a gate to the temple precinct (Neh. 3.1), was the pool of Bethesda, which in this story is associated with healing.[3] This pool was close to five porticoes, a public place where the blind, lame and paralysed gathered. The water of the pool 'is troubled' (John 5.7; cf. 11.33; 12.27; 13.21). The same language is used of the waters in Psalm 77.16 (LXX, Ps. 76.17) when God leads the people 'like a flock by the hand of Moses and Aaron' (Ps. 77.20). There seems to be a hint of Jesus the Good Shepherd being there for the sheep – the poor and afflicted – near the Sheep Gate. Certainly in John 9, the healed man is one of the sheep and Jesus is the sheep gate (10.1–4, 7–9). Does this healing of one who was lame signal the messianic age (Isa. 35.6)?

Once again, we need to let John be John.[4] Many of the ways used to describe sickness in the other Gospels are not found in John.[5] There is no reference to illness through evil spirits. The adjective 'healthy' ('well') is used six times (5.6, 9, 11, 14, 15; 7.23). The word for 'invalids' (5.3) can mean a lack of strength and suggests weakness. It is used for the poor in Proverbs ('If you close your ear to the cry of the poor …' (21.13; cf. 22.22; 31.5, 9)). To describe what the other Gospels call the 'mighty wonders' (miracles), John has the seven 'signs' (2.1–11; 4.46–54; 5.1–15;

6.1–15; 6.16–21; 9.1–41; 11.1–44). Throughout this Gospel, these signs are recalled and referred back to in a kind of refrain, as when in John 6.2 the narrator refers back to the signs of 4.46–54 and to our story of 5.1–15.

Having considered the biblical background to physical disability and John's particular approach to it, we turn to John 5.1–15, where this representative outsider at times parallels, or contrasts, with other characters. As we explore this story, we will discover it is related closely to the story of the beggar born blind in John 9.1–41. There are also some links made with Nicodemus.

'And I am also working' (John 5.17)

Behind the story of this most puzzling of John's characters is the identity of Jesus. The story begins with Jesus healing on the Sabbath and leads to conflict with the authorities. Although the Sabbath is associated with rest, God still has to complete the ongoing work of sustaining creation. God blessed the seventh day and made it holy (Gen. 2.1–3). What the Sabbath represents would only happen in the world-to-come. Until then, that reality is glimpsed tantalizingly in the Sabbath.[6] This links with the biblical 'promises concerning a better future' we discussed in the Overview. While the man would have been excluded from the sacred areas of the temple, he and others like him would have been admitted to some of its precincts. Many similarities exist between the two nameless, poor characters healed by Jesus. Both suffer from long-term disabilities (5.5; 9.1). The settings involve a pool of water in central Jerusalem (5.2; 9.7). Both incidents occur on the Sabbath, lead to disagreement with the religious leadership and discussion about the identity and authority of Jesus, sin and works (5.19–47; 9.9–41). Jesus engages in a follow-up with each one who is healed (5.14; 9.35). Each healed one engages with the Jews (5.10–13; 11.24–34). These obvious similarities between the man by the pool and the poor blind beggar are interwoven with crucial differences.

Jesus takes the initiative by asking the ill man if he wishes to be healed. The man is evasive. He does not state that he wishes to be healed. He blames his condition on others. No one is there to help him into the pool when the water is stirred up. Jesus persists and instructs him, 'Stand up, take your mat and walk.' The man is healed and complies with what Jesus tells him to do (5.9). The sign is verified by a third party when the Jews enter the scene to confront the man for violating the Sabbath by carrying his meagre sleeping mat. The man tells them that he does not know who the one is who had cured him or where he is.

This incident departs from what usually happens in miracle stories. The man is passive. He is not said to believe as do the disciples (2.11) or the official and his household (4.53). Nicodemus and this unnamed man are the only two characters introduced by the formula, 'There was a man' (3.1; 5.5). This suggests that, like that named one of status, this nameless one does not come to faith in Jesus. It is possible that those long 38 years he had lain by the pool parallel the period of the time of the Israelites in Egypt (Deut. 2.14) or even that he had lain there for most of the years it took for the temple construction (5.5; 2.20). This man, like the beggar born blind, is marginalized from the temple cult, which excludes him rather than cares from him. By the time this Gospel is written, the temple has been destroyed. Maybe John's community is being encouraged to reach out to those whose religion and culture are no longer able to care for them.

After Jesus finds him in the temple, the man goes back and tells 'the Jews that it was Jesus who made him well' (5.15). While the previously blind beggar relishes being freed by Jesus and stands up for him against the religious leaders, this healed man does not. He joins forces with them against one who had set him free. This leads to the first open declaration of hostility towards Jesus 'because he was doing such things on the sabbath' (5.16). It is expressed in such a way as to suggest it is not just a single action. Jesus is doing these things repeatedly. At the core of the controversy is that his healing on the Sabbath implies 'a close association – or even an identification – with God's ongoing parental work of sustaining creation in being and bringing it to wholeness' (5.18).[7] The outcome of this incident is that the religious authorities seek to kill Jesus. Two charges of violation of the Sabbath (5.16) and blasphemy (5.18) are made against Jesus. The Evangelist is deeply grounded in reality and is not romantic.[8] Even marginalized characters liberated by Jesus from illness and exclusion are not automatically going to embrace a demanding journey of faith.

'Whatever the father does, the son does likewise' (John 5.19)

The previous two sign stories of 2.1–11 and 4.46–54 are brief and self-contained. In this they are similar to those of the Synoptic Gospels. However, from now onwards, mostly after the accounts of signs, Jesus engages in a discourse (5.19–47; 6.22–59) or series of dialogues (9.9–41; 11.7–37). In a discourse of two parts, Life and Judgement – Jesus' Authority (5.19–30), and Witness and Accusation (5.31–47), which follows the healing of the man at the pool, Jesus responds to charges against him about his authority to heal and his relationship with God.

The Gospel of John's father–son relationship is influenced by, and is embedded in, first-century social conventions. The total dependence of a son on a father socially, economically and culturally in Graeco-Roman and Jewish societies led to the understanding that a son is the most suitable agent to attend to the father's business. By implication, the son's interests are those of the father. The activity of Jesus is portrayed as that of a human agent who acts on behalf of the Father. This understanding is captured in John 5.19–20a, which has been called a hidden parable: 'the son can do nothing on his own, but only what he sees the father doing; for whatever that one does, the son does likewise. The father loves the son and shows him all that he himself is doing.'

In these two verses we have a simple glimpse of a son who is apprenticed to his father's trade. The son watches his father working and imitates him. The background to this is found in a society where crafts are hereditary and passed down from father to son. It would be entirely normal for a father who is an artisan to teach the skills of his trade to his son. These two verses might be called the Parable of the Son as an Apprentice.[9] The apprentice watches his father at work, working with his hands. It describes Jesus, who was himself both a carpenter and a carpenter's son. His words here may echo his experience as a youth working with wood in the workshop at Nazareth. The understanding of kinship that permeates the context of the time of Jesus would see a father as ensuring all that was needed for life. Against the background of the Genesis creation story, this Gospel places great emphasis on God as ongoing creator and sustainer of all life. Creation is unfinished. Biblical 'promises for a better future'[10] unfold as God has promised to create 'new heavens and a new earth' (Isa. 65.17; 66.22). In this context, the image of the father unfolds as an image for God as creator and sustainer of life.[11] The images of God working, of Jesus working (5.17) and of Jesus being shown even greater works (5.20b) frame the parable. Later, Jesus refers to his own works that the Father has given him to do as a witness (5.37–38). He is 'to finish' the works of God (5.36), which includes the work of healing the marginalized, hearing the voice of the poor. What follows in 5.20b–30 is a particular and careful unfolding of the relationship of Jesus the Son and God the Father.

Jesus, having defended his authority to heal on the Sabbath and to call God his Father, now calls witnesses to his defence. Because of this, the discourse has the appearance of a trial scene, which will continue throughout his ministry in both Galilee and Jerusalem. Jesus the accused responds and calls witnesses: John (5.33–35); Jesus' own works (5.36); the Father (5.37–38); the Scriptures (5.39); and Moses (5.45–47). The mention of Moses leads to the allusions to the Exodus in the next scenes about the feeding of the multitude in the wilderness and the crossing of the sea in John 6.

Oratio (Prayer) → *Contemplatio* (Contemplation) →
Actio (Action) →

- Jesus' command to the man who was paralysed, 'Walk!', might well be followed by those of us who live in the wealthy one-third world and overuse our cars.[12] Active transport initiatives such as walking and biking, when linked with other sustainable transport options, are beneficial not only for people but for the wider earth community. The symbolic power of walking in marches attests to the ever-growing global call to seriously address climate justice. As Wangari Maathai, founder of the Green Belt Movement declared, 'We cannot tire or give up. We owe it to the present and the future generations of all species to rise up and walk!'[13]
- Maybe bring to prayer and contemplation a marginalized one today who has 'been there a long time' (5.6). Feelings and thoughts arise by 'sitting with' the reality of this person and some of the 'p' realities – power, privilege and poverty (see Overview). The experience reshapes us. Working with it leads us out of ourselves and often moves our hands and feet to act.
- Dwell on the Sabbath. It is not just about rest. God still had work to do in the ongoing work of sustaining creation. God blessed the seventh day and made it holy (Gen. 2.1–3). The Sabbath gives a glimpse of what will only happen in the world-to-come, that not-yet world we are called to be part of co-creating by taking steps now towards making right relationship happen with God, creation and people.

Notes

1 Stephen Motyer, 1995, 'Jesus and the Marginalised in the Fourth Gospel', in *Mission and Meaning: Essays Presented to Peter Cotterell*, Antony Billington, Tony Lane and Max Turner (eds), Carlisle: Paternoster Press, pp. 81–4.

2 Robert J. Karris, 1990, *Jesus and the Marginalized in John's Gospel*, Collegeville MN: Liturgical Press, pp. 42–3.

3 On water as healing at Bethesda, see Craig S. Keener, 2003, *The Gospel of John: A Commentary*, 2 vols, Peabody MA: Hendrickson Publishers, p. 636.

4 Karris, *Jesus and the Marginalized*, pp. 42–3.

5 On letting 'John be John' and giving attention to the particular way this Gospel describes physical illness, see Karris, *Jesus and the Marginalized*, pp. 44–5. On John 5.1–15, see pp. 50–3. 'Invalids' in the NRSV translates the present participle of *astheneō* (5.3), which is used in various forms for sickness in John.

6 Margaret Daly-Denton, 2017, *John: An Earth Bible Commentary: Supposing Him to be the Gardener*, London: Bloomsbury T&T Clark, p. 100.

7 Daly-Denton, *John*, p. 101.

8 Karris, *Jesus and the Marginalized*, p. 52.

9 Charles H. Dodd, 1968, 'A Hidden Parable in the Fourth Gospel', in Charles H. Dodd (ed.), *More New Testament Studies*, Manchester: Manchester University Press, p. 40.

10 Donald E. Gown, 2000, *Eschatology in the Old Testament*, 2nd edn, Edinburgh: T&T Clark, p. 1.

11 Daly-Denton, *John*, p. 100.

12 Daly-Denton, *John*, p. 102.

13 Quotation from Wangari Maathai, taken from Green Belt Movement, www.greenbeltmovement.org/wangari-maathai/biography (accessed 1.10.19).

Galilee
'Come, Eat of My Bread' – John 6.1–69

'Come, eat of my bread and drink of my wine' (Prov. 9.5)

Seventeenth Sunday in Ordinary Time of Year B (RL)
John 6.1–15
Ninth Sunday after Pentecost of Year B (RCL)
John 6.1–21
Eighteenth Sunday in Ordinary Time of Year B (RL)
Tenth Sunday after Pentecost of Year B (RCL)
John 6.24–35
Nineteenth Sunday in Ordinary Time of Year B (RL)
John 6.41–51
Eleventh Sunday after Pentecost of Year B (RCL)
John 6.35, 41–51
Twentieth Sunday in Ordinary Time of Year B (RL)
Sunday after Trinity Sunday: Body and Blood of Christ of Year A (RL)
Twelfth Sunday after Pentecost of Year B (RCL)
John 6.51–58
Twenty-First Sunday in Ordinary Time of Year B (RL)
John 6.60–69
Thirteenth Sunday after Pentecost of Year B (RCL)
John 6.56–69

As John's Gospel has no narrative of the institution of the Eucharist, John 6 is seen as the counterpart of Last Supper accounts of Matthew, Mark and Luke. The action-narrative pattern of this Gospel unfolds in the actions of the feeding of a large crowd (6.1–15) and a boat trip (6.16–21), followed by the narrative of the 'bread of life' discourse (6.26–71). At the symbolic level, this seemingly simple story has many layers: the bread imagery, Wisdom-Sophia imagery, Passover and Exodus imagery, and imagery evoking suffering and violent death. It is helpful to consider this long sequence under seven headings:

1 The sign of the feeding of the crowd: 6.1–15
2 Jesus comes to the disciples walking on the water: 6.16–21

3 The crowd searches for Jesus: 6.22–24
4 Dialogue between Jesus and the crowd: 6.25–34
5 Discourse on the bread of life – 'Believe': 6.35–50
6 Discourse on the bread of life – 'Eat': 6.51–59
7 Dialogue between Jesus and disciples: 6.60–71[1]

Eight different combinations of the verses from John 6.1–69 are proclaimed throughout the three-year lectionary cycle. In what follows, three reflections are offered: 6.1–21, 6.22–34 and 6.35–71.

Lectio/Reading of John 6.1–21

In reading and rereading John 6.1–21 the reader is invited to imagine and enter into this story by giving attention to the 'where', the 'who' and the 'when'. Consider the bread (food) that we grow or work to buy. We ourselves exist because of a chain of possibilities built upon one other and the gifts of earth in the evolving universe.

Meditatio/Meditation

To prepare for interpreting John 6, let us recall Sandra Schneiders' summary of the three worlds of the text: 'While history lies *behind* the text and theology is expressed *in* the text, spirituality is *called forth by* the text as it engages the reader.'[2] I suggest that there are significant parallels between the situations of those who first heard John 6 and Christians today.

Those earliest Christians were in transition from, and within, Judaism, to be Christians in a world where their world view was not the established one. And Christians today? We are in a changing situation that goes beyond the Church while affecting it radically.[3] The wide-ranging changes over recent decades come from deep shifts that take their origin from Western Europe. The relationship has altered between Christianity and those societies in movement from Christendom to pluralism or pluralistic societies. By Christendom, the Australian theologian Frank O'Loughlin explains,

> We mean that social, cultural and political arrangement by which European society and Christianity were virtually merged into each other. To be one was to be the other ... By 'pluralist' we mean a social, cultural, political arrangement in which in principle no particular religion or worldview is established as an intrinsic part of that society.[4]

In this transition, a long period of Christian history is drawing to an end and a new period is beginning.

The earliest Christians would have identified with the hungry crowd Jesus sees and to whom, after giving thanks (*eucharistein*), he himself distributes the bread (6.11–12). They heard, and we need to discover, the 'hunger' and 'bread' in the feeding of the five thousand (6.1–15) and later in the 'bread of life' discourse (6.22–59). We need to hear and discover, 'It is I; do not be afraid', when Jesus comes to the disciples walking on the sea (6.16–21). We are going to eavesdrop on the conversation between Jesus and the disciples so as to join Peter in his statement of belief in Jesus: 'You have the words of eternal life' (6.60–71). They would have heard echoes of the manna of the desert of the Exodus story; of Wisdom who gathers her disciples, 'Come, eat of my bread and drink of my wine' (Prov. 9.5); and imagery evoking suffering and violent death. Let us consider 'bread', which is at the centre of Jesus' actions and words.

The human speaks of the divine

When Jesus proclaimed 'I am the bread of life', he gave human grounding to the Eucharist. In everyday speech, bread is talked about in a double sense – as a specific element of food and as part-for-the-whole, as in such sayings as 'We earn our bread by the sweat of our brow.' People eat bread (food). We need to eat. There is a very deep dependence at the heart of our existence. We are not able to keep ourselves alive. We must take something from outside ourselves into ourselves so that we can stay alive. Indeed, we are not the source of our own life. When Jesus says 'I am the bread of life', he invites us to consider the very radical nature of bread in our lives. This opens up insight into the meaning of Jesus for human life. In the sign given to us, we go beyond what we see and touch into discovering and celebrating the mystery of Christ.

In the human reality of a family meal, the food on the table is provided by parents.[5] It is there because those parents have worked to give that food. They burn their energy. The very cells of their bodies work. In our living and working, we tire, age and wear out. In a sense, providing food for their children wears parents out and costs them their lives. The meal as a sign of the Eucharist speaks of what Jesus does in his life, his self-giving death and his sacrifice (Latin – to make holy). The bread (food) we grow or work to buy comes, and indeed we ourselves exist, because of a chain of possibilities built upon one other in the evolving universe. Interconnected systems of the heat of the sun and rainfall, plus human interactions such as the tilling of the earth, harvesting, transport, buying, selling and baking, feed our hunger. Enriched by this reflection on bread, we turn now to the seven headings outlined above to consider the 'theology [that] is expressed *in* the text'.

'Come, eat of my bread and drink of my wine' (Prov. 9.5)

A new place is introduced.[6] Jesus goes to the other side of 'the Sea of Galilee of Tiberias' (6.1, literal translation), which is a 12 by 20 kilometre freshwater lake. 'A large crowd kept following him' (6.2). Jesus had disappeared in the Jerusalem crowd (5.13). Now, a new set of characters enters, a crowd from Galilee. So why does the crowd seek out Jesus at Passover time near Tiberias? Perhaps the marginalized crowd could not afford to make the journey to Jerusalem for the Passover during changing times. They come to Jesus, who preaches and heals in the countryside. He avoids the cities of Tiberias and Sepphoris. When a change of values occurs, people and resources are exploited for profit rather than for providing what is needed for subsistence. The works of Jesus resist the changing values and attitudes represented by the rise of Sepphoris and Tiberias. Jesus adapts the Wisdom and Exodus traditions to a new situation in a prophetic critique of the way things were.

The founding of Tiberias and the giving of land to its inhabitants meant displacement of people and pressure on landowners to break up smallholdings. Jesus goes up the mountain and is sitting on the ground with his disciples, when a large crowd comes towards him (6.5). Present-day readers probably miss what John's Jewish original readers would have assumed when Jesus 'sat down'. In adopting that posture, he is characteristically Jewish – Jewish teachers sat down to teach (6.3; 'Moses' seat', Matt. 23.2).[7] Imagine that crowd trailing up, over and down: tax collectors, peasants, artisans, fishers, the sick, small farmers, day labourers, widows, women, children, estate managers and the wealthy. These people are Jews living under the systems of Roman occupation, which include the collaboration of a local king and the upper priestly classes. These people might have included those who earned their living on land, sea or by trade. Some would have been the better-off. Most would have earned a bare subsistence living. All those gathered had a collective history of exile and deportation, of being ruled by nations not their own, of working day and night and of paying huge taxes in a society from which they did not benefit. Jesus understands then, as he does now, that so many are unmoored from the faith of their ancestors.

By John 6, Jesus is established as Wisdom-Sophia and evokes this female figure who gathers her disciples, 'Come, eat of my bread and drink of my wine' (Prov. 9.5). The feeding of the five thousand in John differs from the other three Gospel accounts. Near the time of the Passover (6.4), Jesus takes the initiative. On whose behalf? On behalf of the marginalized. 'He looked up and saw a large crowd' and asked Philip where they are 'to buy bread for these people to eat' (6.5–6). The word used for 'buy' comes from the word for the *agora* (the marketplace). Jesus and his disciples have money, and use some of it for the needs of the poor (12.5–8; 13.29). Philip gives what Karris calls 'a business manager's answer', indicating they have money but not enough to feed this crowd.[8] Throughout this Gospel there is insistence on the 'here-and-now-ness' of the life that Jesus gives.[9] 'Eternal life' is in the now and does not overshadow the materiality of the bread and fish or need for food, which is linked to what Jesus wants to give, 'the food that endures for eternal life' (6.27), which is a new way of life on earth. He gives thanks (*eucharistein*), distributes the bread himself (6.11), as did Wisdom-Sophia. Also evoked here are the Last Supper stories of the Synoptic Gospels, where Jesus himself distributes the bread and acts in this sequence: takes the loaves, gives thanks (*eucharistein*) and distributes them.

'Five barley loaves and two fishes' (John 6.9)

What of the bread used in John, the only Gospel to mention five barley loaves (6.9)? Grain, and the products made from it, was by far the most important of the three staple commodities of grain, oil and wine. Wheat was considered superior to barley, which tasted less desirable and was cheaper. Barley ripened more quickly than wheat, required less water, was less sensitive to soil salinity and so became the major crop in the arid areas of the Mediterranean world. It was the food of the poor and slaves, and was fed to animals. Apart from the hard work to grow barley, it needed to be milled, which could take around three hours to provide about three kilogrammes for a family of five or six.

There is also an echo here of the barley loaves with which Elisha fed a multitude (2 Kings 4.42–44). The 12 baskets for the 'left over' loaves are also anchored in the Scriptures. God said to Elisha, 'Give it to the people and let them eat ... they shall eat and have some left.' In the Exodus wilderness feeding, 12 baskets of left-over manna were gathered. Provision for all gathered and some left over is a recurring description of biblical meals. The description of the food as 'left over' (John 6.12) does not convey the meaning of the Greek word, which has a sense of extraordinary, overflowing abundance.[10] Jesus' words, 'Make the people sit down', use a Greek verb, to stretch out, for meal. Reclining was the customary position for eating. The description of 'a great deal of grass' associates the renewal of Passover with the renewal of spring, when the hill slopes would be covered with lush grass and wild flowers. The assurance of Psalm 23.1

is evoked: 'The Lord is my shepherd; I shall not want. He makes me lie down in green pastures.'

Much movement happens on the mountain, sea and waterfront. Jesus goes up the mountain (John 6.3) and, after feeding the large crowd, 'he withdrew again to the mountain by himself' (6.15). That night the disciples set out in a boat to the busy waterfront fishing town of Capernaum on the northern shore of the Sea of Galilee. Jesus startles them as he comes walking towards them on the stormy sea: 'It is I; do not be afraid' (6.20).

Oratio (Prayer) → *Contemplatio* (Contemplation) → *Actio* (Action) →

- According to the Food and Agricultural Organization of the United Nations, about one-third of the food produced in the world for human consumption every year – approximately 1.3 billion tonnes – gets lost or wasted.[11] What can Christian communities learn from the spirituality of Jesus about completing the works of God when he directs his disciples to gather up the surplus so that nothing is lost? What can Christian communities learn for care of the landscape from the place being cleaned up and restored to how it was found?
- The marketplace (*agora*) comes to the fore when Philip asks Jesus where they can 'buy bread for these people to eat' (6.5–6). The dominant focus of the powerful today is on the market and consumerism. Maximizing economic growth is considered to be their best contribution to improving human welfare. Such an approach is not sustainable in the face of ongoing issues such as global climate change, environmental damage, rising inequality and enduring poverty. A well-being economics framework places well-being at the centre of a nation's life and way forward, rather than gross national product. The focus is on choices made by individuals, households, families, civil society, local government and the global community. The goal is for a sustainable way forward for personal well-being, for community prosperity and for care of the earth.[12]

Lectio/Reading of John 6.22–34

In reading and rereading John 6.22–34, when Jesus proclaims 'I am the bread of life', he invites us to consider the very radical nature of bread in our lives, which opens up insight into the meaning of Jesus for human life.

Meditatio/Meditation

The next day some of the crowd sail from Tiberias, a waterfront city further south named after the Roman emperor, to Capernaum, in order to look for Jesus (6.23). When they find him there 'on the other side of the sea', they question him, and the dialogue begins. The discourses (6.25–59) serve in part to address the mistaken expectations of the Galilean crowd (6.14–15). In a long, intricately structured dialogue, Jesus responds to five questions raised by the crowd (6.25, 30, 34, 42, 52). Some of this teaching takes place in the synagogue (6.59). Sections are addressed to groups who respond in diverse ways to the invitation to 'believe *into*' Jesus – the crowd (6.14–40), 'the Jews' (6.41–59), the disciples (6.60–66) and the Twelve (6.67–71). Views about Jesus and his work unfold, which stretch the faith of disciples who have already followed him.

'This is a work of God ... believe into' Jesus (John 6.29)

The reader knows from the prologue, which provides a summary of the gospel story, that 'in him was life' (1.4). The crowd do not understand that Jesus himself is the bread that sustains life. Other-than-human elements are the agents through which God is revealed in the signs in John: earthen pots filled with water; a mat carried by one who had not been able to walk; and here bread and 12 stout wicker baskets. God encounters persons in unexpected ways.

The crowd asks their first question, 'Rabbi, when did you come here?' (6.25). Characteristically, Jesus does not answer their question but moves the conversation to another level. They just want another meal. Jesus talks of the contrast between physical bread and the bread of life that he offers. This is not to say that Jesus negates the need for the former. There is need for bread for physical hunger and for openness to the One who gives bread (manna), namely God (cf. Exod. 16.4). This is an ongoing need. God *gives* (John 6.32), not in a past event but in a present and ongoing one. Eucharistic tones in this account of the feeding of the five thousand and the bread of life discourse emphasize the Eucharist as meal. The tone changes in John 6.41–69, as we shall see in the next reflection, to the Eucharist as sacrifice and self-giving. This seems to be foreshadowed by the only mention in the New Testament of Tiberias (6.1, 23), a town built by Herod Antipas and named for the emperor Tiberias. In a different vision from that empire, Wisdom-Sophia in the Wisdom creation account is imaged as building her house and filling it with provisions for all (Prov. 9.1–6).

The crowd are seeking Jesus because of the free food. He is straight with

THE MINISTRY OF JESUS

them. They miss 'signs' of what he is really offering: 'Do not *work* for the food that perishes, but for the food that endures for eternal life' (6.27). It seems a bit tough of Jesus to scold people who are probably living on the breadline. Even so, the people seem to understand. A reader familiar with the story world of this Gospel recalls that 'work' evokes the prologue (1.1–18), which inserts Jesus into God's work of creation. The works of God feature often in this Gospel. Here the crowd ask a second question: 'What must we do to work the works of God?' (literal translation). Jesus responds, 'This is the work of God, that you believe *into* the one whom God has sent' (6.28–29). 'Believing *into* Jesus' is a work of God required of all who seek to follow him. It is an all-embracing acceptance of Jesus and of what and who he claims to be. He is the one on whom God has set God's seal (6.27). The crowd then ask Jesus, 'Sir, give us this bread always' (6.34). As yet they do not know who he is. Jesus responds by saying, 'I am the bread of life' (6.35–50).

Oratio (Prayer) → *Contemplatio* (Contemplation) → *Actio* (Action) →

- When the crowd asks, 'What must we do to work the works of God?' (literal translation), Jesus responds, 'This is the work of God, that you believe *into* the one whom God has sent' (6.28–29). 'Believing *into*' Jesus requires a dedication of one's life to him and a commitment to work with him to complete the works of God by hearing *both the cry of the earth and the cry of the marginalized*. In the face of the complexity and vastness of the injustices entrenched in global and in national structures, many people longing for, and working for, change become overwhelmed and burn out. Consider how 'believing *into*' Jesus might offer a spirituality to sustain the Christian community in completing the works of God for environmental and social justice. Prayer is integral. Before his works, Jesus prayed (6.11; 11.41–42; 17.1–26).

Lectio/Reading of John (6.35–71)

The bread discourse consists of two parts (6.35–50; 6.51–59). It is interrupted by some murmuring (6.41–42) and some disputing (6.52). Let us approach a very beautiful, yet multi-layered and complicated section by focusing on two of the words of Jesus: *believe* in 6.35–50 – which we have just referred to – and *eat* in 6.51–59.

Meditatio/Meditation

'Whoever believes into me will never be thirsty' (John 6.35)

Jesus claims, 'I am the bread of life. Whoever comes to me will never be hungry, and whoever believes *into* me will never be thirsty' (6.35). And again, it is the will of God, 'that all who see the Son and believe *into* him may have eternal life' (6.40). 'Believing *into*' Jesus means becoming like him and doing what he does (see the section on John 1.12). He reaches out to those on the fringes of society and religion (7.49); the physically marginalized (the sick man by the pool, 5.1–15; the beggar born blind, 9.1–41); and the geographically marginalized (the official, 4.46–54; the woman of Samaria, 4.4–42). 'Believing *into*' Jesus requires a dedication of one's life to him and working with him to complete the works of God by hearing *both the cry of the earth and the cry of the marginalized*.

Significant shifts happen as Jesus continues to evoke biblical manna and wisdom traditions. The crowd attribute to Moses the feeding with the manna during the Exodus wandering. Jesus points out that God gave their ancestors 'bread from heaven to eat' (6.31). When he declares, 'I am the bread of life' (6.35), Jesus claims to be the manna and, also, Wisdom-Sophia, who invites: 'eat of my bread'. This is consolidated by 'I have come down from heaven' (6.38), as did the manna and Wisdom-Sophia. The response Jesus invites is, 'Whoever comes to me, will never be hungry, and whoever believes *into* me will never be thirsty.' The 'I am' statements are not so much about who Jesus is but about what he does. In response, 'the Jews began to murmur', as did their ancestors in the wilderness.

The crowd had disagreed with Jesus' interpretation of Scripture. A pattern of meal, rejection and betrayal becomes apparent. The words of Jesus lead to division and rejection, as did Wisdom-Sophia's. Now 'the Jews' murmur in a disrespectful tone. This fellow claims, 'I am the bread came down from heaven' (6.41). They know his parents. Who does he think he is? Jesus has stepped out of line, gone beyond his origins by his audacious claims that threaten the established order. Jesus tells them directly to stop murmuring. 'Murmur' evokes the Israelites murmuring in the wilderness (Exod. 16.2, 7–8). Bread in the Scriptures often meant divine instruction. Jesus then quotes Isaiah loosely, 'They shall be taught by God' (54.13), and speaks about being 'drawn by the Father who sent me' (John 6.43–45), using a term that means to be drawn to the Torah. The 'I am' statements of Jesus – in this case, 'I am the bread of life' (6.35, 48) or 'I am the living bread' (6.51) – are not about who Jesus is but about what he does. He nourishes with bread that gives eternal life. I invite my reader to read John 6 reflectively in order to become aware of how strongly 'life' features – 18 times.

THE MINISTRY OF JESUS

'Eat my flesh and drink my blood' (John 6.56)

When reflecting on John 6.35–50 we focused on the first of two words of Jesus, *believe*. We now turn to focus on *eat* in 6.51–59, which comprises the second part of the discourse. There are Eucharistic overtones – 'I am the living bread' that will last for ever, and 'the bread that I will give for the life of the world is my flesh' (6.51). Bread, the staple food of people then and throughout the ages, takes on further symbolic dimensions to reveal Jesus, the Word made flesh (1.14). The word 'flesh' implies human nature in its completeness. In becoming flesh, God's continuing relationship with creation is inclusive of human beings and of all living creatures (Gen. 6.13). Flesh suggests that which perishes and fades like the grass, while blood is the inner life force.

In the image of the vine in John 15, Jesus claims, 'I am the true vine', which parallels 'I am the bread of life'. The language of 'abiding' is found in both passages, 'Those who eat my flesh and drink my blood *abide* in me, and I in them' (6.56). Yet again, the point is made that eucharistic tones flow throughout this Gospel in the actions and words of Jesus and of the disciples. John 6 evokes Eucharist as meal when Jesus as Wisdom-Sophia gathers friends to 'eat of my bread and drink of my wine'. Eating flesh and drinking blood also describes the intimacy and close relationship with Jesus of those who 'believe *into*' him. The Eucharist is placed in the middle of his public life and is linked to his incarnation and ministry. The Eucharist as sacrifice, willing self-giving for others, is evoked when Jesus speaks of his flesh and his blood.

Movement towards the death-resurrection

Tensions rise as 'the Jews' disagree among themselves: 'How can this man give us his flesh to eat?' (6.52). Jesus does not mince words. Using two different verbs for eating, Jesus repeatedly invites those who '*eat* my flesh and drink my blood' to life in its fullness. Four times he repeats a word for an impolite way of eating that means physically crunching food with teeth (6.54, 56–58). Four times Jesus insists that they are not only to eat his flesh but also drink his blood (6.53–58). Drinking of blood was prohibited (Gen. 9.4; Lev. 17.10). Flesh and blood highlight the reality of his incarnation, his humanity and his very real death.

The title 'Son of Man,' found three times in this discourse and which is translated more accurately as 'Son of Humanity', refers to the Word made flesh who will experience death. There is thus another layer to Jesus' speaking about 'flesh' and 'blood'. In the Scriptures and in the Jewish environment of earliest Christianity, these terms refer to a human being who suffers a violent death (Ps. 79.2–3; 1 Macc. 7.17; 4 Macc. 6.6; Ezek. 32.5–6). 'Flesh' and 'blood', therefore, evoke the violent death of Jesus.[13] Here, as in the other discourses in John, there is a movement towards Jesus' death.

'Will you also go away?' (John 6.67)

The words of Jesus create a crisis for many disciples who, having found this teaching too difficult, 'murmur'. They 'turned back and no longer went with him' (John 6.66). Division and rejection by disciples who find this teaching difficult and no longer go with him evoke the rejection of Wisdom-Sophia. After this, Jesus turns to his core group, the Twelve, and asks, 'Will you also go away?' (6.67). The words of Simon Peter echo through the centuries, 'To whom shall we go?' (6.68). For the first time we hear belief expressed in Jesus because of his origins: 'We have come to believe and to know that you are the Holy One of God' (6.69). Further references to Jesus' ultimate betrayal are made. Later, the supper of John 13 will be followed by rejection and betrayal.

Wisdom 'makes them friends of God and prophets' (Wisd. 7.27)

The feeding of the crowd evokes the manna in the desert, and the walking on the water evokes the Exodus. In Jewish understanding, the Passover ritual is not just a memorial. Rather, it brings the living God of the Exodus into the present for a new future. We need to insert ourselves into the prophetic memory of these events.[14] Prophetic memory recalls the past, challenges the present and commits us to a new future. As friends of God and prophets, we are to insert ourselves into the prophetic memory of the living presence of the *sacrifice* of Jesus – that is, the self-gift of his love, which was so great that it leads both to his laying down his life for his friends and to his resurrection – in the eucharistic *meal*.

The emphasis on the community of friends is to strengthen them to be 'friends of God and prophets' (Wisd. 7.27) in their daily lives. As Wisdom-Sophia gathers her friends, so Jesus-Sophia gathers his friends, and the living Jesus gathers twenty-first-century Christians in the Eucharist as meal. As Wisdom-Sophia cries out publicly in the streets, so too the public healings and actions of Jesus result in rejection, suffering and death. Likewise, the living Jesus gathers twenty-first-century Christians in the Eucharist as sacrifice, which implies the self-giving of taking risks, transforming sinful structures, committing to right relationship and celebrating the presence of Jesus with the broken.

In the Synoptic Gospels, Jesus' meal companions cause scandal because they are social outsiders such as tax collectors and sinners. In contrast, in John, meals focus on the community and Jesus' friends. Jesus is with friends near the end of his life. Lazarus, Martha and Mary offer hospitality to their friend and guest and prepare him lovingly for burial (John 12.1–8). The Risen One prepares breakfast for friends on the beach (21.12). Some interpreters find this Gospel inward-looking. The reading of Johannine meals through the lens of Wisdom-Sophia and friendship, however, shows a different story. Meals in the Gospel according to John teach us about Jesus and the continuity of the Church. The motif of friendship found in this Gospel is as much about how we are church together as a community of friends as it is about the living Jesus whom we meet in the Eucharist in meal and in sacrifice, and who makes us friends of God and prophets.

Oratio (Prayer) → *Contemplatio* (Contemplation) → *Actio* (Action) →

- Most of the crowd who heard Jesus would have been illiterate. Their familiarity with Scripture is evident throughout John 6.31–59. They engage passionately in debate – what about today? To what extent do Christian congregations and individuals access, study and engage deeply with Scripture from the perspective of being conscious of both the earth and the marginalized in order to complete the works of God by responding to *both the cry of the earth and the cry of the marginalized*?

Notes

1 For a very helpful overview of John 6, see Brendan Byrne SJ, 2014, *Life Abounding: A Reading of John's Gospel*, Collegeville MN: Liturgical Press, pp. 108–28.

2 Sandra M. Schneiders, 1999, 'The Community of Eternal Life (John 11:1–53)', in *Written that You May Believe: Encountering Jesus in the Fourth Gospel*, New York: Crossroad, p. 151 (italics hers).

3 On this time of transition in the Church from Christendom to pluralism or pluralistic societies and the implications of interpreting this change, see Frank O'Loughlin, 2012, *This Time of the Church*, Mulgrave, Vic: Garratt, pp. 9–28; on evangelization in this new situation, see pp. 62–75; on bread as 'a reality of our human life', see pp. 70–2.

4 O'Loughlin, *This Time*, p. 11.

5 O'Loughlin, *This Time*, p. 71.

6 This draws on my articles, Kathleen P. Rushton, 2006, 'Eucharistic Wisdom

and Friendship in the Gospel according to John', in Helen Bergen and Susan Smith (eds), *Whangaia ki te Taro o te Ora. Nourished by the Eucharist: New Thoughts on an Ancient Theme*, Auckland: Accent Publications, 2006, pp. 45–53; 2018, 'Completing God's Work (John 6:1–21)', *Tui Motu InterIslands*, July, pp. 20–1; and 2018, 'Being a Disciple (John 6:24–69)', *Tui Motu InterIslands*, August, pp. 22–3.

7 Ronald J. Allen and Clark M. Williamson, 2015 [2004], *Preaching the Gospels without Blaming the Jews: A Lectionary Commentary*, Louisville KY: Westminster John Knox Press, p. xvii.

8 Robert J. Karris, 1990, *Jesus and the Marginalized in John's Gospel*, Collegeville MN: Liturgical Press, p. 31.

9 Margaret Daly-Denton, 2017, *John: An Earth Bible Commentary: Supposing Him be to the Gardener*, London: Bloomsbury T&T Clark, p. 107.

10 Both NRSV and JB have 'left over'. The Greek word is *perisseusanta*.

11 Food and Agricultural Organization of the United Nations, 2019, 'SAVE FOOD: Global Initiative on Food Loss and Waste Reduction', www.fao.org/save-food/resources/keyfindings/en/ (accessed 10.07.19).

12 Paul Dalziel, Caroline Saunders and Joe Saunders, 2018, *Wellbeing Economics: The Capabilities Approach to Prosperity*, Basingstoke: Palgrave MacMillan. Open Access EBook: www.palgrave.com/gp/book/9783319931937 (accessed 10.07.19).

13 On flesh and blood evoking violent death, see Maarten J. J. Menken, 1993, 'John 6.51c–58: Eucharist or Christology?' *Biblica* 74.1, pp. 1–26.

14 On prophetic memory and the Hebrew understanding of *zikaron*, see Francis Moloney, 2005, 'Christ in the Eucharist', Address at Lay Centre, Rome, in John R. Allen, 2005, 'The Word from Rome', *National Catholic Reporter*, 21 October, http://nationalcatholicreporter.org/word/word102105.htm (accessed 6.04.19)

Jerusalem
'Rivers of Living Water' – John 7.37–39

'Rivers of living water' (John 7.39)

Pentecost Sunday Vigil of Years ABC (RL)
Day of Pentecost of Year A (RCL)
John 7.37–39

Lectio/Reading of John 7.37–39

In our *meditatio*/meditation on the woman at the well (4.5–42), the motif of water was described as being like a stream on a hillside that flows through the narrative of this Gospel. Be aware of how water streams again in John 7.37–39, 'rivers of living water' flowing from the rock.

Meditatio/Meditation

We have followed the path to the source of the north branch of the Riwaka River, South Island (Aotearoa New Zealand). Towering above us are huge moss-covered rocks that had tumbled down from the Takaka Hill face thousands of years ago. Below is the Spring of Riwaka, sacred place of the two local Māori tribes (Te Atiawa and Ngāti Rārua), which has special status, for from here spring the waters of life. For generations this has been a place of healing. Water emerges from the rock through a cave into this deep, clear, astonishingly beautiful spring-fed pool. If what can be seen filled me with awe, so does what cannot be seen. In 1963, five divers first charted what lies beyond the spring. After descending into the pool, they entered a hole, swam about 30 metres, rounded a corner, surfaced, climbed up a waterfall and dived down again to swim a further 50 metres.[1] Reaching a ledge, they climbed up into a huge cathedral-like space about 30 metres in diameter and six to seven storeys high. Then they plunged through waist-high water until, after about 40 metres, the cavern narrows into tiny unpassable passages.

Rock, spring, source, water flowing, what is unseen; all these evoke a favourite passage in John's Gospel – those mysterious verses of John 7.37–39. Traditional interpretation translates 7.38 as if the believer is the source of living water (e.g. Jerusalem Bible in the RL). Another possible way, called the christological interpretation, sees the living water flowing from within Jesus. If this water symbol is interpreted within the two-fold pattern of symbols in John, the first level of meaning concerns Jesus and the second level concerns disciples. 'I am the light of the world', for example, applies to Jesus and then says something about disciples, 'Whoever follows me ... will have the light of life' (8.12).

'The Jewish festival of Booths was near' (John 7.2)

Rich symbolism surrounds the Festival of Tabernacles (in Hebrew, *sukkoth*; in English, shelters, booths, tabernacles or huts). Small flimsy huts featured, in which people slept and ate in memory of the 40 years they lived in tents in the wilderness.[2] There is a special relationship to the temple in Jerusalem, since the dedication of the first temple built by Solomon took place at Tabernacles (1 Kings 8.2). The natural world and the agricultural rhythm of life were integral as this festival was celebrated in the season of autumn (September–October) with festivities that accompanied the grape and olive harvests.

Prayers were offered for winter rains (water) so necessary for fertile crops the following year, and for the renewal of sunlight (light). If early rain fell during this time, it was regarded as an assurance of the abundant rain that God would send. This hope was acted out in a solemn ceremony. On the seven mornings of the festival, a procession set out for the nearby temple mount to the fountain of Gihon, the source of the Pool of Siloam. A priest filled a golden pitcher with water while a choir repeated, 'With joy you shall draw water from the wells of salvation' (Isa. 12.3). The procession returned to the temple through the Water Gate, accompanied by crowds carrying festival symbols: in their right hand twigs tied with a palm (representing branches used to build the huts) and in their left hand symbols of the harvest. In the temple, the priest poured the water into a special funnel from which it flowed into the ground.

While Jesus is in Galilee, the Festival of Tabernacles is near (John 7.2). At the middle of the festival he goes up to the temple and teaches (7.14); he cries out as he teaches there (7.28); and yet again he cries out (7.37). Later, Jesus says to them, 'I am the light of the world' (8.12). He is teaching in the treasury of the temple (8.20) and goes out of the temple (8.59). So the temple and Tabernacles, with its symbolism of water and light, are the background for John 7.1—8.59.

'Rivers of living water' (John 7.39)

On the last day of the festival, Jesus cries out, 'Let anyone who is thirsty come to me' (7.37). The imagery of thirst as longing for God is well known (Ps. 42.1–2; 63.1). In John 7.38, translations use 'heart' or 'side' or 'breast' for what means literally 'out of his belly' (*koilia*). For the Hebrews, the belly was the seat of deep human emotions. Jesus as the giver of living water (4.13–14) and as the rock (19.34) are suggested by a whole series of Old Testament images in which God gives water to the people from the rock (Exod. 17.6; Ps. 105.41). Water comes out of the temple (Ezek. 47.1–12) and heals the holy land, while living water comes out of Jerusalem, the holy city, and heals the whole earth (Zech. 14.6–11). Against this background, Jesus 'cried out' claiming to be the life-nurturing living water for which the pilgrims pray. He stands and cries out (John 7.37), as does Wisdom, who in Proverbs sings out her invitation (1.20) and yet again stands and sings out (8.2–3).

The gift of the Holy Spirit poured out is identified with 'rivers of living water', which believers in Jesus are to receive. At this stage, however, they are not yet ready because he had not been glorified (John 7.39). John the Baptizer reports that Jesus had received the Spirit already (1.32–33). Jesus assures the woman of Samaria that the hour for 'worship in spirit and truth' was already at hand (4.23–24). In the farewell discourses, Jesus promises the Spirit (15.26–27; 16.12–15), which is given when 'he bowed his head and handed over the Spirit' (19.30) to the women and the Beloved Disciple near the cross. Evoking the 'rivers of living water' flowing from the rock, water flows from the pierced side of Jesus, creating the new people of God, the Church. Later re-creation continues when Jesus 'breathed on them', saying, 'Receive the Holy Spirit' (20.22).

Imagery of springs of living water flowing from the rock leads deeply into the mystery of Jesus who gives the Spirit. Interconnected with the preciousness and sacredness of earth, living water is necessary to sustain all forms of life. As Linda Gibler sums up, 'Creation is water-drenched. All living beings on Earth are born of water – in oceans or ponds, within eggs, seeds or wombs.'[3] The sacredness of water permeates the world of the Māori, the indigenous people of Aotearoa New Zealand. Every river has its mauri or life force. Its waters are the veins of papatūānuku (earth) and water is her life blood. Rivers link with the ancestors. Māori people use the term *tangata whenua* (literally, 'people of the land') to express their relationship with a particular area of land. They identify themselves by referring to the *marae* (meeting house), *maunga* (mountain), *awa* (river) and *waka* (ancestral canoe) with which they are affiliated. By identifying with the particular local river of their ancestors, Māori people know who they are and where they stand in the world.

Oratio (Prayer) → *Contemplatio* (Contemplation) → *Actio* (Action) →

- In the face of climate change and the accelerating loss of biodiversity, scientists around the globe are turning to what is known as Traditional Ecological Knowledge (TEK) to learn from indigenous peoples about their deep knowledge of place and the natural world that has been acquired over hundreds and thousands of years.[4] This knowledge comes from their dependence on local ecosystems and 'observations and interpretations of change generated and passed down over many generations, and yet adapted and enriched over time'.[5] They are affected directly by expanding agricultural frontiers and production, such as logging, mining and energy. Indigenous communities and their cultural traditions 'are not merely one minority among others, but should be the principal dialogue partners' (*LS* §146). I experienced the difference that explicit attention to the interconnection between human persons and the land makes when people gather. A recent conference on spirituality and place began with a traditional Māori welcome. In the customary way, the Māori elder identified himself by naming his mountain and his river; that is, the mountain and river of ancestral tribal region. He invited participants to introduce themselves by naming their mountain and river. This caused consternation, especially among overseas participants. People took time to prepare. The introductions began: I am ... my mountain is ... my river is ... What a contrast to how introductions usually begin with: a person's name, I am from such and such an institution and my occupation is ... The effect on the atmosphere of the conference after beginning in this way was remarkable. Many participants became aware of their place of origin in a new way. Relationship with land and river emerged in new ways. So too did the relationships among participants flourish with new connections made. Some participants discovered they had the same place of origins.
- How does the gift of the Spirit, imaged as 'rivers of living water' poured out, inspire Christians to live in ways that value the vital gift of water as a symbol of their longing for God and as free gift of the planet – endangered and necessary to sustain all life?

Notes

1 For a diagram, film clips and description of Te Puna (Spring) of Riwaka, see www.stuff.co.nz/nelson-mail/news/9503621/Diving-into-darkness (accessed 6.06.19).

2 For an overview of the Feast of Tabernacles, which is the background festival for John 7—8, see Francis J. Moloney, 1998, *The Gospel of John*, Sacra Pagina Series 4, Collegeville MN: Liturgical Press, pp. 232–6.

3 Linda Gibler, 2010, *From the Beginning to Baptism: Scientific and Sacred Stories of Water, Oil, and Fire*, Collegeville MN: Liturgical Press, p. 2.

4 Jim Robbins, 2018, 'Native Knowledge: What Ecologists are Learning from Indigenous People', *Yale Environment 360*, 26 April, https://e360.yale.edu/features/native-knowledge-what-ecologists-are-learning-from-indigenous-people (accessed 12.10.19).

5 Intergovernmental Science-Policy Platform on Biodiversity and Ecosystem Services (IPBES), www.ipbes.net/deliverables/1c-ilk (accessed 12.10.19).

Jerusalem
Jesus, the Scribes, the Pharisees and the Woman – John 8.1–11

'In the middle' (John 8.3)

Fifth Sunday of Lent of Year C (RL)
John 8.1–11

Lectio/Reading of John 8.1–11

In reading and rereading John 8.1–11, it could be helpful to be aware that perceptions of this story may be shaped by the history of interpretation, which has given it titles such as 'The woman taken in adultery' or 'The adulterous woman', or similar titles that focus on the woman alone. Recall the invitation extended in the Overview to be aware of 'p' codes within a text – power, privilege, property, poverty and persecution.

Meditatio/Meditation

Although the story of Jesus, the woman and her accusers is considered to go back to the life of Jesus, it was not until the third century that it found its way into the canonical tradition.[1] Even then, this incident took a long time to settle where we find it today in John's Gospel. Some ancient manuscripts place it in two other places in John, others in Luke's Gospel and some omit it altogether.

The content of this story was opposed and suppressed because the forgiving words of Jesus were at odds with the ancient Church's penitential discipline. Augustine, for example, writes about men's fears that this story would 'make their women immune to punishment for their sins'.[2] The essence of the story is summed up by Raymond Brown as a 'succinct expression of the mercy of Jesus'. The woman there with Jesus is captured by Augustine: 'only two remain, the wretched one and the incarnation of mercy'.[3] The delicate balance between the justice of Jesus in not condoning the sin and his mercy towards the woman make this incident a rich reflection on mercy.

Scene one: 'To stone such women' (John 8.5)

It is early morning, 'All the people' come to Jesus, who begins teaching in the temple (8.1–2). Then three scenes feature the Scribes, the Pharisees and the woman (8.3–6a; 8.6b–7; 8.8–11). A careful reading of the text shows that the title 'Jesus, the Scribes, the Pharisees and the woman' fits better than 'The adulterous woman', which focuses on the woman alone. In the first scene, the Scribes and Pharisees lead a woman caught in adultery to Jesus to ask him to join in condemning her because, in the Torah, 'Moses commanded us to stone such women' (8.5).

Stoning is referred to by Geraldine Brooks in *The Secret Chord*, her novel about the morally complex King David. Batsheva, his eighth wife, is given voice to tell her story to Natan. She was the wife of Uriah when David watched her bathing during her ritual purification and desired her. He sent for her to come to his palace and raped her. Batsheva asks:

> Have you ever seen a woman stoned to death, Natan? I have. My father made me watch when I was a girl so I would know what became of faithless wives. And when my monthly signs did not come, I thought of that woman, the sounds of her moans, her mashed flesh, her shattered bone … At the end she had no face.[4]

It is important not to pit Jesus against Judaism by seeing the stoning of women as unique to the Jewish Torah. At that time, under Roman law, the position of women was worse than in Judaism, for it allowed for the immediate murder of a woman alleged to have committed adultery. According to Luise Schottroff, 'Every legal system of antiquity threatens women, whose sexuality is the possession of a man (father or husband), with severe punishment or death in the case of adultery or premarital intercourse.'[5]

Stoning is an execution performed by a group or community that is threatened by a certain deed. Men carry it out by throwing stones at the victim in a specific order that indicates the rank of those who were injured or alleged to be so. An account of the stoning of an allegedly adulterous Iranian woman in 1990 has her father throwing the first stone, followed by her husband, the imam and her sons.[6] Men followed according to rank. Each man was plaintiff, judge and executioner. Crowds were present at this collective rage. The woman was buried in a hole up to her shoulders. The mayor drew a chalk circle around her. She was in the middle.

'In the middle' (John 8.3)

The situation facing Jesus is not a theoretical debate. The stoning is about to happen. The woman is placed literally 'in the middle' (8.3), which is the beginning of stoning (translations have 'in full view of everyone' or 'before them all'). She is facing death. For these Scribes and Pharisees, Jesus as a Jewish male has the responsibility to join them in condemning her and in punishing her.

Not all Scribes and Pharisees (or imams and their communities referred to above) behave in this way. Some, those in this story, were zealots who take on themselves the indignant enforcement of the Torah. They are intent on finding fault with Jesus by pitting him against the Torah. They are not interested in the woman or her allegedly wronged husband or even the other man. Indeed, both the man and woman caught in adultery should die (Lev. 20.10; Deut. 22.22).

Scene two: 'They kept on questioning him' (John 8.7)

The collective nature of the seizing of the woman and her punishment requires Jesus to take his place in the male hierarchy to stone her. He is to join the collective of men as judge and as executioner. In the face of this, he does not answer. Jesus bends down and writes on the ground with his finger. Whatever the meaning of his action, it replaces the condemnation demanded of him and his part in her execution. The Scribes and the Pharisees continue to press for an answer, so Jesus stands and addresses them directly: 'Let anyone among you who is without sin be the first to throw a stone at her' (John 8.7).

Scene three: 'Jesus was left alone with the woman' (John 8.9)

Then Jesus bends down and writes on the ground again. The crowd departs. Jesus speaks to the woman twice. One by one, according to rank, the woman's accusers leave. Then Jesus says, 'Woman, where are they? Has no one condemned you?' He addresses the woman as 'you' (8.10). She is no longer an object. Through unconditional forgiveness, she was able to enter into a relationship with Jesus. On the basis of this relationship, Jesus can challenge her to sin no more. 'From this moment on' (8.11;

literally, 'from this now on'), the moment of her encounter with Jesus, she is offered the possibility of new life: physical life and a life of right relationship with God.

Civic moral courage

In an act of what Luise Schottroff calls civic moral courage, Jesus, as an independent interpreter of the Torah, places adultery, an offence that in a patriarchal society made women vulnerable to unjust allegations and treatment, on the level of other offences such as theft and defamation.[7] He disputes the status of adultery (shared with idolatry) as a crime requiring death. This story is underpinned by gender, which Yves Charbit describes as:

> the array of 'socially constructed' roles, behaviours, attributes, aptitudes and relative powers linked with being a woman or a man in a society at any given time. The term 'socially constructed' means that they are not 'innate' or 'natural' characteristics but constructions and products of a society and, as such, can be modified and transformed.[8]

According the Pope Francis, 'Mercy is the force that reawakens us to new life and instils in us courage to look to the future.'[9] This new life is at the heart of Maria Boulding's comment:

> The Pharisees are tense, but [Jesus] is calm and relaxed throughout; he accepts the woman openly and lovingly, as an adult and as a person. He has a sureness of touch; he can handle the situation with her because he has nothing to be afraid of in himself ... He must have completely accepted and integrated his own sexuality. Only a man who has done so, or at least begun to do so, can relate properly to women.[10]

Oratio (Prayer) → *Contemplatio* (Contemplation) → *Actio* (Action) →

- In the Overview, the reader was invited to be 'on the move' with Jesus in his barrier-crossing ministry as he completes the works of God, and to be aware of the 'p' codes within a text – power, privilege, property, poverty and persecution. These 'p' codes permeate 'the behaviours, attributes, aptitudes and relative powers' (see Charbit above), which are acted out in the story of John 8.1–11. Jesus disrupts and transforms the socially constructed role he is expected to assume. He refuses to take his place in the male hierarchy. He addresses the woman as 'you', as a person rather than from a position of male power or privilege or as the personal property of an allegedly aggrieved male. For disciples today, the 'p' codes operate at many levels of human culture and global systems. The Anti-Human Trafficking Coalition, which works to eliminate the exploitation of women, youth and girls, lists climate change among '14 Things You Need to Know about Human Trafficking'. Climate change affects the most vulnerable and is 'one of the causes of poverty and forced migration, which are breeding grounds for human trafficking, forced labour, prostitution and organ trafficking'.[11] The power and privilege of wealthy countries, particularly in the Global North, means 'a true "ecological debt"' exists with poor countries 'connected to commercial imbalances with effects on the environment, and the disproportionate use of natural resources by certain countries over long periods of time' (*LS* §51).

Notes

1 On authorship and place in the canon, see Raymond E. Brown, 1966–1970, *The Gospel According to John*, 2 vols, The Anchor Bible 29–29A, Garden City NY: Doubleday 1966, pp. 335–6.

2 Luise Schottroff, 1995, *Lydia's Impatient Sisters: A Feminist Social History of Early Christianity*, Barbara and Martin Rumscheidt (trans.), Louisville KY: Westminster John Knox Press, pp. 181–5. On Augustine and the fears of men about this text found in his *De adulterinis coniugii* 2.6, see p. 180.

3 Brown, 1966, *Gospel According to John*, on Augustine, p. 337. Augustine, *In Iohannis Evangelium* 33.5 CCSL XXXVI, 309: *Relicti sunt duo, misera et misericordia*.

4 Geraldine Brooks, 2015, *The Secret Chord*, Sydney: Hachette Australia, p. 268. She transliterates the spelling of names according to Hebrew rather than as in English renderings: Batsheva for Bathsheba and Natan for Nathan.

5 Schottroff, *Lydia's Impatient Sisters*, p. 182.

6 Schottroff, *Lydia's Impatient Sisters*, p. 183.

7 Schottroff, *Lydia's Impatient Sisters*, p. 185.

8 Yves Charbit, 2018, 'Women as Actors in Addressing Climate Change', in Nancy E. Riley and Jan Branson (eds), *International Handbook on Gender and Demographic Processes*, International Handbook of Population Series, No. 8, Dordrecht: Springer, p. 317.

9 Francis, 2015, *Misericordiae Vultus: Bull of Indiction of the Extraordinary Jubilee of Mercy*, Strathfield NSW: St Paul's Publications, §10.

10 Maria Boulding, in D. Rees et al., 1978, *Consider Your Call. A Theology of Monastic Life Today*, London: SPCK, 1978, p. 169, quoted by Francis J. Moloney, 1998, *The Gospel of John*, Sacra Pagina Series 4, Collegeville MN: Liturgical Press, p. 262.

11 Anti-Human Trafficking Coalition, http://thetraffickedhuman.org/get-informed/get-informed (accessed 10.10.19).

Jerusalem
The Beggar Born Blind – John 9.1–41

'We must work the works of the One who sent me' (John 9.4)

Fourth Sunday of Lent of Years ABC (RL)
Fourth Sunday in Lent of Year A (RCL)
John 9.1–41

Lectio/Reading of John 9.1–41

In reading and rereading John 9.1–41, be aware of the repetition of the words 'opened' and 'eyes' and of what this may mean for the reader of this text.

Meditatio/Meditation

Jesus' barrier-crossing ministry of reconciliation across social barriers creating a new community continues in John 9.1–41.[1] In the narrative world of this Gospel, the story of the man who is lame of 5.1–18 prepared the reader for similarities that exist between this character who used to sit by the pool and the beggar born blind. The background context, in which the majority of the people were marginalized physically and religiously, is brought into the foreground by the hostility of the marginalizers. As we shall see, the attitudes expressed towards those who are ignorant of the Torah in John 7.48–49 are acted out in story form in John 9.

'This crowd ... does not know the law' (John 7.48)

The temple police sent to arrest Jesus return to the chief priests empty-handed. Some Pharisees accuse them of being deceived: 'Has any one of the authorities or of the Pharisees believed in him? But this crowd, which does not know the law – they are accursed' (7.48–49). The references to 'the crowd' (7.40, 43) are among 20 similar uses throughout John, which represent the struggle of those who are open to believing but cannot quite get there. They are representative, too, of those held in low esteem and marginalized by the religious leaders. Old Testament and early Jewish writings tell of religious leaders who felt superior to the common people and regarded them as 'people of the land'.[2] A distinction existed between the leaders and the common people. A further distinction was made between those who know and observe the law and those who do not. In short, the leaders are saying two things to 'the crowd'. First, look at us, we know God's Torah. We do not believe in Jesus. Second, 'the crowd' cannot be trusted in their belief in Jesus because they are ignorant of God's revelation in the Torah.

'The man who used to sit and beg' (John 9.8)

The story of this plucky man is remarkable and has inspired such music as Elgar's 'The Light of Life' (Opus 29). There is a significant element in the story, however, that is given little attention.[3] The man whom Jesus and his disciples meet in the streets of Jerusalem is 'a beggar ... who used to sit and beg' (9.8). Maybe he is waiting near the temple for alms from those who worship there. The marginalization, outlined above, has another layer – that of the physically incapacitated. This man's physical weakness is that he is blind from birth. Incapacitated, his circumstances reduce him to begging. Along with the chronically ill man (5.1–15), he is on the margins of society and religion (Lev. 21.17–23).

Creation – 'opening of the eyes'

The sixth-century Rossano Codex and other early illuminations of John 9 depict in two moments the 'opening of the eyes' of the beggar born blind. Jesus' anointing of his eyes with clay is set alongside his washing in the waters of the Pool of Siloam that was fed by the Gihon spring east of Jerusalem. Clay from the ground and water are elements of earth through which body healing and the healing power of God are shown. The focus on clay and water, the detail of the beggar blind from birth and the repetition of 'to open eyes' (9.10, 14, 17, 21, 30, 32; and also 10.21; 11.37), are found only in John, even though the other three Gospels tell of five stories about healing the blind.

The beggar was blind from birth. The story is, therefore, not a restoration of sight, as the man never had the gift of sight (9.2). Sight is a gift of creation. This is suggested by the clay (9.6), which evokes 'the dust of the ground' in Genesis 2.7 from which God creates Adam (*ādām*), who is said to be formed from the earth (*hā-adāma*). Creation is evoked in this Gospel's very first words, 'In the beginning'. Creation motifs, such as light and darkness, continue. Jesus as Wisdom-Sophia is with God in the beginning. Through him 'all things came into being' (John 1.3). Jesus is buried and is raised in a garden (19.41). In his post-resurrection appearance to his disciples, Jesus breathes on them as the Spirit of God breathes over the primal waters (20.22). A cosmic struggle ensues between light and darkness. Jesus speaks of working the works of God while it is still day, as when night comes no one can work (9.4). Here, the natural rhythm of night and day indicate times for labour and rest.

'I am light of the world' (John 9.5)

According to an ancient saying, no more than two active characters would usually appear on stage at one time. Scenes were divided by following that rule.[4] John 9, one of the jewels of John's storytelling, may be divided into eight scenes (9.1–5; 9.6–7; 9.8–12; 9.13–17; 9.18–23; 9.24–34; 9.35–38; 9.39–41) on that basis. In Scene One (9.1–5), Jesus and his disciples see a man blind from birth. The disciples' interest is in the question, 'Who sinned?' For them, suffering is an occasion to moralize about the victim. For Jesus, it is an occasion to do the work of God; that is, to relieve suffering and marginalization.

Jesus declares, 'I am light of the world' (9.5). All scenes take place near the temple during the Festival of Tabernacles, which celebrates God's care for the people who lived in tents during the Exodus. The words and actions of Jesus evoke its symbols of light and water. In the modern lit-up world, darkness is avoided through electric lights, inside and outside, enabling people to work and play sport under floodlights. In the ancient world, darkness at night was usual. When Jesus claims, 'I am the light of the world' (8.12), he evokes Scripture passages about light as well as the festival ceremony of light. At the latter, four youths climbed ladders to light four huge candlesticks topped with golden bowls filled with oil and wicks made from the worn-out clothing of the priests.[5] Dancing and singing lasted most of the night on each of the seven days of the festival. It is said that there was not a courtyard in Jerusalem that did not reflect the light of those candles. Those lights, however, are only a memory for John's community, as the temple had already been destroyed. For them, Jesus is present as light to the world (9.5).

In Scene Two (9.6–7), Jesus tells the man to wash in the Pool of Siloam. On each festival day, a procession led by the priests goes there to bring back water in a golden container. This evokes the gift of rain and also the gift of God's well of the Torah. Jesus' claim to be the source of living water causes consternation (7.40–44). In Scene Three (9.8–12), the man is questioned by friends and neighbours, who in Scene Four (9.13–17) bring him to the Pharisees. In Scene Five (9.18–23), he is abandoned by his parents and questioned, insulted and cast out by 'the Jews'. Perhaps the most shocking aspect of the story is the action of his parents. Their '[h]e is of age, ask him' turns their questioners' attention to their son, knowing that he will have to endure treatment that they are too afraid to face. Self-protection involves the betrayal of another.

Jesus is absent – the struggle of John's community

The absence of Jesus in Scenes Three to Six (9.8–34) is for a greater span than any other in this Gospel. What is going on here for events to be recounted without Jesus as a character in the drama? This beggar's story reflects the situation of John's community.[6] When they come to believe in Jesus a couple of generations after his death, they are alienated from family, friends and the synagogues. They face three difficult choices because Jesus has broken into their lives. First, they could remain in their local synagogue as members of a religious group that had official recognition in the empire and avoid the scrutiny of its officials. Second, they could stay with the synagogue, while at the same time also worshipping secretly as Christians, as did Nicodemus. (The man's parents may be in one of these two situations.) Third, John's people could worship openly as Christians and risk the consequences.

In his physical absence, Jesus is present in the experience and witness of this poor marginalized beggar who has grown in faith, has openly become a disciple of Jesus and has been 'put out of the synagogue' (9.22; also 12.42 and 16.2). Like him, John's community receive their sight from the one who is the Light of the World. Like him, John's community suffer for confessing it. The man's daring attitude to the Pharisees contrasts with that of his parents, the healed lame man (5.1–18) and Nicodemus (7.50–51). Nearest to the man's attitude is that of Jesus before the high priest (18.19–23). Jesus can be absent because his role is taken over by the beggar born blind.

'He is of age' (John 9.21)

The irony is that this outcast has his eyes opened to believe in Jesus. As others move to darkness and blindness, the beggar becomes not only a sighted but an enlightened disciple who moves from belief in Jesus as a person (9.11), as a prophet (9.17), to proclaiming him to be from God (9.33), to confessing 'Lord, I believe' (9.38). Thomas Brodie finds in his story, 'the complex process whereby a person is created, comes to birth, grows up and matures'. He is an 'emerging person'.[7] Margaret Daly-Denton highlights his growth in confidence and knowledge.[8] The learned ones regress. They shift from asserting that Jesus may be a sinner or be from God (9.16) to 'We know this person is a sinner' (9.24), and then to 'We know that God has spoken to Moses, but as for this one, we do not know where he comes from' (9.29). Two journeys go in opposite directions. Supposed ignorance of the Torah (7.49; 9.34) leads to his believing *into* Jesus (9.36); presumed knowledge of the Torah blocks recognition of Jesus (7.48; 9.34; 9.40–41; 3.10).

The significance of the beggar's progress to faith in Jesus is the circumstances under which it develops. He comes to knowledge and grows in confidence, not as do Thomas and the Samaritan woman in reflective conversation with Jesus, but in the process of *confrontation* with the Pharisees in Scene Four (9.13–17) and Scene Six (9.24–34). He has to struggle for his understanding, which came in the process of confession, rebuke and stubbornly continued confession.[9] Like the woman of Samaria, he could be said to be Jesus' co-worker. Those facing a similar choice are to be confident that their choice is not a disaster but a way to a deepened encounter with the One who gives sight. In Scene Seven (9.35–38), the beggar is asked by Jesus to take a further step in his journey into true light and sight. Is he able to accept that in Jesus, the one standing before him and whom he hears and now sees, he will find the revelation of God? He replies, 'Lord, I believe', and worships him.

Our progress to faith

This story begins with the question, 'Who sinned?' Words relating to sin occur more often in John 9 than anywhere else in this Gospel. In Scene Eight (9.39–41), Jesus makes clear that it is no sin to be blind. Sin comes from rejecting the works of God. It is not the Pharisees who see what is most important to see but a beggar born blind who sees more and more as he takes his stand against them.

In John there is a significant link between the action of Jesus and disciples imitating his action. Jesus describes one significant action of his as being exemplary when, in 13.14–15, he states, 'So if I, your Lord and Teacher, have washed your feet, you also ought to wash one another's feet. For I have set you an example, that you also should do as I have done to you.' While this action of Jesus is not a work of mercy for the poor it is surely typical of the understanding of discipleship in John. Disciples and the Church today are to imitate *all* the actions of Jesus, Master and Teacher. Jesus speaks of the works he does and of the greater works of those who believe into him would do (14.12). 'Works' include the healings of the marginalized poor in John 5 and John 9. The expectation is that 'greater works' would mark the life of the Church. All disciples are included in the remarkable emphatic 'we', whereby Jesus associates his disciples with the healing of the beggar: 'We must work the works of the One who sent me' (9.4).[10]

Oratio (Prayer) → *Contemplatio* (Contemplation) → *Actio* (Action) →

- This story begins with the question, 'Who sinned?' Words relating to sin occur more often in John 9 than anywhere else in this Gospel. This invites us to consider sin from the perspective of responding or failing to respond *to both the cry of the earth and the cry of the marginalized*. The Genesis creation accounts contain deep truths about human reality, which is grounded 'in three fundamental and closely intertwined relationships: with God, with our neighbour and with the earth itself. According to the Bible, these three vital relationships have been broken, both outwardly and within us. This rupture is sin' (*LS* §66). Steps are required for disciples to come 'to see', to come to be 'opened', to confront 'blindness' when right relationship with God, with people and with the earth is ruptured. 'We confess', says the WCC in 'Economy of Life', that churches and members 'are complicit in the unjust system when they partake in unsustainable lifestyles and patterns of consumption and remain entangled in the economy of greed'. Some even preach 'theologies of prosperity, self-righteousness, domination, individualism and convenience'. Some affirm 'theologies of charity' rather than justice for the impoverished. Others do not question and go as far as legitimatizing ideologies and systems based on unlimited growth and 'ignore the reality of ecological destruction and the plights of the victims of globalization'. Short-term, quantifiable results are focused on at the expense of 'deep-seated, qualitative changes' (§17). The WCC is also aware of the increasing number of churches in all continents that are 'stepping up their efforts and expressing their belief that transformation is possible' (§17).[11] 'We must work the work of the One who sent me' (9.4) – *we* disciples are drawn into this story to grow up, become adults with a mature knowledge of God and draw on our rebirth through 'water and Spirit' (3.5).

Notes

1 Stephen Motyer, 1995, 'Jesus and the Marginalised in the Fourth Gospel', in *Mission and Meaning: Essays Presented to Peter Cotterell*, Antony Billington, Tony Lane and Max Turner (eds), Carlisle: Paternoster Press, pp. 70–89.

2 Robert J. Karris, 1990, *Jesus and the Marginalized in John's Gospel*, Collegeville MN: Liturgical Press, p. 35. On 'the people of the land' (*am haartz*), see pp. 33–41.

3 Karris, *Jesus and the Marginalized*, p. 48. On the physically marginalized, see pp. 42–5; on the beggar born blind, pp. 46–50.

4 Francis J. Moloney, 1998, *The Gospel of John*, Sacra Pagina Series 4, Collegeville MN: Liturgical Press. For the structure of the eight scenes, see pp. 290–1; for an overview of the Feast of Tabernacles, pp. 232–6; and on translation of John 9.4, p. 297.

5 R. Alan Culpepper, 1998, *The Gospel and Letters of John*, Nashville TN: Abingdon Press, p. 171.

6 Raymond E. Brown, 1979, *The Community of the Beloved Disciple: The Life, Loves, Hates of an Individual Church in New Testament Times*, Mahwah NJ: Paulist Press, p. 72.

7 Thomas L. Brodie, 1993, *The Gospel According to John: A Literary and Theological Commentary*, Oxford: Oxford University Press, pp. 346–7, 350.

8 Margaret Daly-Denton, 2017, *John: An Earth Bible Commentary: Supposing Him to be the Gardener*, London: Bloomsbury T&T Clark, pp. 136–7.

9 David Rensberger, 1998, *Johannine Faith and Liberating Community*, Philadelphia PA: Westminster, pp. 41–8.

10 On the emphatic 'we', see Motyer, 'Jesus and the Marginalised', p. 80.

11 WCC, 'Economy of Life', §17, in Rogate R. Mshana and Athena Peralta (eds), 2015, *Economy of Life: Linking Poverty, Wealth and Ecology*, Geneva: WCC Publications.

Jerusalem
The Good Shepherd – John 10.1–30

'He goes ahead of them' (John 10.4)

Fourth Sunday of Easter of Year A
John 10.1–10

'The good shepherd lays down his life for the sheep' (John 10.11)

Fourth Sunday of Easter of Year B
John 10.11–18

'Jesus was walking in the temple' (John 10.22)

Fourth Sunday of Easter of Year C (RL)
10.27–30
Fourth Sunday of Easter of Year C (RCL)
John 10.22–30

Lectio/Reading of John 10.1–30

In reading and rereading John 10.1–30, be aware of its links with the story of Jesus and the beggar born blind (9.1–41). How are the words and actions of Jesus towards this person further expanded in John 10 to draw disciples into completing the works of God by responding *to both the cry of the earth and the cry of the marginalized*?

Meditatio/Meditation

'Those were shepherds' cottages' is how as a child I first learnt about shepherds. This was my father's explanation to my question about who used to live in two abandoned cottages in isolated spots on our hill country farm. Later, I associated a shepherd with my gentle strong father, sunshine or rain, combing the hillsides tending sheep. While the 'good' of the Good Shepherd was no surprise to my young mind, it would not have been so for those who first heard the extended image of the Good Shepherd in the words of Jesus in John 10.1–21. They knew of local shepherds and shepherds in the Scriptures, but there are startling differences. Shepherds are presented as abandoning and exploiting their sheep. No 'good' shepherd is found in the Scriptures.

Jesus coming up once again as a pilgrim to Jerusalem (7.14) for the Festival of Booths is the background for the long sequence of John 7.1—10.21. John 10 follows the story of the beggar born blind without any mention of a change of place, time or introduction of characters. Jesus has found the beggar 'they had driven out' (9.35). The words of Jesus about his being the Good Shepherd have been acted out in his words and actions with the beggar whose sight he restores (10.1–21; 9.1–41; Ezek. 34.12) and contrast with the religious leaders' treatment of this outcast. John 10 has four parts: the sheepfold (10.1–6); Jesus, the gate (10.7–10); Jesus, the Good Shepherd (10.11–21); and the division among the 'Jews' (10.22–42).[1]

'The shepherd of the sheep' (10.2)

The opening verses of John 10 present a new set of images in the words of Jesus: the shepherd, the gate, the thief, the gatekeeper and the sheep. Jesus draws on the daily life of shepherds who return to the sheepfold each morning and call to their sheep, who follow them out through the gate (10.1–5). The work of shepherds included moving sheep for grazing, protecting them from wandering off and from predators and thieves, caring for them at lambing time, shearing, and taking measures against disease and injury. Sheep were not only milked but killed for food and their skins used for clothing and for leather such as the sandals of Jesus (1.27). Human connectivity with the eco- and biospheres would have been Jesus' inherited tradition. Old Testament ecological images centre on the land, its diverse landscapes, its varied flora and fauna.

Jesus begins his discourse with a solemn 'Amen, Amen'. John 10.1–5 is concerned with the two different ways to enter the sheepfold and the response of the sheep to each of those two ways. Jesus starts in the negative. The 'anyone' who climbs over the wall, rather than enters through the gate, is a thief and a bandit. The real shepherd comes to the gate, which the gatekeeper will open for such a one (10.2–3). The focus moves to the response of the sheep. They recognize the voice of their shepherd who will lead them out through the gate. Jesus returns again to the negative. The sheep will not follow a stranger whose voice they do not know. Mention of a thief points to Judas, who later, at the anointing at Bethany, objects to the cost of the nard not because he cares for the poor but because he is a thief (12.6).

The word translated as a 'figure of speech' or parable in John 10.6 can have a wider meaning. This is a way of communicating through similes, images and metaphors. It is not plain or direct speech. It is full of movement. Multiple shades of meaning evoke many images. Even though readers' expectations tend to lean towards a particular understanding, Jesus takes us in another direction.

'That they may have life, and have it abundantly' (John 10.10)

Jesus will not be the one to lead the sheep through the gate as, surprisingly, he declares, 'I am the gate' (10.7, 9). Our understanding of 'the gate' is enhanced when placed in the setting of circular shapes with narrow entrances and funnel-shaped approaches, which archaeologists have identified as sheepfolds into which several shepherds would guide their flocks for protection at night. A shepherd would then lie across the narrow entrance, becoming a gate to protect the sheep from intruders. Jesus identifies himself with the gate.

Like his two earlier claims, 'I am the bread of life' (6.35, 41, 48, 51) and 'I am the light of the world' (8.12; 9.5), this claim of Jesus, 'I am the gate', is made with the temple in the background and during a festival. The temple, entered through its gates, was the symbolic gathering place for Israel and the nations. By the time this Gospel was written, it had been destroyed. Jesus is the new temple. His words and deeds in 10.1–18 do not remove him from his tradition. At least three biblical traditions are embodied in Jesus.

In the traditions of Matthew, Mark and Luke there are several references to the lost sheep of the house of Israel (Matt. 10.6; 18.10–14; Luke 15.3–7) or to sheep without a shepherd (Matt. 9.36). There are tirades against bad shepherds. These represent the compromised leadership of Israel, who abandon their flocks to wolves (Jer. 23.1–8) and exploit and marginalize the poor. There are calls for a leader who would ensure that the people are not like sheep without a shepherd (Num. 27.16–17). Two other traditions come together. Through his concern for the poor, marginalized by the religious leadership, Jesus participates in God's ongoing creation and re-creation by finishing the works of God. In the public space of the temple, Jesus evokes the biblical figure of Wisdom crying out for justice for the marginalized. Jesus as Wisdom is the one who gives life: 'I came that they may have life, and have it abundantly' (John 10.10).

THE MINISTRY OF JESUS

'I am the good shepherd' (John 10.11)

In John 10.11–18, we come to perhaps the most loved image and title of Jesus and the one most depicted in art since the earliest times. This is the image he gives to himself – the Good Shepherd (10.11). While the image of the Good Shepherd links Jesus with the longing of the people for the messianic shepherd of the biblical tradition, there is an image of his self-revelation that is unique: 'the Good Shepherd lays down his life for the sheep' (10.11). The self-giving of the shepherd to the point of death for the sheep is found nowhere else in the Scriptures. Ancient readers would, however, make other links that are lost on us because the word 'good' is the adjective describing the Shepherd. The original word means 'noble'. In this sense, Jesus is the best possible shepherd, a shepherd beyond all others. By applying 'noble' to Jesus as shepherd, links are made with ancient Greek writings, in which there are many references to 'noble death'.[2] Nobility is associated with those who give their lives freely for the benefit of others and triumph paradoxically through their death.

Jesus is no hireling who runs away in the face of danger. He does not abandon his flock even when in the preceding gospel story there are so many incidents that point to a violent end to his life because of his words and actions (2.20–22; 3.13–14; 5.16–18; 6.27, 51, 53–57; 7.30; 8.20). Jesus insists that his laying down of his life and taking it up again is an act of freedom (10.17). His death is a deliberate act of self-giving love. This is emphasized as Jesus refers to laying down his life five times in 10.11–18. He is not a victim. There is a link, too, with ancient ideals of friendship.[3] The true friends are willing to lay down their lives for their friends (15.13). Jesus' free offer of his life is shown, also, at his arrest (18.4–6, 11; and in 12.27 and 19.28–30).

The desire of Jesus, who has 'other sheep that do not belong to this fold', for 'one flock, one shepherd' (10.16) recalls when the people were exiled in Babylon. In the hardships of those times, the prophet Ezekiel speaks of God as the future shepherd who will gather the flock (34.11–16). After the fall of the monarchy, prophets speak of a future Davidic figure who will shepherd the people (Micah 5.4; Jer. 3.15). The sense of 'one shepherd' and 'one flock' emerges in Ezekiel (34.23–24; 37.24). Jesus in his boundary-crossing ministry gathers the people together.

A way of understanding John 10 that we shall explore further is as a trial scene. The 'noble shepherd' testifies. Sequences continue relentlessly in which those who hear him must decide for or against him (7.12, 25–27, 40–41; 9.8–9, 16; 12.29). A division occurs. Some accuse Jesus of 'having a demon', which suggests witchcraft. They consider he is 'out of his mind' (10.20). They have not heard his voice. Others show to some degree that they have heard the shepherd and 'know' him. They allude to the argument of the healed beggar born blind (9.31–33) and join with that brave marginalized one in bold defence of Jesus (10.21).

We turn now to John 10.22–42, which begins with a description of the setting (10.22–23). Two confrontations follow between Jesus and 'the Jews' (10.24–30, 32–38), separated by an attempt to stone him (10.31). This scene closes with an attempt to arrest him (10.39), after which Jesus returns to the Jordan area (10.40–41).

'Tell us plainly' (John 10.24)

A new scene- and a time-change mark the end of Jesus' ministry in Jerusalem (John 10.22–42). It is the Festival of Dedication or Hanukkah (10.22). This comparatively recent feast celebrated the rededication of the temple in 164 CE (1 Macc. 4.52–59). After being away for some time, Jesus returned, as a pilgrim, to hostile territory for this festival celebrated in the middle of winter, some three months after the Festival of Booths (John 7.2). He is walking in the portico of Solomon, where groups met to study, talk and debate (Acts 3.11; 5.12). Clearly, the authorities know what he is up to and opposition builds to the point that, as Jerome Neyrey suggests, this scene is patterned on a court trial.[4] There are remarkable parallels between John 10.22–39 and the Judean trial scenes of Matthew, Mark and Luke. In summary, in John there is an assembled elite who demand testimony from Jesus about his critical claim, 'If you are the Messiah, tell us plainly' (John 10.24). Jesus charges his questioners, 'I have told you and you do not believe' (10.25). His accusers deliver a judgement of blasphemy (10.33). We shall look, now, more closely at some aspects of this trial.

'My sheep hear my voice' (John 10.27)

From John 5, Jesus has been on trial by leaders, courts and crowds. Many times, he has been sentenced to death (5.18; 7.1; 8.20, 37, 40, 59). All this happens in Jerusalem, which is a place of hostility and rejection. Because of his words and actions over a considerable time, those putting Jesus on trial demand that he speaks to them 'plainly' about his claim to be the Messiah (10.24). Returning to the sheep/shepherd image (10.1–16), Jesus accuses his questioners of refusing to believe in him and of 'not hearing his voice'. This is a very serious matter as previously he stresses that those who do not believe in him will die in their sins (8.24). A contributing factor to their increasing hostility may well have been that the title and role of shepherd belonged traditionally to Israel's king.

Jesus spells out the criteria for being 'my sheep' in order to explain why his questioners do not recognize him. They do not belong to his sheep because the sheep of the Noble Shepherd hear his voice and respond to it (10.3, 4, 14, 16). The image of the sheep who hear his voice and follow him so that he may give them life and they may never be lost evokes the true believing disciple in this Gospel. A believing disciple 'hears' (10.3, 16; cf. 1.41; 3.8, 29; 4.42; 5.24, 28; 6.45; 8.38, 43;), has 'eternal life' (3.15–16, 36; 4.14, 36; 5.24, 39; 6.27, 40, 47, 54, 68), 'follows' Jesus (10.4–5; cf. 1.37, 43; 8.12;) and 'is not lost' (10.10; cf. 3.16; 6.12, 27, 39).

'The works that I do ... testify to me' (John 10.25)

Some acknowledge Jesus has spoken plainly (7.26) and understand that he is the Messiah. Some support the testimony of the beggar born blind (10.21). Jesus adds further testimony: 'The works that I do in my Father's name testify to me' (10.25). Among these works, as we have seen, are the healing of two of the marginalized poor. It is not, however, 'a good work' that is beneficial for others that is at issue. His questioners go directly to blasphemy. The issue is Jesus' relationship with God, 'you, though only a human being, are making yourself God' (10.33), and 'the Jews' attempt to stone Jesus for blasphemy (10.31–33; cf. 8.59). Later, some try to arrest him but he escapes (10.39).

Jesus is 'not making [himself] God' (10.33). It is very significant that Jesus speaks of himself as 'the one the Father consecrated (RSV, NAB, JB; NRSV has 'sanctified') and sent into the world' (10.36). Brendan Byrne points out that since the mention of 'consecration' is placed before 'sending', this implies the pre-existence of Jesus.[5] Evoked here is the opening verse of this Gospel: 'In the beginning was the Word, and the Word was with God, and the Word was God' (1.1). Jesus Wisdom-Sophia was with God at the beginning. 'Consecration' suggests being set apart for God's purpose (cf. 17.17, 19). Jesus continues the ongoing work of God's mission to bring life to the world. The setting, in the context of the Festival of Dedication, suggests that Jesus is not only the new temple, which is the seat of God's presence, 'but also its altar as the locus from now on of worship'.[6]

'And he remained there' (John 10.40)

Now Jesus leaves Judea and 'went away again across the Jordan' to a place of safety where he 'remained' (10.40; that is, abided) and many 'believe *into*' him (10.42). This suggests a situation of close relationships of friendship.

Oratio (Prayer) → *Contemplatio* (Contemplation) → *Actio* (Action) →

- In the two shepherd parables, Jesus the Good Shepherd is contrasted with 'a thief or a bandit' (10.1) and with 'a hired hand who does not care for the sheep' (10.13). This comparison invites disciples to extend these parables to a consideration of greed and its consequences today. The World Council of Churches initiated the Greed Line Study Group (2009–11) to work out how greed could be measured and monitored; to draw up ethical, theological and moral guidelines for just and sustainable consumption; and to outline proposals to avert greed in our economic systems. Greed could be defined 'as the desire to have more than one's legitimate share of wealth and power'.[7] The Greed Line Study establishes that the problem is greed that is 'a highly damaging form of desire' that has negative consequences not only for vulnerable communities and peoples but also for increasingly fragile ecosystems. Complex dynamics drive greed, which has to be interrogated individually, institutionally, structurally and culturally. Structural arrangements exist that facilitate, foster, demand and presuppose 'the development of greedy desires on the part of individuals or societies'. We can speak of 'structural greed' or 'institutional greed' with structural consequences. It works hand in hand with a 'culture of greed' or 'habitual greed' that shapes collective thinking and behaviour.[8] Disciples live in this tension and are called to interrogate this 'culture of greed' and not to be thieves who 'constantly consume and destroy, while others are not yet able to live in a way worthy of their human dignity' (*LS* §193).

Notes

1 Brendan Byrne SJ, 2014, *Life Abounding: A Reading of John's Gospel*, Collegeville MN: Liturgical Press, pp. 169–82.

2 Jerome H. Neyrey, 2007, *The Gospel of John*, New York: Cambridge University Press; on ancient funeral orations and 'noble' death, see pp. 180–4; on the trial of Jesus, pp. 185–91.

3 Gail R. O'Day, 2004, 'Jesus as Friend in the Gospel of John', *Interpretation: A Journal of Bible and Theology* 58.2, pp. 145–57.

4 Neyrey, *The Gospel of John*, pp. 180–1.

5 Byrne, *Life Abounding*, p. 181.

6 Byrne, *Life Abounding*, p. 181.

7 Rogate R. Mshana and Athena Peralta (eds), 2015, *Economy of Life: Linking Poverty, Wealth and Ecology*, Geneva: WCC Publications, p. 29.

8 Mshana and Peralta, *Economy of Life*, p. 30.

Bethany
Martha, Mary and Lazarus – John 11.1–45

'I am the resurrection and the life' (John 11.25)

Fifth Sunday of Lent of Years ABC (RL)
Fifth Sunday in Easter of Year A (RCL)
John 11.1–45

Lectio/Reading of John 11.1–45

In reading and rereading John 11.1–45, be attentive to how this story calls disciples to face the realities of the death and the decay of all life on earth, of human emotions and of Jesus' absence and presence.

Meditatio/Meditation

Martha and Mary are found at the turning point of this Gospel when the anointing of Jesus (12.1–8), and the death and raising of Lazarus (11.1–44), foreshadow what will happen to Jesus. A community's tragedy, the untimely death of Lazarus (history), is framed by two dialogues that explore the meaning of life/death and presence/absence (theology). The reader is drawn first with Martha and then with Mary into a new horizon of experience in which the reality of death is not denied but is transfigured.

These two chapters between the ministry of Jesus and his passion and death-resurrection are often called hinge chapters. They expand Jesus' promise that he 'came that they may have life and have it abundantly' (10.10). With all creation, the human community shares the abundance and interconnection of the life and death-resurrection of Jesus, which is expressed in the tension of both his absence and his abiding presence in the mystery of physical death (11.1–44), the abundance of the fragrance of the costly nard (12.5) and the image of the grain of wheat (12.24).

The last of three Passover festivals, found at three key points of Jesus' public life (2.13–23; 6.4–14), draws near (11.55) and is the recurring background of 11.55—19.14. Ironically, the raising of Lazarus leads to the resolve of the religious leaders to arrest Jesus (11.57). When a message comes from Martha and Mary to Jesus to go to Bethany of Judea, a short distance away from Jerusalem (11.3), he is 'across the Jordan' (10.40), where he is remaining (abiding). Jesus escapes an attempt to arrest him when he was last in Jerusalem (10.39). Serious risk lies behind his words, 'Let us go to Judea again' (11.7).

The paradox of life/death and presence/absence

No matter how 'prepared' one is for the passing of a loved one, when it happens, the experience of death shatters. My mother died just before her ninetieth birthday. Nothing prepared me for her absence and yet, paradoxically, for her presence. The paradox of life/death and presence/absence is explored in the narrative of the raising of Lazarus, which Sandra Schneiders points out integrates history, theology and spirituality.[1] The story of a community's tragedy, the untimely death of Lazarus (history), is framed by two dialogues that explore the meaning of life/death and presence/absence (theology). In offering 'eternal life' to his friends, Jesus does not shield them from the reality of death, which is the lot of all life on earth. In the face of death, the reader is drawn, first with Martha and then with Mary, into a new horizon of experience in which the reality of death is not denied but transfigured. We are helped to unite the ever-ambiguous experience of death – that of our loved ones, that of ourselves and that of all the universe – in our faith vision (spirituality). Schneiders summarizes this as, 'While history lies *behind* the text and theology is expressed *in* the text, spirituality is *called forth by* the text as it engages the reader.'[2] In John 11, the community experiences the death of a member, Lazarus, the brother of Martha and Mary, whom Jesus loved and called 'friend' (11.5; 11.11; cf. 3.29; 15.13–15). This is the community of eternal life, yet a loved member has died. The need to make meaning of this tragedy is explored in two theological dialogues.

'I believe that you are the Messiah' (John 11.27)

When Jesus comes eventually after Lazarus has died, Martha goes out to meet him. The first dialogue (11.17–27) is between Martha and Jesus. They talk about the meaning of life and death. Jesus proclaims, 'I am the resurrection and the life ... Do you believe this?' (11.25–26). Martha replies, 'Yes, Lord, I have believed that you are the Messiah (*christos*), the Son of God, the one coming into the world' (11.27). Her confession of faith is remarkable in itself and also in the context of this Gospel for three reasons. First, there are several confessions of faith: Nathanael (1.49), many Samaritans (4.42), Peter (6.69), the beggar born blind (9.38) and Thomas (20.28). Martha's is the most complete and reflects most closely the purpose of the gospel, 'that you may come to believe that Jesus is the Messiah, the Son of God, and that through believing you may have life in his name' (20.31). Second, her expression of faith is threefold. She acknowledges Jesus as 'the Messiah', 'the Son of God' and 'the one coming into the world'. Finally, most remarkably, Martha's confession echoes that of Peter in Matthew's Gospel. In the context of receiving the keys of the kingdom, Jesus proclaims him to be the rock on which he will build the Church. Peter confesses, 'You are the Messiah, the Son of the living God' (Matt. 16.16). Only on the lips of Martha is found such a similar confession in John.

'When she heard it, she got up quickly and went to him' (John 11.29)

The second theological dialogue is between Jesus and Mary (John 11.28–37), who is described as having 'anointed the Lord with perfume and wiped his feet with her hair', an event found later in 12.1–11. Mary hears that Jesus 'is calling for you' (11.28). In John, the phrase 'his own' is a special one used for Jesus' relationship with his loved ones who hear the voice of the Good Shepherd calling and follow him. Mary is cast as such a one. She hears his call and goes out to meet him on the way.

'The Jews ... were with her in the house consoling her' (John 11.31)

The two sisters are depicted as friends and followers of Jesus, yet they are in a good relationship with the general Jewish community, who are in their house consoling them in their grief (11.19, 31) and weeping with them (11.33). The sisters do not distance themselves from the mourners when Jesus arrives (11.32ff.). According to the Jewish scholar of John, Adele Reinhartz, these two women who had made choices that set them aside from the larger Jewish community 'continued to reside within it and relate themselves to it'.[3] In their grief, they draw support from that community. Reinhartz sees that the sisters are engaged in traditional mourning rites of first-century CE Palestine. It would seem that there are women disciples of Jesus who are integrated into Jewish communities, certainly in the time of Jesus and possibly in the time of John's communities. This family is clearly and openly attached to Jesus and integrated into Jewish life. This goes against the usual picture of the hostility assumed to exist between 'the Jews' and Jews who confess that Jesus is the Messiah, as presented elsewhere (9.22; 12.42; 16.2). It is extraordinary, to say the least, and unnoticed by most commentators.

'Greatly disturbed in spirit' (John 11.33)

There are four references to Jesus' emotional response to the grief around him and to his own grief. He 'was greatly troubled in spirit and deeply moved' (11.33). 'Jesus wept' (11.35, NAB, JB, NJB translations) and again he is 'greatly troubled in himself' (11.38). Later, he is 'troubled' at his impending death (12.27) and 'troubled' that one of his disciples will betray him (13.21). That same word for 'troubled' describes the movement of the water at the pool of Bethesda (5.7). Later, Jesus is mindful of his disciples' feelings and responses to their fears and hard times. He will assure them, 'Do not let your hearts be troubled' (14.1, 27; cf. 16.6, 22). There may be many possible reasons for Jesus' emotional response just before he raises Lazarus, among which surely is his awareness of the cost of what he is about to do. Part of the healing in John 9 and the raising from death in John 11 is Jesus' extended dialogue and interaction with those healed and those who stand by. This makes healing and the raising from the dead an act of friendship. These actions, however, place Jesus the healer in danger. His love for his friends, Lazarus, Mary and Martha, leads to increased hostility towards him, and the authorities plan his death (11.45–47). Later, Nicodemus' act of friendship in requesting the body of one executed by the Roman authorities possibly incurs considerable political risk.

Oratio (Prayer) ▸ *Contemplatio* (Contemplation) → *Actio* (Action) →

- Before Lazarus' open tomb, Jesus 'looked upwards' and prayed (11.41–42), as he had previously before his works (6.11) and as he will do later (17.1–26). The paradox of the life/death and presence/absence of Jesus opened up by this narrative's integration of history, theology and spirituality resonates with the ever-ambiguous experience of the death of our loved ones and the shadow of our own death. John's Gospel insists that resurrection happens for believers in the here and now. 'Eternal life' is experienced in the here and now. Our faith vision is stretched to encompass the paradox of the life/death and presence/absence of Jesus in the immense suffering of death in such events as earthquakes and the appalling ongoing aftermath. We can ponder the suffering of people and lands devastated by war, forests burnt for pastoral development, oceans used for waste disposal, species' habitats ruined, and imagine a restored world. We can learn from the ignorance of the past, the abuse of power and wilful destruction, and work together now to halt the damage and restore health within earth. So too, our faith vision stretches to encompass the paradox of the life/death and presence/absence of Jesus in the death and catastrophic extinctions built into the evolution of life in all its forms over billions of years. How is Jesus' death-resurrection foreshadowed symbolically in this story, in my life, in the world and in the expanding and unfolding universe? How is Jesus' presence found in his absence and how in his absence is he present? How might Martha's dialogue with Jesus and Mary's dialogue with him on the mystery of his presence in absence reflect the situation of John's community and the Christian community today?

- Imagine you are at Martha and Mary's house. Many of the Jews come to console them (11.19, 31). Pray and reflect on this family, which is clearly and openly attached to Jesus and integrated into Jewish life even though they have made other choices. This Gospel was written after the traumas of the destruction of the temple. They, along with other Jews, would have engaged in controversies over the proper direction that faith in God needs to take. The situation is rather like siblings in family disagreements. The Gospels repeatedly express that the early Christian communities are to be faithful to expressions of Judaism.[4] John's Gospel constantly draws on Jewish and biblical imagery and echoes. Jesus and his disciples give arms to the poor, an essential part of Jewish religious tradition (12.5; 6.8; 13.29). John's understanding of eternal life (11.24–25) is in sympathy with Hellenistic Judaism in that it presents Jesus' resurrecting power as already at work: 'I *am* [present tense] the resurrection and the life.' Resurrection is not 'a single future event but a quality of existence characterized by life that begins now'.[5] Maybe look back over times 'the Jews' are referred to in John's Gospel and bring to prayer your self-judgement of how you have responded. What changes may need to be made? Is access to informed information on the relationship between Jesus and his own Jewish people needed?

Notes

1 Sandra M. Schneiders, 1999, 'The Community of Eternal Life (John 11:1–53)', in *Written that You May Believe: Encountering Jesus in the Fourth Gospel*, New York: Crossroad, p. 161.

2 Schneiders, 'Community of Eternal Life', p. 151 (italics hers).

3 Adele Reinhartz, 1994, 'The Gospel of John', in Elisabeth Schüssler Fiorenza

(ed.), *Searching the Scriptures, Vol. 2: A Feminist Commentary*, Crossroad: New York, p. 597.

4 Ronald J. Allen and Clark M. Williamson, 2015 [2004], *Preaching the Gospels without Blaming the Jews: A Lectionary Commentary*, Louisville KY: Westminster John Knox Press, p. xxvi.

5 Allen and Williamson, *Preaching the Gospels*, p. 34.

Bethany
Mary Anoints Jesus – John 12.1–8

'Filled with the fragrance of the perfume' (John 12.3)

Fifth Sunday in Lent Year C (RCL)
John 12.1–8

Lectio/Reading of John 12.1–8

In reading and rereading John 12.1–8, be aware that perceptions of Mary of Bethany may be shaped by the history of interpretation that identifies her with the anointing woman in Luke's account and with other non-biblically based interpretations. Let John be John!

Meditatio/Meditation

In John's Gospel, the rivalry that generations of interpreters have assumed to exist between the two sisters in Luke 10.38–42 does not arise. Both are portrayed as exercising leadership differently in the two episodes. In John 11.1–45, Martha's leadership is displayed in her initiating action and participating in a theological discussion.[1] There, Mary's function is mainly to lead the Jews to the tomb and view the sign of Lazarus' raising, which leads some Jews to believe in Jesus and others to report him to the Pharisees, thus beginning the events that precipitate his death.

In this scene, Mary's leadership is highlighted. Two announcements about what is going on among the hostile Jerusalem elite (11.55–57 and 12.9–11) frame the story of Mary's anointing of the feet of Jesus. In this wider context, pilgrims are coming to prepare for the third Passover mentioned in John (12.1; 2.13; 6.4). We have seen how John 11 connects with 12.1–11. Six days before the Passover, Jesus and some disciples 'came to Bethany, where Lazarus was' (12.1, as translated literally in RSV, JB, NAB). In calling Lazarus 'our friend' (11.11), Jesus confirms that he is a disciple (15.13, 14, 15; 3.29). This indicates too that Jesus often enjoyed the hospitality of Mary, Martha and Lazarus. Mary has been introduced as the one who anoints Jesus and wipes his feet with her hair (11.2). The mention of Lazarus, whom Jesus raises from the dead (12.1), foreshadows Jesus' resurrection and recalls that this event leads to his own death. Even in this house of friends and in the company of his disciples, the nearness of the Passover and of Jerusalem, the knowledge of the plans of Pharisees (11.53), and the fact that Jesus no longer goes openly among the Jews (11.54), prepare the reader for further events that foreshadow his future. Martha and Mary have been part of the movement from death to life. Now they are present in the movement from death to eternal life. What glimpses emerge from this episode into women in John's community?

'Martha ministers' (John 12.2)

According to Schneiders, this scene seems 'to be evocative of the Eucharist'.[2] There would also seem to be a fusing of times – the time of the actual Jesus and the time of John's community, as happens so often in this Gospel. This meal is six days before the Passover. In John's sequence of time, the passion happens on the following Saturday (see 19.31). This would mean the meal at Bethany happens on a Sunday, which was the usual day of the Eucharist in the early Church. People believe the risen Jesus is among them. It is also possible that the washing of the feet is part of the liturgy of John's community. The activity of Martha is more often than not translated as 'Martha served' (12.2). The original word means 'ministered', which at the end of the first century was related to the ministry of those described by the term 'deacon' (Phil. 1.1; 1 Tim. 3.8, 12–13; Rom. 16.1). This understanding relies on whether the technical usage found in Paul, Luke and Acts was current in John's context.[3] Jesus tells us that 'whoever ministers to me must follow me ... Whoever ministers to me, the Father will honour' (12.26). Martha is the only person who 'ministers' in John's Gospel (12.2).

'The house was filled with the fragrance' (John 12.3)

Mary anoints Jesus with 'a pound of costly perfume made of pure nard' (12.3). The word translated as 'pure' means 'true' or 'genuine'.[4] John's original readers would have recognized that it is related to 'believing' (20.27) and to the verb used throughout the Gospel for to 'believe *into* Jesus' (see Appendix 2). Her anointing both anticipates and is performed for his burial (12.7). It is significant that Mary anoints Jesus' feet as opposed to anointing his head (Matt. 26.7; Mark 14.3). This alludes to the understanding that a disciple would sometimes wash the feet of a teacher or rabbi as an act of devotion and, therefore, suggests that Mary is a disciple of Jesus.[5] More significantly, it also links her action to Jesus' washing of the feet of his disciples (John 13.1–20) and his command that disciples imitate him in ministering to each other (13.14–16). 'During the supper' (13.2), Jesus does not talk about love, he washes feet. Likewise, the focus is on Mary's actions, for she speaks no words. Mary's action of great and extravagant love anticipates the love command of Jesus that is to be the measure of discipleship (13.34–35) and that all disciples are to imitate. Mary participates in three profound meanings of that action. First, she models the love and discipleship that Jesus seeks to show to the disciples (13.12–16). Second, Mary's action signals her participation in Jesus' suffering and death in a way that is integral to understanding Jesus' own action and words (13.3–11). Third, the word 'house' (*oikos* 12.3) is often used in biblical texts for the temple, which is associated with the fragrance of precious spices as is the Garden of Eden. Mary is honouring the temple of Jesus' body. Temple incense also evoked the divine presence.[6]

The fragrance and quantity of the nard fill the house, enabling all present to share in Mary's action. She asks no one's permission but is clearly portrayed as having independent access to resources to dispose of nard to the equivalent value of the yearly wage of a labourer. Mary acts autonomously and initiates her generous, loving, open action that contrasts with the dishonest, greedy, unfaithful, male disciple Judas.

'He kept the common purse' (John 12.6)

This meal with friends gives a glimpse into the practice of Jesus and his disciples concerning giving alms to the poor, an essential part of the Jewish religious tradition, as shown in Matthew 6.1–4. As we look at the word for 'the poor', which is used in several ways in the Synoptics (five times in Matthew, five times in Mark and eleven times in Luke), we must again 'let John be John'. In John, this word is used four times in the context of Judas and care of the poor on two different occasions (12.5, 6, 8; 13.29).[7] Judas was the keeper of the money box from which Jesus and his disciples gave money to the poor.[8]

John gives two details about Judas not found elsewhere. 'The disciples'' (Matt. 26.8) and 'some' (Mark 14.4) objected to the waste involved in the cost of the nard or ointment used to anoint Jesus' feet, which could have been sold and the money given to the poor. In John, Judas is the one who objects: 'Why was this perfume not sold for three hundred denarii and the money given to the poor?' (John 12.5). Three hundred denarii was a large sum of money. A denarius was a day's wage, so the total of 300 denarii was a year's wages for a labourer. The second detail about Judas is the reason given for his asking that question: 'He said this *not because he cared about* the poor, but because he was a thief; he kept the common purse and used to steal what was put into it' (12.6). The words in italics were used of the hireling who 'runs away because a hired hand *does not care for* the sheep' (10.11). Judas is portrayed as self-interested. Generous Mary is contrasted with greedy Judas. Jesus defends her action against Judas' complaint of waste.

Jesus and his disciples observe the Jewish tradition of almsgiving by caring for the marginalized needy. Much of the Jewish tradition had to be abandoned because of the destruction of the temple. However, in John's Gospel many of the functions of the temple are now centred in Jesus, the new temple of God. The tradition of almsgiving for the poor, especially for those suffering in their post-Jewish war situation, continues. This may well be another example of John telling us that Jesus and his disciples observe certain Jewish practices. Unlike Jesus and the disciples in the Synoptic Gospels, who had nowhere to lay their heads, had no money and were ministered to by women, Jesus and his disciples have money and give alms to the poor.

Some attention needs to be given to words of Jesus that are so often repeated and can overshadow the whole of 12.1–8: 'You always have the poor with you' (12.8). These words have been misinterpreted across the generations to preserve the status quo and to take the view that it is not possible to eliminate poverty. Even Jesus said it is not possible to do so! It is hard to find commentaries that deal with this sentence, so to quote Pheme Perkins, who corrects commonly held views of 12.8, 'Jesus' saying, then, does not reject the principle of concern for the poor; he merely rejects the attempt to invoke it against the woman.'[9]

Being disciples is for both women and men. This vision is underscored when the only other character who washes feet is Jesus' friend Mary of Bethany. She recognizes who Jesus is and that his hour is coming when 'having loved his own ... he loved them to the end' (13.1) by laying down his life. The noun 'the end' here links Jesus to his death; that is, his laying down of his life for his friends because his last words on the cross contain the verb, 'It is finished' (19.30). Mary's washing of Jesus' feet foreshadows the eucharistic love commandment in action. Jesus calls the disciples his 'friends' if they live according to his commandments and love one another as he loves them. This implies willingness for self-gift, for sacrifice, for laying down one's life for one's friends.

Oratio (Prayer) → *Contemplatio* (Contemplation) → *Actio* (Action) →

- The fragrance of Mary's 'true' or 'genuine' nard invites us to become aware of our sense of smell, which is one of five ways in which we connect with the earth and people around us. The sense of smell is very much linked with memory, emotion and mood.[10] Smell is connected with memory probably more than any other sense. Memories of childhood can surface. The fragrance of a lilac bush in spring can trigger a long-forgotten experience of a childhood home. Perhaps of all the senses, smell has been neglected. It does not have a precise vocabulary. When describing a smell, we say that it is 'like' or 'a bit like' another smell. Smell can warn us of danger, such as the smell of smoke or of rotten food. We share our sense of smell with other living creatures. Loss of the sense of smell can affect a person's capacity to make and sustain close personal relationships and can lead to depression. Loss of smell, a condition called anosmia, is unknown and invisible to all but the person without it. Because of collective and individual irresponsibility in our world today, earth's gifts of fragrance are being increasingly lost and often overwhelmed by pollution of the atmosphere, waters and the land. People are cut off from the smell of freshly turned soil in a vegetable garden; the smell of sheep in a paddock or field; and the fragrance of a rose.
- 'The common purse' held by Jesus and the disciples (12.6; 13.29) and from which Judas steals (12.6) can be extended to 'the commons', which refers to a shared resource held in common today – rivers, land, especially the air and atmosphere polluted and resulting in global warming and climate change. The World Council of Churches refers to the 'ecological commons', which 'through the use of military force, by the political and economic elites', have been degraded and appropriated.[11] The wealthy, developed one-third nations steal from the common purse. The ecologist and philosopher Garret Hardin named this situation as 'the tragedy of the freedom of the commons'. A shared resource cannot support the individuals who depend on it because of the collective effect of individuals who make independent and often well-intended decisions that lead to its degradation.[12] Wisdom invites reverence and respect for our planet: 'When I was born, I began to breathe the common air and fell upon the kindred earth' (Wisd. 7.3). 'The natural environment is a collective good, the patrimony of all humanity and the responsibility of everyone' (*LS* §95).

Notes

1 Sandra M. Schneiders, 1999, 'Women in the Fourth Gospel', in *Written that You May Believe: Encountering Jesus in the Fourth Gospel*, New York: Crossroad, pp. 93–114; on John 12.1–8, see pp. 107–10.

2 Schneiders, 'Women in the Fourth Gospel', p. 107.

3 The word *diakoneō* is used of Martha: 'There they gave a dinner for him. Martha served (*diakoneō*), and Lazarus was one of those at the table with him' (12.2). Otherwise in John's Gospel, it is used only of Jesus: 'Whoever serves (*diakoneō*) me must follow me, and where I am, there will my servant (*diakonos*) be also. Whoever serves (*diakoneō*) me, the Father will honour' (12.26). See 'The Diakonia of Jesus and the Early Church', in John Collins, 2002, *Deacons and the Church: Making Connections between Old and New*, Harrisburg PA: Morehouse, pp. 27–58. In John, Jesus uses the servant/to serve language (12.26), which is more accurately translated as minister/to minister.

4 Margaret Daly-Denton, 2017, *John: An Earth Bible Commentary: Supposing Him to be the Gardener*, London: Bloomsbury T&T Clark, p. 153. The word usually translated as 'pure' is *pistikē*, which is similar to *pistos*, believing (20.27), and the verb *pisteuō*, which is used for believing *into* Jesus.

5 Raymond E. Brown, 1966–1970, *The Gospel According to John*, 2 vols, The Anchor Bible 29–29A, Garden City: Doubleday, p. 564.

6 Daly-Denton, *John*, p. 155.

7 The Greek word for 'the poor' used in John 12.5, 6, 8 and 13.29 is *ptōchos*.

8 Robert J. Karris, 1990, *Jesus and the Marginalized in John's Gospel*, Collegeville MN: Liturgical Press, pp. 22–32.

9 Pheme Perkins, 1978, *The Gospel According to St. John: A Theological Commentary* (Herald Scripture Library), Chicago IL: Franciscan Herald Press, p. 133, quoted in Karris, *Jesus and the Marginalized*, p. 24.

10 On the sense of smell, 'Fifth Sense', see www.fifthsense.org.uk (accessed 10.10.19).

11 WCC, 'Economy of Life', §1, in Rogate R. Mshana and Athena Peralta (eds), 2015, *Economy of Life: Linking Poverty, Wealth and Ecology*, Geneva: WCC Publications.

12 Garrett Hardin, 1968, 'The Tragedy of the Commons', *Science*, 162 3859, pp. 1243–48, https://science.sciencemag.org/content/sci/162/3859/1243.full.pdf (accessed 10.10.19).

Jerusalem
'The Hour' Approaches
– John 12.12–16, 20–33

'Then they remembered these things had been written of him'
(John 12.16)

Palm Sunday Procession of Palms of Year B (RL Option 2)
Liturgy of Palms of Year B (RCL Alternative)
John 12.12–16

'Unless a grain of wheat falls into the earth' (John 12.24)

Fifth Sunday of Lent of Year B (RL)
Fifth Sunday in Lent of Year B (RCL)
John 12.20–33

'Then they remembered these things had been written of him'
(John 12.16)

Jesus' entry into Jerusalem (12.12–16), in what was to be the last week of his life, is essentially the same in the four Gospels. That said, there are details described as happening in John 12.12–15 and in surrounding events that are found only in John. It is Jesus' third journey to Jerusalem (2.13; 7.10). He appears to enter the city by walking from nearby Bethany. Crowds go to meet him. They carry palm branches, which were a traditional way of expressing triumph and joy, especially when welcoming a ruler (1 Macc. 13.51; 2 Macc. 10.7). Their shouting out 'Hosanna! Blessed is the one who comes in the name of the Lord – the King of Israel' (John 12.13; Nathanael uses this title in 1.49) expresses their hope for a royal messianic king. Many welcoming Jesus may have been present at an earlier Passover time in Galilee where he fed the hungry crowd and they tried to make him king (6.14–15).

In the other Gospels, Jesus asks disciples to make preparations for his entry into Jerusalem by arranging for a colt or donkey for him to ride. In

John, Jesus himself finds a young donkey (12.14) and sits on it, recalling Zechariah 9.9. His action of riding into Jerusalem on a young donkey speaks louder than words. In the face of the crowd's messianic expectation of his being a glorious king who will drive out the Romans, it is a critique of their expectation – he is not that kind of Messiah. Yet this action affirms him as 'the one who comes' (John 12.13), not as triumphant warrior king but as one who is 'humble and riding on a donkey, on a colt, the foal of a donkey' (Zech. 9.9–10). Jesus does not go to cleanse or close down the temple – that was done at the beginning of his ministry (John 2.13–22). The discussion about Jesus' raising Lazarus (12.17–19) leads the chief priests to plan his death (12.10). Jesus responds by proclaiming that his 'hour has come' and then speaks of his death-resurrection using the image of the grain of wheat that must fall into the ground and die (12.23–24).

Lectio/Reading of John 12.20–33

In reading and rereading John 12.20–33, many features found earlier in this Gospel emerge. Pilgrims 'going up' for the festival include Greeks who are presented as seeking Jesus through the Johannine pattern of approaching another person. Ways of speaking about Jesus' death recur along with a new image.

Meditatio/Meditation

'Unless a grain of wheat falls into the earth' (John 12.24)

Jesus' inherited belief in the gift of the land was the backdrop to his role in God's call.[1] The grain of wheat image in John is an example of how Jesus' imagination is grounded deeply in the natural world and in the human struggle with it. Many who first heard this image would have known that wheat is listed in God's promise of 'a land with flowing streams, with springs and underground waters welling up in hills and valleys, a land of wheat and barley, of vines and fig trees' (Deut. 8.7–15). A rich scriptural tradition associates God with creation. The prologue of John inserts Jesus into this scriptural tradition: 'In the beginning was the Word ... All things came into being through him' (John 1.1–3). In the cosmology of the time when this Gospel was written, the word for 'all things' was one of the terms used for what we understand to be the universe. The scriptural tradition accepts that mortality is integral to God's order of creation and humans share this with all living things (Ps. 104.29; Ecclus. 17.1–2).

While this image of the grain of wheat had rich connotations for those versed in Scripture, it was a familiar natural image that resonated with those who did not share that tradition.

Gift of long processes

Imagine you are holding a grain of wheat in your hand. Take time. Consider its size, shape, colour, texture, its potential for new life, its journey from the soil to your hand. This gift of earth evolved through long processes. Some 3.9 billion years ago, for example, photosynthesis emerged; 335 million years ago, the first forests emerged; 114 million years ago, flowers evolved with their colour, perfumes, nectars and seeds. This grain is descended from the family of grasses that evolved some 50–70 million years ago and from which, about 20 million years ago, came the sub-family that includes wheat.[2] The story of its ancestry is complex and includes gene flow from wild cereals. Early evidence suggests that it is possible that hunter-gatherers collected and used this grain's ancestors on the south-western shore of the Sea of Galilee about 19,000 years ago. The domestication of wheat took several thousand years, as in many locations spike, grain and plant size evolved to enable cultivation some 5,000–10,000 years ago.

For agrarian peoples, the repetitive organic nature of the processes of planting and harvesting, grinding and milling, baking and cooking were linked inextricably to the natural world. In all of this, God is in some way present and also present in the organic processes of the cosmos that are controlled by the wider-than-human. Life was hard in the face of drought and famine. Farmers knew that wheat depletes the soil and needs to be integrated within a crop rotation cycle and other measures for restoration of soil fertility. The cycle of the seasons – the death and renewal of nature – was at the basis of local fertility and mystery religions, and associated with the death and resurrection of a god. Karen Armstrong, in her book *Fields of Blood*, traces how settled agriculture introduced institutional or structural violence as elites began to control land and force others into subjection.[3] As Thomas Merton pointed out, all of us who have benefitted from this systemic violence are implicated in the suffering inflicted for over 5,000 years on the majority of people.[4] The earth has suffered from this systemic violence as resources of land and water have been relentlessly exploited.

The harvest imagery of 'the hour'

Let us look at what has happened just prior to John 12.20–33 (Fourth Sunday in Lent of Year B).[5] This wider context shows that several strands of this Gospel have come together. Jesus enters into Jerusalem amid cheering crowds. Those who oppose him are enraged. A real sense of building up to a crisis prevails. Up until now, 'the hour' of Jesus – his glorification and death – has not arrived (2.4; 4.21, 23; 7.30; 8.20). The arrival of the Greeks suggests that 'his hour' is imminent (12.20–22). Jesus' words with the crowds fall into three main sections: the necessity of his death (12.23–26); Jesus' struggle with his coming death (12.27–30); and the response of people to his coming death (12.31–36).

Disciples network to provide access to Jesus (12.20–22). Some Greeks approach. These most likely represent all the Gentiles who will come not to 'worship at the festival' but to worship the One who replaces the now destroyed temple as the presence of God on the earth. These Greeks 'desiring to see Jesus' (12.22) come to Philip, one with a Greek name from Bethsaida, who takes their request to Jesus. A pattern is repeated. Persons come to Jesus through another (1.40–42; 4.29–30). Jesus' invitation to the first called Jewish disciples (1.39) now extends to Gentiles who 'desire to see'. From the text, it is not clear whether or not the Greeks come to Jesus because his response appears to be made to Philip and Andrew: 'The hour has come for the Son of Humanity to be glorified' (12.23). The interconnectedness of his suffering and death-resurrection – how he is 'glorified' – is expressed in the agricultural image of the grain of wheat (12.22). This one verse has signals that alert the reader to other significant threads in this Gospel. The verse begins with 'Amen, amen I say to you' ('I tell you, most solemnly', JB), highlighting the authority with which Jesus is accustomed to speak (used 25 times in John). Demands for discipleship begin with 'unless' and preface rites of transformation: the grain dies that it might live and bear much fruit (also 3.3; 8.24; 13.8).

In the Scriptures, the image of harvest is used for several aspects of God's intervention in the world. One aspect particularly related to John is that when 'the harvest' comes, God will gather, redeem and heal God's scattered people (Isa. 27.12–13). In three images, in this Gospel, harvest is evoked by the gathering and bearing of fruit. The grain of wheat 'bears much fruit'. The vine and branches image refers to 'fruit' (John 15.2, 4, 5, 8, 16). The fields, which Jesus declares are ripe for harvesting even though it is four months away, have a reaper who is 'gathering fruit'. John's community are reapers of a harvest sown by Jesus (4.35–38). All these images rely on the soil, to which we now turn.

Down-to-earth God

Now hold a handful of soil. Take time. Touch and smell the soil formed by endless cycles of the weathering of rocks and necessary for all ecosystems.[6] Recall the words of Joel:

> 'Do not fear, O soil;
>   be glad and rejoice,
>   for the LORD has done great things!' (Joel 2.21)

Into the soil, the grain of wheat falls. Jesus, the self-revelation of God in our world, became flesh (John 1.14), a term that includes all living creatures. The Holy One, in embracing materiality, enters into the evolutionary process of becoming in which death is an integral part. God is with creation in process, in evolution, and is revealed in humility, a word derived from the Latin *humus*, referring to earth, soil or ground. Humble, then, may mean 'from the earth', 'down to earth' or 'grounded'. God hears the groan of creation, embraces the world of all living creatures in the incarnation and the cross, and promises re-creation in the risen Christ. In Jesus' resurrection, evolution reaches a new stage.[7]

The transcendent God enters into the evolutionary process in the unimaginable nearness of a down-to-earth, grounded God imaged by the grain that we can imagine falling into the ground and being separated from all in which it had lived. This is simultaneously a sowing and a falling and a dying. The Unshakeable One is shaken. Jesus' whole being (translated as 'soul') is 'troubled' (12.27; cf. 13.21; 11.33). In John's version of the agony in the garden, Jesus prays to be saved from 'this hour' and then praises God. He is affirmed by a voice from heaven (12.28). Jesus enters into the evolutionary process of death-resurrection to finish the work of God. He proclaims on the cross, 'It is finished' (19.30). The scattered people in the image of the harvest are gathered: 'And I, when I am lifted up from the earth, will draw all people to myself' (12.32). Significant for *hearing the cry of the earth* as we read this verse is a footnote in some Bible translations (e.g. NRSV) that points out that instead of 'all people' some ancient manuscripts have 'all things', which is one of terms for 'the universe' (1.3, see section on the prologue; 3.35; 13.3). This 'all things' reading suggests that Jesus lifted up on the cross draws the whole created world, not only human persons. Elsewhere, mission is shown to be the work of God, the Son and the disciples, as found in Jesus' prayer of John 17. All three parties are involved in 'the drawing' of people (6.44; 12.32; 21.6, 11). This is also suggested in 15.16: 'And I appointed you to go and bear fruit, fruit that will last, so that the Father will give you whatever you ask in my name.'

Oratio (Prayer) → *Contemplatio* (Contemplation) →
Actio (Action) →

- How does this image enable disciples to enter into the evolutionary process of the death-resurrection of Jesus? At two points of the *meditatio* (meditation) above there is an invitation to hold a grain of wheat in your hand and later some soil. It could be helpful to return and combine those invitations. Imagine the grain of wheat being planted in the darkness of the earth where all seeds grow. There in the womb of earth, new life emerges. Dying and death are the way of all living matter. In deep incarnation, Jesus, 'a grain of wheat', in embracing materiality enters into the evolutionary process of becoming in which death is an integral part. He invites his disciples to follow his example (13.15). Jesus the Christ is in process along with all living things. He is humble and returns us to the origins of that word *humus* – 'from the earth', 'down to earth' or 'grounded'. This involves a rite of transformation: the grain dies that it might live and bear much fruit (cf. 3.3; 8.24; 13.8). How does this down-to-earth image of the grain of wheat bring greater awareness of the gift of the earth? An aspect of bringing about transformation is environmental education. We 'are faced with an educational challenge' (*LS* §209) of broadening goals to include 'a critique of the "myths" of modernity grounded in a utilitarian mindset (individualism, unlimited progress, competition, consumerism, the unregulated market)' (*LS* §210). Sound virtues need to be cultivated to enable people to make a selfless ecological commitment 'to care for creation through little daily actions' that can bring real changes such as:

> avoiding the use of plastic and paper
> reducing water consumption
> separating refuse
> cooking only what can be reasonably consumed
> showing care for other living beings
> using public transport or car-pooling
> planting trees
> turning off electric lights
> or any number of other practices. (*LS* §211)

Notes

1 In what follows I draw on Kathleen P. Rushton, 2015, 'The Implications of an Eschatological, Cosmological Reading of the Prologue for Johannine Harvest Imagery', unpublished paper given at Australian Catholic Biblical Association Conference, Sydney (2–5 July).

2 On the evolution of wheat and its domestication, see Junhua H. Peng, Dongfa Sun and Eviatar Nevo, 2011, 'Domestication, Evolution, Genetics and Genomics in Wheat', *Molecular Breeding* 28.3, pp. 281–301.

3 Karen Armstrong, 2014, *Fields of Blood: Religion and the History of Violence*, London: The Bodley Head, pp. 10–13, gives an overview of how settled agriculture introduced structural violence. For more detail, see her Parts One and Two.

4 Thomas Merton, 1968, *Faith and Violence*, Notre Dame IN: University of Notre Dame Press, pp. 7–8.

5 On John 12.20–33, see Brendan Byrne SJ, 2014, *Life Abounding: A Reading of John's Gospel*, Collegeville MN: Liturgical Press, pp. 210–12.

6 Food and Agriculture Organization of the United Nations, 2015, 'Soils and Diversity', International Year of Soils. www.fao.org/documents/card/en/c/43b565e7-57c2-43c6-b4f0-812091486ed3/ (accessed 14.08.09).

7 On deep incarnation, see the section on John 1.1.

PART 3

The 'Hour' of Jesus: Last Night, Passion and Resurrection 13.1—21.25

Jerusalem
The Last Supper – 13.1—17.26

We move now to what is regarded as the second part of the Gospel. After the first part, known as the 'Book of Signs', which looks forward to the glorification of Jesus, comes the 'Book of Glory', in which the glorification of Jesus happens and is described. This movement is not sudden or unexpected. Until now, Jesus has moved among his own people, the Jews (1.11) – 'his own' in the widest sense. In finishing the works of God through his boundary-crossing mission of reconciliation across social barriers, he created conflict because he insists on including the marginalized among 'his own'. All 'his own' who 'received him, who believed *into* his name', were born of God into his new community (1.12–13). The prologue, also, prepared us for what was to happen, 'He came to what was his own and his own people did not receive him' (1.11). Over and over again, we have seen that most reject him or respond with inadequate faith (2.23–24; 6.66; 12.33–37). In John 13—17, 'his own' are restricted to his chosen group of disciples.

There is an obvious change of tone here. The harshness that colours the exchanges with those who have opposed Jesus gives way to the intimacy of the farewell meal. There is intimacy between Jesus and his disciples. There is the profound intimacy between Jesus and the Father. The disciples, as we recalled in the prologue, are drawn into this intimacy as children of God who are 'born ... of God' (1.13). In an awe-inspiring way found nowhere else, John 13—17 presents profound insights into Jesus' intimacy with God, which he shares with the disciples and into which they are drawn.

There are many ways of approaching John's Last Supper, in which interrelated images and themes appear and reappear and criss-cross. Three main units are offered below as a structure to approach this rich sublime section:

1. The foot washing and following dialogue: 13.1–30
2. The farewell discourse of Jesus: 13.31—16.33
3. The prayer of Jesus: 17.1–26

If the entire Last Supper is approached in this way, foot washing with its dialogue (13.1–13) and the long discourse of 13.31—16.33 comprise five major blocks about equal in length, as shown in the structure below.[1]

Structure of John 13—17

Discourse: Second Part: 15.1—16.4a:
'Abide in my love': 15.1–17
The world's hatred: 15.18—16.4a

Discourse: First Part
13.31—14.31

Discourse: Third Part
16.4b–33

Foot washing and following dialogue:
13.1–30

Jesus' prayer to the Father:
17.1–26

This scene happens at an evening meal just before the Passover. Note that Jesus is not celebrating the Passover meal with disciples as in the other Gospels. In John's time frame, Jesus dies on Passover Preparation Day, the day before the Passover (19.14, 31, 42), at the same time as the Passover lambs are killed in the temple in preparation for the Passover meal celebrated the following evening. In John, Jesus dies as the Passover lambs are being sacrificed. The link between the Eucharist and the Passover are found in an earlier Passover context in John 6. In what follows, the focus is on those passages proclaimed in the lectionary cycle.

Notes

1 On the farewell discourses, which many readers may find difficult to approach, I recommend the insights and clarity found in Brendan Byrne SJ, 2014, *Life Abounding: A Reading of John's Gospel*, Collegeville MN: Liturgical Press, especially the overview, pp. 225–8. My diagram is adapted from that book (p. 227).

Jerusalem
Jesus Washes Feet – 13.1–17

'I have set you an example' (John 13.15)

Holy Thursday Mass of the Lord's Supper of Years ABC (RL)
John 13.1–15
Maundy Thursday of Years ABC (RCL)
John 13.1–17, 31b–35 (for 13.31b–35, see John 14)

'I give you a new commandment' (John 13.34)

Fifth Sunday of Easter of Year C
John 13.31–35 (see John 14)

Lectio/Reading of John 13.1–17

In reading and rereading John 13.1–17 we find, at the place in the supper where Matthew, Mark and Luke tell of the Eucharist meal, that John presents Jesus as stripping to his waist and washing his disciples' feet, which was the work of a slave.

Meditatio/Meditation

'Jesus knew his hour had come' (John 13.1)

In the farewell meal, where we would expect to find the account of Jesus instituting the Eucharist, we find him taking a towel and washing the feet of his disciples.[1] This can be looked at in one of three ways: first, as an action that must be done and that places one person in a position of basic inequality; second, as an action that a person can do freely while the server remains superior; and third, as an action that a person can do in friendship and which is based on equality. New perspectives open up when this action is considered against the background of the grim reality of the institution of slavery on which the Roman Empire was structured. A great example of friendship is found when Jesus, the master (*kyrios*), washed the feet of his slaves (*douloi*, 13.4–6), to whom he gave the status of friends (*philoi*, 15.12–15).

The English artist Ford Madox Brown's painting, *Jesus Washing Peter's Feet* (1852–6), captures the Evangelist's characteristic way of telling the story of Jesus through vivid, concrete images that *embody* the Word made flesh (John 1.14). Jesus does not just talk.[2] He washes feet. There is a back story to this remarkable pre-Raphaelite painting. Madox Brown's original version caused outrage. Critics were offended by his coarse depiction of Jesus nude to the waist with leg exposed. The painting remained unsold for several years until Madox Brown retouched it several times and clothed the figure of Jesus in green robes. His original inspiration, which he returned to paint again in 1876, peels away layers that obscure the ancient context (world *behind* the text), the radical Jesus of John's gospel story (world *of* the text) and the transformation we are called to today (world *in front of* the text). Holy Thursday/Maundy Thursday offers an opportunity to look anew at Jesus' astonishing action and his example.

'The slave does not have a permanent place' (John 8.35)

John's Gospel was written somewhere in the Roman Empire, which was undergirded by the system of slavery. If written in Ephesus, it came from the 'hub' of Roman slavery. Slaves were brought from Asia Minor (modern Turkey) and Syria to the *statarion*, the slave market of Ephesus, where they were auctioned and transported to places of demand, especially Rome.[3] The focus of the auction process was a raised wooden platform. At the direction of the auctioneer, the naked or almost naked slave – sometimes with placard on which was written his/her notable features – stepped up on to it to be looked over and often probed by potential buyers. Spouses could be sold to different buyers. Children could be sold separately from their parents.[4]

All slaves were the property of their 'master' who bought them. They had no rights. Children born of slave or owner–slave unions became the property of the owner and, like all slaves, passed on usually to the next of kin through inheritance. At the order of their owners, slaves could be beaten, chained, imprisoned and even crucified. Any task could be assigned to them, including the lowly task of washing feet soiled by dust and travel filth. At the master's whim and with a moment's notice, slaves could be sold. The words of Jesus highlight the precariousness of a slave's position in a household in contrast to that of a son (8.35). When John 13.1–17 is considered in the context of slavery, new perspectives open up.

'Jesus ... got up from the table' (John 13.4)

The Evangelist tells us that choices had to be made about what was included in this gospel story (20.30–31; 21.25). This implies selecting how the story is told and where to put what is included. The foot washing is clearly central to the supper (13.4; 13.23–26). Things are going on here at many levels. In place of the institution of the Eucharist narrative told in the other Gospels, this Gospel images Jesus as the master who washed the feet of his slaves (13.4–6), whom he elevated to the status of friends (5.12–15). Usually, foot washing was done on arrival, yet we are told that 'during supper Jesus ... got up from the table' (13.2–4). Assuming the appearance of a slave, he 'took off his outer robe' (*ta himatia*), stripping down to his waist cloth, wrapped a towel around his waist and began to wash and dry his disciples' feet. Jesus' disrobing links the foot washing with his forced disrobing at his crucifixion, when Roman soldiers 'took his clothes' (*ta himatia*; 19.23). Crucifixion was considered to be the appropriate death sentence for a slave.

'Do you know what I have done?' (John 13.12)

Jesus' commandment to love one another as I have loved you (known in the Christian tradition as the *mandatum*, 15.12–13) is expressed in his example of foot washing (13.15) done from the motivation of love and friendship. This is found nowhere else in ancient literature. Jesus is not explicitly called 'friend' in this Gospel. His life, however, is the incarnation of the ancient ideal of friendship concerning love and death (15.13; 10.11). This ideal is described by Plato and Aristotle as the love that leads one to lay down one's life for friends.[5] According to Plato, 'Only those who love wish to die for others.' The disciples are to imitate Jesus, to wash one another's feet and to carry out his love commandment – even to the point of laying down their lives for others as Jesus does (15.13).

The washing of the feet may be understood in three ways.[6] First, one person is in a situation of inequality as in a master–slave relationship. This lingers in the liturgical washing of the feet on Holy Thursday. The 1956 Roman reform was an innovation that turned the washing of the feet into a clericalized, hierarchical, male-centred sacred drama.[7] Earlier Christians had rites in which they washed each other's feet (*Mandatum Fratrum*) and those of guests, and of the poor (*Mandatum Pauperum*). Further, uncritical appropriation has led to sincere church talk about so-called 'servant leadership' in a manner that theologizes away and obscures ancient slavery, which was intrinsically oppressive and maintained only for the benefit of the privileged slave owners. Second, foot washing can be done as an action that one does freely as in a mother–child relationship. One person remains superior. In the idealized image of Mother-Church and her children-members, the latter can be regarded as being eternally infants.[8] Unlike real mothers and real children, Mother-Church's children are often not encouraged or expected to grow up. Third, footwashing can be regarded as an action of friendship based on equality. It seems Peter knew that this would mean a whole new way of transformative relating and was unwilling to change.[9] Perhaps he understood that to let Jesus wash his feet would mean a conversion he was not willing to undergo. In other words, Peter's 'refusal of Jesus' act of service was equivalent, then, to a rejection of the death of Jesus understood as the laying down of his life for those he loved and implying a radically new order of human relationships'.[10]

The new commandment of this Gospel is about mutual love (13.34–35). Jesus uses the word *doulos* (slave, 13.16) here and also later in the farewell discourse in a way that offers a different nuance (15.15).[11] In this Gospel, Jesus never uses the term 'disciples' for his followers. Only in 15.15 does he address them by the term 'slaves', which he transforms to 'friends'. Translations of *doulos* in 15.15 and 13.16 as 'servant/s' (NRSV, JB), and on which the servant leadership motif is based, sanitize and obscure the master–slave relationship evoked by both foot washing and the prevailing practice of slavery.[12] Also obscured by this translation is the Jesus–friends relationship, which is the basis of transformative leadership. The meaning of the foot washing for us today is not about self-humiliation.[13] It is about participating in Jesus' work in order to change and transform sinful structures of domination in our society and church into a model of friendship that is lived in joyful mutual service unto death.

'I have set you an example' (John 13.15)

In his painting, Maddox Brown captures the shock and dismay of Peter and the disciples. We have seen that foot washing is central to John's supper – some suggest it was part of that community's Eucharist. How would the Christians of Ephesus and the empire have heard this story? They knew the reality of slavery and the cultural value of friendship – both expressed in the flesh of Jesus. Some Christians may have owned slaves. Should they wash their feet? The example of Jesus makes flesh/incarnates a whole new order of human relationships and self-giving. In his foot washing, Jesus calls disciples to participate in his work of transforming relationships, making right relationship happen with God, the earth and people in the Church and the world God so loves (3.16). Sandra Schneiders suggests that 'the "world" with which we are concerned ...

[is] the *good world* to which we are missioned, the *evil world* which we confront, and the *alternative* world'[14] we are called into with Jesus in the ongoing creation of finishing the works of God (John 4.34; 5.36; 14.12).

Oratio (Prayer) → *Contemplatio* (Contemplation) → *Actio* (Action) →

- '[S]pirituality is *called forth by* the text as it engages the reader'[15] in transformation. Our dialogue with John's Gospel is grounded in faith when we, with others, face slavery, which is a global threat touching nearly every corner of the world. The 2018 *Trafficking in Persons Report (TIP)* observes: 'Despite its global reach, human trafficking takes place locally – in a favorite nail salon or restaurant; in a neighborhood home or popular hotel; on a city street or rural farm.' The *TIP June 2019 Report* recalls that the *2018 TIP Report* covered the issue of supporting community efforts to find local solutions because local communities are full of partners in the fight against modern human slavery. How the public sees human trafficking has an impact on how governments act to address it. A well-informed public 'can be the eyes and ears of their communities and can put pressure on law enforcement to make it a priority'.[16] What does it mean 'to be the eyes and ears of [our] communities' in our world today as followers of the One, imaged as subverting contemptible slavery, around which the world of the time was organized? All have a role to play in bringing modern human slavery to an end. About 40 million people are enslaved worldwide, including an estimated 800 in my nation of Aotearoa New Zealand. We are implicated in a global lifestyle that demands cheap clothing, goods, services and food made available by exploited labour. We need to be informed, to buy fair trade, to be aware of people and to befriend them. The first human slavery conviction that happened in my country came about because a woman at a church service noticed a very upset woman, invited her for a cup of coffee and listened to her story. We need to learn to see the links between slavery and the degradation of the earth, as Kevin Bales explains in his remarkable, hopeful and accessible book, *Blood and Earth: Modern Slavery, Ecocide, and the Secret to Saving the World.*[17]

Notes

1 This section draws on Kathleen P. Rushton, 2013, 'Rediscovering Forgotten Features: Scripture, Tradition and Whose Feet May Be Washed on Holy Thursday Night', in Anne Elvey, Carol Hogan, Kim Power and Claire Renkin (eds), *Reinterpreting the Eucharist: Explorations in Feminist Theology and Ethics*, Sheffield: Equinox Publishing, pp. 91–112, and Kathleen P. Rushton, 2006, 'Eucharistic Wisdom and Friendship in the Gospel according to John', in Helen Bergen and Susan Smith (eds), *Whangaia ki te Taro o te Ora. Nourished by the Eucharist: New Thoughts on an Ancient Theme*, Auckland: Accent Publications, pp. 45–53.

2 For copies of Ford Madox Brown's paintings, see my article, Kathleen P. Rushton, 2018, 'Jesus Washed Feet: John 13.1–17', *Tui Motu InterIslands*, Dunedin, New Zealand, Issue 224, March, pp. 22–3, https://hail.to/tui-motu-interislands-magazine/publication/ak395Yu/article/koov4AD (accessed 10.08.19).

3 W. V. Harris, 1999, 'Demography, Geography and the Source of Roman Slaves', *Journal of Roman Studies*, 89, p. 74.

4 For an accessible overview of slavery at this time, see Richard J. Cassidy, 2015, *John's Gospel in New Perspective: Christology and the Realities of Roman Power, With the New Essay, 'Johannine Footwashing and Roman Slavery'*, first published 1992, Eugene OR: Wipf & Stock, pp. 119–23.

5 Gail R. O'Day, 2004, 'Jesus as Friend in the Gospel of John', *Interpretation: A Journal of Bible and Theology* 58.2, pp. 144–57. See pp. 146 and 156 for references to Plato, *Symposium* (*Symp*.179B), who records that 'only those who love wish to die for others'. Cf. Aristotle, *Nicomachean Ethics* (*Eth. Nic*. 9.8.9), 'it is also true the virtuous man's conduct is often guided by the interests of his friends and of his country, and that he will if necessary, lay down his life in their behalf ... And this is doubtless the case with those who give their lives for others' (LCL translation).

6 Sandra M. Schneiders, 1999, 'A Community of Friends (John 13:1–20)', in *Written that You May Believe: Encountering Jesus in the Fourth Gospel*, New York: Crossroad, pp. 170–2.

7 Rushton, 'Rediscovering Forgotten Features', pp. 102–9.

8 Cristina Lledo Gomez, 2015, 'The Motherhood of the Church: Mary, the Quotidian and the People of God', in Catholic Women Speak Network (eds), *Catholic Women Speak*, Mahwah NJ: Paulist Press, pp. 32–6.

9 Schneiders, 'Community of Friends', p. 169.

10 Schneiders, 'Community of Friends', pp. 169, 173, 176.

11 The disciples are no longer slaves (*doulos*) but friends (*philos*): 'This is my commandment, that you love one another as I have loved you. No one has greater love than this, to lay down one's life for one's friends (*philos*). You are my friends (*philos*) if you do what I command you. I do not call you slaves (*doulos*) any longer, because the slave (*doulos*) does not know what the master is doing; but I have called you friends (*philos*), because I have made known to you everything that I have heard from my Father' (John 15.13–15, NRSV). On Wisdom and friendship in John, see Sharon H. Ringe, 1999, *Wisdom's Friends: Community and Christology in the Fourth Gospel*, Louisville KY: Westminster John Knox Press.

12 'So if I, your Lord and Teacher, have washed your feet, you also ought to wash one another's feet. For I have set you an example (*hupodeigma*), that you also should do as I have done to you. Very truly, I tell you, slaves (*doulos*) are not greater than their master' (13.14–16). Jesus uses *diakonein/diakonos*: 'Whoever serves (*diakonein*) me must follow me, and where I am, there will my servant (*diakonos*)

be also. Whoever serves (*diakonein*) me, the Father will honour' (12.26). The New American Bible translates *doulos* as 'slaves' in 13.16 and 15.15. Other translations – The Douay-Rheims, New Revised Standard Version, Revised Standard Version, Jerusalem Bible, New Jerusalem Bible, Good News Bible and Christian Community Bible – all have 'servants'; see *The Catholic Comparative New Testament*, Oxford: Oxford University Press, 2006. 'Servant' is an appropriate translation for *pais*, which is a collective term for all members of a household subordinate to the master, for example servant, child, son (found only in Matthew, Luke-Acts). I have reservations about translating *diakonos* as servant, but space does not permit discussion here.

13 Schneiders, 'Community of Friends', pp. 176.

14 Sandra M. Schneiders, 2013, *Buying the Field: Catholic Religious Life in the Mission to the World*, Mahwah NJ: Paulist Press, p. 37 (italics hers).

15 Schneiders, 'Community of Friends', p. 151 (italics hers).

16 Department of State, United States of America, 2018, *Trafficking in Persons Report (TIP)*, 2018, www.state.gov/trafficking-in-persons-report-2018/ (accessed 21.07.19); Department of State, United States of America, 2019, *Trafficking in Persons Report (TIP)*, p. 12, www.state.gov/wp-content/uploads/2019/06/2019-Trafficking-in-Persons-Report.pdf (accessed 21.07.19).

17 Kevin Bales, 2016, *Blood and Earth: Modern Slavery, Ecocide, and the Secret to Saving the World*, New York: Spiegel & Grau.

Jerusalem
First Part of the Last Supper Discourse – John 13.31—14.31

'I give you a new commandment' (John 13.34)

> Fifth Sunday of Easter of Year C
> John 13.31-35

'The one who believes into me will also do the works that I do'
(John 14.12)

> Fifth Sunday of Easter of Year A (RL)
> John 14.1-12
> Fifth Sunday of Easter of Year A (RCL)
> John 14.1-14

'The Spirit of Truth ... abides with you' (John 14.17)

> Pentecost Sunday Vigil of Year C (RL option)
> John 14.15-16, 23b-26
> Day of Pentecost of Year C (RCL)
> John 14.8-17 (25-27)
> Sixth Sunday of Easter of Year A
> John 14.15-21
> Sixth Sunday of Easter of Year C
> John 14.23-29

The foot washing and following dialogue (13.1–30), the first of the three main units in the scene of the Last Supper (John 13—17), ends when Judas goes out and 'it was night' (13.30). It may be helpful to return and look at the 'Structure of John 13—17' diagram set out at the beginning of Part 3. After Judas leaves, a new atmosphere is created. Jesus begins a long discourse (second main unit: 13.31—16.33), which we shall consider in three parts. The First Part of his discourse comprises 13.31—14.31. In the centre is the Second Part, which consists of 15.1—16.4a, where Jesus encourages his disciples 'to abide in his love' (15.1-17) and afterwards prepares them for the hatred and persecution they will experience from the world (15.18—16.4a). The Third Part, which comprises 16.4b-33, is similar to the First Part of Jesus' discourse but less positive in tone.

The earliest Christians would have recognized this seemingly repetitive talk by Jesus as a farewell address. In this genre or type of literature, a well-known leader or teacher gave instructions before death. Both Jacob (Gen. 49) and Moses (Deut. 31—33) do so. In the ancient world, a dying leader or teacher delivered a farewell address containing a last will and testament.[1] Today, many would associate a will with goods and property. It was not so in the time of Jesus. The leader about to die expressed deep concern for the well-being of the group in general and for individuals after his death. He announced that his death was about to happen, reviewed his life to set the record straight, stressed that relationships were to continue and talked about the good things that were to happen as well as the hard times ahead. He encouraged his followers to practise virtues and to avoid vices, named a successor, gave a legacy and usually finished with a final prayer.

These purposes permeate the Evangelist's creative presentation of the teaching of Jesus in the form of the farewell address found in John 13.31—16.33. His final words of consolation and encouragement to his disciples need to be understood within this cultural framework. In his farewell discourse, the words of Jesus move between two levels of time. On the one hand, today's readers are taken back to the Last Supper and the end of Jesus' life on earth, where what comes into view is the actual situation of the disciples. Jesus talks of 'going away' and 'coming to you'. 'Going away' refers to his disciples when he dies on the cross. 'Coming to you' refers to when Jesus 'returns' to them after his resurrection. On the other hand, the situation of the disciples after Jesus has departed this earth is put before us.

Lectio/Reading of John 13.31-35

In reading and rereading John 13.31-35, it is helpful to consider it as part of the long farewell discourse Jesus presents to the disciples. He knows 'his hour' is approaching because his barrier-crossing ministry of completing the works of God has upset the status quo and enraged both the leaders of his own people and those of the empire of Rome. In completing the works of God, disciples face similar or different opposition.

Meditatio/Meditation

'Just as I have loved you, you also should love one another'
(John 13.34)

The Gospel reading proclaimed on the Fifth Sunday after Easter in Year C, John 13.31–35, forms the first five verses of 13.31—14.31, which we have called the First Part of Jesus' long discourse. The lectionaries in Easter continue to focus on the risen Jesus who empowers the people of God every day of the year. Unlike the gospel characters, who did not have this Gospel in written form, the early Christian communities, from which this Gospel arose probably in the 90s, knew and experienced the risen Jesus. The post-Easter Gospel readings of Year C show two ways in which Jesus is present and through which people came into the family of faith after the resurrection. The first is through the Holy Spirit (e.g. 14.23–29; 20.21–22). The second way, through the work of the disciples, will be explored in our reflection on John 13.31–35, which we shall first place in the context of Judas' leaving the supper (13.26–31). Then we shall consider the new commandment.

'He should give something to the poor' (John 13.29)

Judas went out into the night (13.31). In order to hear the cry of the marginalized in this Gospel, we shall turn briefly to one of the reasons why some disciples assume he leaves. Judas keeps their common purse (13.29; 12.6). They think that Jesus is telling him to act quickly so that 'he should give something to the poor'. This is the last of the four times when 'the poor' are referred to in John (12.5, 6, 8) and the second incident that indicates that Jesus and his disciples have money in a common purse from which, according to the Jewish custom, they give alms to the poor. Jesus and the disciples, here and at the meal at Bethany (12.5–8), continue this Jewish practice. This was especially so at this festival time because it was customary to give something to the poor on Passover night.[2] After Judas leaves, Jesus is with his disciples who, despite their weakness, which will soon be revealed, have the intention of remaining true and loyal. Judas' departure ushers in the process of the movement towards the death of Jesus. Remember that this time, too, hovers between the time of Jesus and the time of John's community. In 13.31–35, a new phase begins in the supper scene, which moves now into the intimate atmosphere of Jesus' farewell discourse.

'Having loved his own' (John 13.1)

Throughout John, Jesus speaks of his death-resurrection in many images. Some are material images taken from creation or daily life, such as the grain of wheat or the shepherd laying down his life for his sheep. Other images are abstract ones, such as glorification, which indicates that his death-resurrection was underway. In 13.31–32, five references are found to the mutual glorification of God and Jesus, which span the past, present and future in ways it is hard to unravel. In the biblical tradition, 'glorify' is associated with the glory of the unseen presence of God in the saving event of the Exodus. While his glorification is being brought about by betrayal and execution as a criminal, the core of 'glory/glorify' centres on the revelation of God in the person and life of Jesus.

'Just as I have loved you' (13.34)

The intimacy and love that exists between Jesus and 'his own' – his disciples – is expressed by his addressing them by the endearing term, 'little children' (13.33). Repetition of such experiences as 'only a little longer' and 'I am going' away suggests a sense of loss and grief. He is returning to God. They cannot follow and will experience his absence keenly. As the discourse unfolds, we learn what is being done to meet this new situation.

Jesus gives the disciples a new commandment of love (13.34–35). The loss of the love of the physical presence of Jesus is to be compensated for by the love they are to have for one another.[3] Jesus gives them love in action as an example of how they are to love. Rather than just speak about love, Jesus acts. He washes their feet (13.1–17). Disciples are to do likewise. The commandment of love is already in place (Lev. 19.18). It is new in that now it is to be lived out in the new situation of the departure of Jesus to such a degree that, by this love, 'everyone will know that you are my disciples, if you have love for one another' (John 13.35). New too is the measure of this love, 'just as I have love you' (13.34). The conjunction 'as' is found 31 times in this Gospel. Sometimes it simply means 'as' in the sense of 'for example' ('as it is written' 6.31). Several times it is used in a 'see-and-do-likewise' dynamic in the relationship between Jesus and his disciples, as in 'just as I have loved you' (13.34; cf. 15.10; 17.11, 21, 22; and 17.18; 20.21).[4] Jesus' new commandment shows a three-phase dynamic or movement in this Gospel's ethics: as the Father has loved Jesus, Jesus has loved the disciples (15.9; 17.23), and the disciples are to love one another *as* Jesus has loved them (13.34).

Loving one another is integral to the ethical dimension found in the link between cosmology and the human person in the prologue of this Gospel, and is in direct continuity with the love that they receive from Jesus who speaks about finishing the works of God (4.34; 5.36; 19.28, 30). In his barrier-crossing ministry of reconciliation, he moves across frontiers to create a new community to participate with him in completing the works of God. In action, he seeks to bring into practice what he is to pray later, 'that they may be one' (17.21). Disciples are to continue this work by their love for each other. People would come to faith through this work of the disciples.

Oratio (Prayer) → *Contemplatio* (Contemplation) → *Actio* (Action) →

- There is a new situation in Aotearoa New Zealand and for many around the world following the massacre of 51 innocent people worshipping in two mosques in Christchurch on 15 March 2019. At the National Remembrance Service, Prime Minister Jacinda Ardern urged, 'We each hold the power [to combat hate], in our words and our actions, in daily acts of kindness. Let that be the legacy of the 15th March.' A survivor, Farid Ahmed, whose wife Husna was killed at the Masjid Al Noor Mosque, spoke tenderly: 'I don't want to have a heart that is boiling like a volcano ... I want a heart that is full of love and care, and full of mercy, a heart that will forgive lavishly.'[5] In this new situation, we are to move on to complete the works of God by creating new ways in word and action to 'love one another just as I have loved you' and care for our common home.

Lectio/Reading of John 14.1–31

In reading and rereading John 14.1–31, which is part of the farewell discourse, it could be helpful to be aware of how the purposes of such a farewell, outlined above, influence the words of Jesus who expresses his deep concern for the well-being of the group of disciples in general and for individuals.

Meditatio/Meditation

'The one who believes in me will also do the works that I do' (John 14.12)

Various passages of John 14 are proclaimed five times in the three-year lectionary cycle after Easter and around Pentecost. This parallels John's intention. The Evangelist is not just recording what happened at that supper in the month of Nisan in the early 30s CE. What is being told is the story of the life and death-resurrection of Jesus and its significance for a community in another time and place – probably in the 90s and probably in the Roman city of Ephesus. By then, many had suffered for their belief in Jesus, 'for the Jews had already agreed that anyone who confessed Jesus to be the Messiah would be put out of the synagogue' (John 9.22; also 12.42; 16.2). This significance of the death-resurrection of Jesus continues wherever Christians today, in their particular life situations, assemble at the Eucharist or for worship to hear the Word of God proclaimed. Our exploration will attempt to give an overview of John 14, which has many parallels with John 16.

While the atmosphere of intimacy at the supper is pierced by Jesus' repetition of phrases like having 'only a little longer' and 'I am going', perhaps there was another problem troubling the disciples. This is hinted at in the dialogue between Jesus and Peter (13.36–38). The love required by the new commandment is the means by which the love of the physical presence of Jesus is to be compensated for by the love that disciples are to have for one another – 'just as I have loved you' (13.31–35). This following of Jesus in the biblical sense of discipleship may mean laying down one's life. Earlier at the foot washing, Peter seems to understand that a whole new way of transformation is required. His assertion that he would lay down his life for Jesus echoes the Good Shepherd (10.11, 15, 17–18). This is brought to ground by Jesus' declaring solemnly ('Amen, Amen') that Peter would deny him three times (13.38). In the rest of this part of his discourse (14.1–31), Jesus addresses the disciples' lack of understanding. Jesus is speaking to them in the midst of the hard times they are facing. Be aware also of the other elements of a farewell discourse that influenced the way the Evangelist wrote John 13.31—16.33.

'Do not let your hearts be troubled' (John 14.1)

Now, mindful of their feelings and responses, Jesus begins and ends by assuring them, 'Do not let your hearts be troubled' (14.1, 27; cf. 16.6, 22). He is intent on forming their hearts. He is aware of their emotions.

The word translated as 'troubled' means literally 'stirred up'. It describes the movement of the water at the pool of Bethesda (5.7) and Jesus' own inner agitation and emotional distress at the death of his friend Lazarus and at the prospects of his own death (11.33; 12.27; 13.21). The emphasis on their 'hearts' continues as Jesus uses more imperatives: 'Believe *into* God, believe *into* me' (14.1). Here again we find this Gospel's much used unique expression, 'believe *into*', which comes from the heart, the centre of one's being and suggests the fidelity and faithfulness that bound one person to another. This is a dynamic and an active commitment. This Evangelist prefers verbs – doing words and actions. 'Believing *into* Jesus' is a work of God required of all who seek to follow him who repeats yet again, 'I am going away' (14.2–3, 28).

'Many dwelling places' (John 14.2)

After reassuring the disciples, 'Do not let your hearts be troubled. Believe *into* God, believe *into* me' (14.1), Jesus explains that even though he would not be present physically for some time, it is for their benefit (14.2–4). In his Father's house, there are 'many dwelling places'. Dwelling place and house suggest a place of belonging and of being at home. The purpose of his going away is to 'prepare' a place for them. This text is often chosen for funerals because of a popular view of 'heaven' in which 'rooms' are provided for the faithful departed to live for all eternity. To consider John 14.2 in terms of buildings or space is a limiting view that undermines the theological depth of Jesus' words. No fixed sacred space or temple on earth made sacred by God's dwelling exists (4.21). The body of Jesus is the new temple. The Greek word translated as 'dwelling places' (NRSV) and 'rooms' (JB) is one of a cluster of words found in this Gospel that have the sense of the divine 'abiding', 'remaining' or 'dwelling'.[6] The whole purpose of Jesus' coming into the world to finish the works of God is that human persons may share in the status of becoming 'children of God' (1.12). This means living the eternal life that Jesus had with God from the beginning (1.1). Jesus is 'going away' to 'prepare', through his life and death-resurrection, 'dwelling places' for them to dwell as children of God so that 'where he is' – not just spatially but by right and privilege – they also may be (14.3).[7] Significantly, the dwelling places are 'many' because in a number of ways Jesus would remain present with his disciples through the love they have for one another (13.34), through keeping his word, through Jesus and the Father dwelling in them (14.22–24) and through the presence of the Holy Spirit.

We have seen how John 14 begins with the phrase, 'Let not your heart be troubled' (plus reasons, 14.1–4), and ends with the same imperative

(14.27–31). The body of this passage is structured around questions, as is often the case in John. A pattern recurs. Jesus makes a statement that provokes misunderstanding, and then a question is asked of him or a statement made. Further explanations follow. Here, the questions of three named disciples – Thomas (14.5), Philip (14.8) and Judas not Iscariot (14.22) – structure the discourse.

'I am the way, and the truth, and the life' (John 14.6)

Jesus' assurance to his disciples that 'you know the way to where I am going' gives rise to the question of the ever-inquiring Thomas, who objects that because they do not know where he was going, how could they know 'the way' (14.5; 11.16; 20.24). To Thomas' question, which is most likely also the question of all present, Jesus replies, 'I am the way, and the truth, and the life' (14.6). This very dense claim is made at a time of crisis. Jesus is 'going away' and the disciples face uncertainty and impending persecution. This is the first and only time this key term, 'the way', is introduced by Jesus (14.4, 5, 6). It evokes being earthed, embodied and walking. There are rich biblical connections here, such as Isaiah's 'preparing the way of the Lord', which was quoted previously by John the Baptizer (John 1.23), the only other time we hear of 'the way' in this Gospel. Jesus continues to give the disciples knowledge and reveals further aspects about himself in relationship to them. This statement and the other 'I am' sayings (6.35, 41, 48, 51; 8.12; 10.7, 9; 15.1, 5) are more about what Jesus brings uniquely to the world, how he benefits the world, rather than being just about himself.

The links between the claims of 'I am the way, and the truth, and the life' (14.6) are very clear. In this Gospel, one of the central issues is the identity of Jesus. Integral to his identity is his relationship with God. Jesus is 'the way' because he is 'the word made flesh' who reveals who God is ('truth'), and when people come to believe *into* him, they share in eternal 'life'. Jesus has been imaged repeatedly as biblical divine Wisdom. In describing himself as 'the way', he takes to himself an aspect of how Wisdom is named in the Jewish biblical tradition (Prov. 4.11; 8.32; 23.19; Wisd. 10.17–18). After the destruction of the temple, emphasis was given to Wisdom now being found in the Torah. In his claim, 'I am the way', Jesus sets himself against many of his contemporaries who believe that Torah is 'the way', as found in Psalm 119 (119.1, 14, 27, 32, 33, 128). The earliest name of the Christian movement is the 'Way' (Acts 9.2; 19.9, 23; 22.4; 24.14, 22). Jesus embodies the truth (John 1.14, 17). Knowing Jesus sets one free (8.32) but not everyone accepts the truth (18.38). Acceptance or rejection of Jesus as 'the truth' reflects the constant refrain of the rejection of the 'the way' of Wisdom (John 1.10-11; 5.43; 7.19; 8.37; 9.22; 10.31; Prov. 1.20-23; Bar. 3.9-24). 'Life' is a persistent thread throughout this Gospel. At the heart of Jesus' finishing the works of God is the sharing of eternal life (1.4; 3.16; 5.24-26; 11.25).

'And still you do not know me?' (John 14.9)

Immediately after Jesus tells the disciples that he is 'the way' to the Father and that anyone who knows Jesus comes to know and see the Father, Philip asks him to 'show us the Father' (14.8). After rebuking Philip, Jesus states that it is not necessary for anyone to show them the Father because Jesus is in their midst. Later, Judas (not Iscariot) asks about how it is that he reveals himself to them and not to the world (14.22). These interruptions indicate that the disciples still do not understand. In what follows, we shall return to tracing how that presence of Jesus would continue in the world and that people would come into his new family in two ways: first, through the Holy Spirit, and, second, through the works of the disciples. In these two strands of presence, John's earliest hearers/readers would recognize features of a farewell address as described above.

'Another Paraclete to be with you forever' (John 14.16)

Jesus assures the disciples that they will not be alone because he will ask the Father to give them another Advocate, the Holy Spirit of Truth (14.16-17, 25-26). Jesus names the one who will succeed him to guide the disciples, who are to continue the works of God. John 14 offers a springboard to consider further the Spirit in John. First, we shall situate the Spirit within what we have learnt so far and look forward to John 19—20. As we do so, let us be aware of our earlier reflection on 'the Spirit as the *Breath of God who always accompanies the Word*' and 'of God creating *with two hands, that of the Word and that of the Spirit*'.[8]

Earlier, Jesus has said, 'The wind (*pneuma*) blows where it chooses, and you hear the sound of it, but you do not know where it comes from or where it goes. So it is with everyone who is born of the Spirit (*pneuma*)' (3.8). Wind and breath are beautiful images that describe the Spirit as an unseen wonder known by what it does, the effect it has and how it feels. The Spirit flows through all creation bringing life and love. Creation is evoked in the first words of John, 'In the beginning' (1.1), which here refers to the period before creation, what we would call before the Big Bang. The Spirit broods over our universe from the beginning. For John, the beginning of creation is when 'all things came into being' through the Word (1.3). Later, we shall see that the climax of the passion is not the death of Jesus but a giving of the Spirit: 'When Jesus had received the wine, he said, "It is finished."' Then he bowed his head and 'handed over the Spirit' (19.30).[9] The Spirit remains with the Church, the new family of God created when blood and water flowed from the pierced side of Jesus (19.34). That Jesus was buried and raised in a garden evokes new creation. After his resurrection, Jesus breathes on the disciples (20.22) as God breathes on 'the dust of the ground' in Genesis 2.7, creating Adam (*ādām*) who was formed from the earth (*hā-adāma*). After this overview, we return to the Spirit in John 14.

'The Spirit ... abides with you' (14.17)

True to the emphasis in a farewell discourse on relationships continuing, the departing Jesus insisted that three interconnected relationships are to continue: the relationship of Jesus and God (14.8–11, 20), the relationship of Jesus and the disciples, and the relationship of Jesus, God and the disciples (14.6–7, 13, 23). Being with Jesus is about relationships of 'abiding' (14.10; 15.4–10). In the outpouring of the Holy Spirit, who 'abides with you and will be in you' (14.17), and the work of the disciples, the risen Jesus continues to abide with people in the world God so loved. This is shown in the intimacy and mutuality of the relationship between God and Jesus, and then in this relationship that the disciples enter through the Spirit-Paraclete. To be disciples is to be in relationship with and through the risen Jesus, with God, the community and the world ('I am the way, the truth, and the life', 14.6). The Spirit is the Paraclete, who is presented as a person (14.15–16, 25–26; 15.26–27; 16.13–14) and is the one who will be with disciples who do God's works. Under the term 'paraclete' many meanings come together in a rich all-embracing picture of the Spirit as: presence, teacher, comforter, guide, helper, friend, advocate, one who intercedes, consoler, spokesperson, witness and companion. As Brown summarizes, 'the one who Jesus calls "another Paraclete" is really another Jesus. Since the Paraclete can only come when Jesus departs, the Paraclete is the presence of Jesus when Jesus is absent.'[10] The Paraclete-Spirit is a bridge between the past of the historical life of Jesus and the post-Easter life of the Church. Later, the Spirit will teach them everything and remind them of all Jesus had said to them while he was remaining/abiding with them (14.26). Jesus gives his peace to the disciples and, therefore, with his departure, he can repeat his assurance of 14.1: 'Do not let your hearts be troubled' (14.27).

'Greater works than I do' (John 14.12)

Having considered how Jesus would continue in the world and how people will come into his new family through the Holy Spirit, we now turn to the works of the disciples, which the Spirit will guide. Jesus has been in the midst of the disciples. In John 2—12, he is shown doing the works of God and speaks often of God as 'still working' and of himself, 'I am still working' (5.17). He speaks of finishing the works God gives him to do. Jesus' last words are, 'It is finished' (19.30). Jesus speaks of God doing works through him (14.10), and those who believe in Jesus 'will do the works that I do and, in fact, greater works than I do' (14.12–14). A farewell address indicates that a legacy is being given by the departing one. The legacy that disciples who believe will receive is the promise of doing even greater works. Underlying the words of Jesus in John 14 is the assurance that when he is absent, he is present through the Holy Spirit. Now those earliest disciples, as we have seen, do not understand. Jesus' talk is interrupted by the questions of Thomas, Philip and Judas (not Iscariot). Jesus talks about future hard times when he repeats that he is going away and that he will come to them, emphasizing that he has told them about this before it occurs so that 'when it does occur, you may believe' (14.28–29). They are encouraged to believe him (14.10–11, 29). Yet again Jesus sums up his life to set the record straight, 'I do as the Father has commanded me, so that world may know that I love the Father' (14.31). He who is 'the way' ends the first part of his farewell (13.31—14.31) with, 'Arise, let us leave' (14.31).

Oratio (Prayer) → *Contemplatio* (Contemplation) → *Actio* (Action) →

- And what is God's work that is also Jesus' work and our work? We heard Jesus speak about how God works through him and how those who believe in Jesus will do even greater works than he does (14.12). These references echo Genesis, where 'God rested from all the work that [God] had done in creation' (Gen. 2.2). A completed creation is sealed by Sabbath rest, yet God's work is incomplete. Jesus continues God's work. Underlying the words of Jesus in John 14 is the assurance that when he is absent he is present through the Spirit. Further, uniquely, this Gospel tells of eternal life being experienced *now*, in the world God so loved. In relationship to the world in all its senses, humankind has the potential to respond with awe and wonder. Such a response to beauty changes those who see *the now* in a new perspective and fires the human imagination to make connections, to abide in, to care for and protect the earth and the whole earth community by completing the works of God. Pope Francis reminds us that in the Bible, 'the God who liberates and saves is the same God who created the universe, and these two divine ways of acting are intimately and inseparably connected' (*LS* §73). That this Gospel has no description of Jesus' return in the future or of the heavens opening or Jesus' coming down on the cloud from heaven in judgement is striking. Instead the language is relational: 'I ... will take you to *myself*' (14.3). This promise centres on a person, on a relationship and on finding Jesus in the present, in this world. In our plunging into the world to finish God's work in God's ongoing creation and re-creation (salvation), '[t]he Spirit, infinite bond of love, is intimately present at the very heart of the universe, inspiring and bringing new pathways' (*LS* §238).

Notes

1 On the nine elements found in ancient farewell discourses, see Jerome H. Neyrey, 2007, *The Gospel of John*, New York: Cambridge University Press, pp. 239–40.

2 Robert J. Karris, 1990, *Jesus and the Marginalized in John's Gospel*, Collegeville MN: Liturgical Press, p. 28.

3 Brendan Byrne SJ, 2014, *Life Abounding: A Reading of John's Gospel*, Collegeville MN: Liturgical Press, p. 240.

4 Margaret Daly-Denton, 2017, *John: An Earth Bible Commentary: Supposing Him to be the Gardener*, London: Bloomsbury T&T Clark, p. 180. The Greek word for 'as' is *kathōs*.

5 Jacinda Ardern and Farid Ahmed, 29 March 2019, National Remembrance Service, Christchurch, www.stuff.co.nz/national/christchurchshooting/111638469/christchurch-memorial-all-eyes-on-nz-for-national-remembrance-service (accessed 10.09.19).

6 *Monai* is translated as 'dwelling places' (NRSV), and 'rooms' (JB) is one of a cluster of words from the verb 'abide' (*menein*).

7 Byrne SJ, *Life Abounding*, p. 242.

8 Denis Edwards, 2004, *Breath of Life: A Theology of the Creator Spirit*, Maryknoll NY: Orbis, pp. 26, 40 (italics his).

9 The NRSV translation has 'gave up his spirit'. For reasons I explain on pages 184–5 below, I prefer the translation 'handed over the Spirit'.

10 Raymond E. Brown, 1966–1970, *The Gospel According to John*, 2 vols, The Anchor Bible 29–29A, Garden City NY: Doubleday, pp. 1140–1.

Jerusalem
Second Part of the Last Supper Discourse
– John 15.1 – 16.4a

'I am the vine, you are the branches' (John 15.5)

Fifth Sunday of Easter of Year B
John 15.1–8

'But I have called you friends' (John 15.15)

Sixth Sunday of Easter of Year B
John 15.9–17

'When the Advocate comes' (John 15.26)

Pentecost Sunday Vigil of Year B (RL Option B)
John 15.26–27; 16.12–15 (see John 16)
Day of Pentecost of Year B (RCL)
John 15.26–27; 16.4b–15 (see John 16)

Lectio/Reading of John 15.1–8

In reading and rereading John 15.1–8 we discover another image drawn from the agricultural world that invites us to enter into the everyday reality of the earth and of human work.

Meditatio/Meditation

'I am the vine, you are the branches' (John 15.5)

Jesus has talked to his disciples about their 'dwelling' in him after he returns to the Father to send the Holy Spirit (John 14.23). Now, the 'dwelling place' image is expanded through the image of the vine and the branches (15.1–8). The fruit of abiding in the vine is the love they have for one another (15.9–17). Jesus then prepares them for the hatred and persecution they will experience from the world (15.18—16.4a). He is the only speaker in this section of the discourse. There is no explicit reference to the disciples. It may be helpful to return to the 'Structure of John 13—17' diagram set out at the beginning of Part 3 and review the farewell discourse of Jesus. Notice we enter into a new phase in this central part of his discourse, which we have named the Second Part (15.1—16.4a). This flows into another section of the discourse that is similar to the first one (First Part, 13.31—14.31) but less positive in tone (Third Part, 16.4b–33).

Vine imagery has the potential to hold together joy and suffering. Of all the plants that provide food, grapevines can grow in the most adverse places. The agricultural image of the vine (15.1–11) suggests growth, fruitfulness and self-giving. Yet this life-giving image does not bypass suffering and death, thereby offering a different ethical language from that of self-sacrifice and self-denial. In this Gospel, disciples are not invited 'to take up their cross'. Instead, God the vinedresser prunes in order to promote life.

The Hebrew culture was deeply rooted within an agricultural world. The people were familiar with wine making and the delight of wine. Viticulture and wine were so much part of daily life that they were sources of rich imagery to describe the relationship of God with people and land. Israel is the vine God brought out of Egypt, planted in cleared ground. Yet it was burnt with fire and cut down (Ps. 80.8–16). Jeremiah tells us that Israel, the vine planted by God as 'a choice vine from purest stock', degenerated and became 'a wild vine' (2.21). God is the keeper of the vineyard (Isa. 27.2–3). Jesus' last 'I am' statement, expressed as 'I am the true vine, and my Father is the vine-grower' (John 15.1) and then as 'I am the vine, you are the branches' (15.5), describes his relationship with God and with his disciples. Jesus makes a very strong claim since the vine is a well-known biblical symbol for Israel. It is also likely that as Jesus is the true Israel, so too are his followers. Jesus' claim may be even stronger. Margaret Daly-Denton offers another translation, 'I am vineyard, you are the vines', because by the third century BCE the Greek word translated as 'vine' referred to the plot of land, the vineyard, and that translated as 'branches' referred not just to a branch or twig but to the whole vine.[1] The vine-grower would uproot the unproductive vines and burn them. The fruit-bearing vine would be pruned to bear more fruit. Jesus knows his audience would not only understand agricultural language and its implications but would also be reminded of many biblical associations.

Biblical vine imagery is a challenge for today's readers, surrounded as they are by large commercial vineyards and supermarkets where the focus is on mass production, economic investment and profit. In *A Spiritual-*

ity of Wine, the theologian Gisela Kreglinger writes of her experience of growing up on a family winery where wine, characteristic of their Bavarian region, has been crafted for centuries. She insists on using the term 'viticulture' for the process of wine making, and 'vintner' rather than wine maker for the one who tends to the beauty of growing well-crafted wine, in order to honour the expertise of this traditional craft.

We have already noted how the grapevine is able to grow and be productive in adverse conditions. Many other plants cannot flourish in stony soils and on steep hillsides. Where little else grows, vines are most productive. Natural and living organisms of root and soil interact to produce fruit. It is a great mystery how the combination of sun, soil, rain and vines are able to produce eventually such a delightful liquid. Likewise, the great mystery of Jesus' fruitfulness – his finishing the works of God, 'handing over the Spirit' (John 19.30) to the women and to the Beloved Disciple – peaks in a situation where seemingly no life can be found, namely the cross.[2]

'Prunes to make it bear more fruit' (John 15.2)

Pruning is an unsettling image. Its purpose is not the cutting back in itself but the hope for fine, abundant fruit. Persons, like the branches of the vine, are pruned in order to bear fruit. This promise of abundance (John 10.10) is not without the pruning of our addictions. A journey of pruning and healing is a life-giving practice of restraint and cutting back. 'Abiding' also offers a language of love and fullness to describe discipleship. This differs from the self-sacrifice and self-denial language of the Synoptic Gospels, which requires taking up one's cross to follow Jesus (Mark 8.34; Matt. 16.24; Luke 9.23). 'Abiding' suggests a community of interrelationship, mutuality and indwelling. It expresses Jesus' relationship with God (John 15.10), Jesus' relationship with the community (15.4, 9) and the community's relationship with Jesus (15.1, 7). For Dorothy Lee, 'abiding' is 'an icon of wholeness and intimacy', which moves 'through suffering, to accept the reality that life and fecundity come through pain and death, through pruning and the pierced side (7.38; 19.34)'.[3]

When pruned, the vines are tied to wires supported by poles spread throughout the vineyard. The vines are supported by this wiring structure (called 'trellising') and directed in their growth.[4] These vineyard wire structures are like the structures and rules in a community that guide, support and give stability to the common life. When we live independently without such structures, we easily become hurt and have no direction. We wither and bear no fruit. Vine and branches constitute a group of friends. Disciples are friends of Jesus, not slaves (15.13–15). The directness with which he speaks about pruning is in line with the ancient ideal of the true friend. The opposite was the flatterer who sought to curry favour by not commenting on another's faults. Jesus' authentic friendship is both the source and norm for disciples' relationships with others.

The image of the vine is very much tied to the seasons. Pruning suggests the chill and dying of winter, which looks forward to the new buds of spring and the fruitfulness of late summer and early autumn. When we open ourselves to the love of God in Jesus, when we permit God the vintner to prune our lives in order that we might bear fruit, we become free to love one another. As a vineyard produces good grapes for good wine to bring joy to humanity, so the members of the Church are to love one another, discover true joy and share this with the world.

God's garden and economy

Disciples are to be grounded in God's economy, which is not based on competition and maximum profit but on mercy, forgiveness and love. Persons are not autonomous and isolated consumers but branches connected together and nurtured by Jesus and cared for by the vintner God. God tends the vineyard by watering, pruning and protecting it day and night (Isa. 27.2–3), and guiding it to thrive and be fruitful (Hos. 14.7), to grow into being a fruitful nation and a blessing to others (Isa. 27.2–6). The vine and the practices of viticulture were used metaphorically to describe training in philosophy. Pupils were to be shaped, like young vine shoots tended by others. The vine is associated with Divine Wisdom: 'Like the vine I bud forth delights, and blossoms become glorious and abundant fruit' (Ecclus. 24.17). Withered branches were gathered and their dry, sapless wood easily burnt. Through this aspect of the image, Jesus warns about the reality of the failure of members of the community who do 'not abide in me' (John 15.6).

The viticulture image conveys the biblical hope of transformation through justice for all. The neglect of the poor affects the whole vineyard. God, Isaiah warns, 'enters into judgement with the elders and princes ... you who have devoured the vineyard; the spoil [Hebrew word means 'stolen things'] of the poor is in your houses. What do you mean by crushing my people, by grinding the face of the poor?' (Isa. 3.14–15). God's vineyard will only flourish if the powerful and strong stop exploiting the poor and vulnerable. The image of vines declares that wars will cease. Soldiers are to 'beat their swords into ploughshares and their spears into pruning hooks'. The Hebrew word for the latter refers to the special knife a vintner used to prune vines. People 'shall all sit under their own vines ... and no one shall make them afraid' (Micah 4.3–4).

In presenting Jesus as the true vine (or vineyard?), John may have been calling into question an aspect of contemporary temple practice. Over the time that Herod the Great was rebuilding the temple, a huge golden vine was set up at the entrance to the sanctuary.[5] The clusters of grapes were as tall as a human person. People could donate a golden leaf or even a whole bunch of grapes. The priests could call on the gold to supplement the temple treasury. Margaret Daly-Denton further explains:

> The golden vine was intended to represent the Israel, the vine planted by God on Mount Sion (Exod. 15.17; Ezek. 19.10–11 ...), its roots going down to the waters of the cosmic abyss beneath the temple's foundations and its branches reaching up to the heavens, a unifying force in the created order.[6]

Instead, visible in this golden vine was the extravagant wealth and greed of the privileged Judean elites.

Oratio (Prayer) → *Contemplatio* (Contemplation) → *Actio* (Action) →

- The understanding of human flourishing we have considered is very different from our contemporary focus on maximizing production and profit. The use of chemicals and fertilizers in the production of wine now often interferes with natural organisms. This can tend towards a posture of working 'against' something – against nature, against problems – rather than working as *part of* creation. For many people consumerism is like a spirituality that gives a sense of identity, comfort and a brand. Vines are an interconnected and dynamic reality. The language of viticulture can refresh the Christian imagination and reinvigorate what it means to be church today. Creation and redemption are intertwined. The vine offers a rich and organic view of the Christian life through a spirituality of joy in the earth and in our senses.

Lectio/Reading of John 15.9–17 and 15.26–27

In reading and rereading, it would be helpful to read the whole of John 15.9–27. In the context of the purposes of Jesus' farewell discourse it functions to sustain and to encourage the disciples for the hard times they will experience (15.18–25; omitted in the lectionaries). We see how John 15 links back to John 14, where we discussed how the presence of Jesus in completing the works of God continues through the work of the Holy

Spirit (see below, 15.26–27) and through the works of the disciples (John 15.9–17).

Meditatio/Meditation

'but I have called you my friends' (John 15.15)

In John 15.9–17 the imagery of the vine and the branches appears to fade into the background. Jesus extends the image to pick up on and strengthen two recurring and interrelated motifs, namely 'remaining/ abiding' and disciples as friends. The Scriptures, as we have seen, are a treasure trove of symbols and images mined by early Christians to explain Jesus' relationship with God and Jesus' continuity with biblical traditions. Evoked again and again in John is the biblical figure of Wisdom-Sophia, who is associated with 'abiding' and friendship. Wisdom tells of how 'I came forth from the mouth of the Most High ... Among all these [every people and nation] I sought a resting place; in whose territory should I abide?' (Ecclus. 24.7).[7] Wisdom 'is an image of God's goodness ... she can do all things, and while abiding in herself, she renews all thing ... passes into holy souls and makes them friends of God, and prophets' (Wisd. 7.26–27).

The image of 'abiding'

This Wisdom relational quality suggested by the word 'abide' occurs over 40 times in John. Its nuances are found in such words as stay, continue, remain, endure, live or dwell, which Bible translations use for this one Greek word (see Appendix 2). However, the practice of using various translations obscures the powerful poetic image of Jesus' invitation to those seeking him (John 1.38–39); the relationship between Jesus and the Spirit (1.32–33); the reciprocal abiding between Jesus and the disciples; the relationship between Jesus and God (14.10); and the many dwelling places in God's house (14.2). The word 'abide' is best known from 15.1–17, where it is found 15 times to suggest that deep, continuous union with Jesus is always present. Previously, Jesus had given the assurance that he would always be present in the community. Now, he explains how this will be so.

'Just as I have loved you' (John 13.35)

The language of 'abiding' suggests a community of interrelationship, mutuality and indwelling. We find that 'abide' expresses Jesus' relationship with God (15.10), Jesus' relationship with the community (15.4, 9) and the community's relationship with Jesus (15.1, 7). 'Abiding', along with the vine and pruning, offers a language of love (13.35), which suggests a language of discipleship as a language of fullness. Jesus links abiding in his love with the keeping of the commandments (15.10). He had spoken earlier of 'a new commandment', that they should love one another *as* he had loved them (13.34). Jesus restates his new commandment (15.12). We have seen how this conjunction 'as' suggests a 'see-and-do-likewise' dynamic in the relationship between Jesus and his disciples (see the section on John 13.31–35). Its newness and challenge lie in that little connecting word 'as'. The life work of Jesus' followers is to love '*as* I have loved you'.[8] The love required of the disciples for each other is to reflect the love between Jesus and the Father. For the Evangelist, the joy and virtue summed up in John 15.13 comes from friendship with Jesus who lays down his life for his friends (cf. Good Shepherd, 10.11; Peter, 'I shall lay down my life for you', 13.37).

Wisdom declares that 'in every generation she passes into holy souls and makes them friends of God and prophets' (Wisd. 7.27). The Johannine Christians not only evoke this aspect of the Wisdom tradition but also tell the story of Jesus by using aspects of the highly valued ideal of friendship that gave cohesion to ancient society. In ancient Hellenistic culture, friendship was regarded as a relationship between equals who together contributed to the public ethos of citizenship.[9] The virtues of courage and justice were required. In both classical philosophy and in popular thought, noble death was held to be the ultimate act of friendship. According to Plato, 'only those who love wish to die for others'. Similarly, for Aristotle, 'it is also true the virtuous man's conduct is often guided by the interests of his friends and of his country, and that he will, if necessary, lay down his life in their behalf'.[10] While Jesus is not explicitly called 'friend' in John, his life is the incarnation of the ancient ideal of friendship concerning love and death (15.13). He speaks about the good shepherd laying down his life for the sheep (10.11). Later, when they come to arrest him in the garden, he demonstrates his willingness to die for others. Jesus comes forward and asks, 'Who are you looking for?' (18.5). When they answer 'Jesus of Nazareth', he replies, 'I am' (there is no 'he' in the Greek).

THE 'HOUR' OF JESUS

'Not slaves any longer ... I have called you friends' (John 15.15)

Jesus explains further the implications for the disciples of the image of the branch that abides in the vine. Abiding in Jesus leads to a radical change that takes place in the relationship between him and them. In this Gospel, Jesus does not use the term 'disciples' of his followers. He calls them by two terms. The first is 'slaves' (often translated as 'servants'), which he no longer calls them (15.15). Then follows 'friends' – the only name Jesus gives them. They are named explicitly as friends three times (15.13, 14, 15). Why? Jesus calls them 'friends because I have made known to you everything that I have heard from my Father' (15.15).

Behind Jesus' *mandatum* (commandment, 15.13) is the example of foot washing (13.15), which is done from the motivation of love and is unparalleled in ancient literature. In Jewish and Graeco-Roman environments, as we have seen in John 13, the slave motif would have been associated with the action of foot washing. While cultural norms emphasize superior–inferior social status, in the farewell discourses John offers a different nuance. The action of Jesus is paradigmatic. The disciples are to imitate Jesus because, 'I tell you, slaves are not greater than their master' (13.14–16). They are to wash one another's feet; to carry out this love commandment even to the point of laying down their lives for others, as Jesus does (15.12–15). Amazingly, Jesus hides nothing from the believers who are his friends of what he has learnt from his Father. Nothing is to be hidden. There is no sense of the vertical or hierarchical. Friendship is a model of John's community, as is oneness – one vine, one shepherd, one sheepfold, one seamless garment.

'If the world hates you' (John 15.18)

Jesus moves from the love the disciples received from God and from one another to the very opposite, which is the persecution and hatred that they will experience from the world. John 15.18—16.4a contains some very difficult and troubling views of the world. This section may be divided into three parts: 15.18–25, through which runs the motif of hatred; 15.26–27, which contains an assurance of the Holy Spirit; and 16.1–4a, with its warning of persecution resulting in expulsion from the synagogue. Of these three sections, only 15.26–27, to which we now turn briefly, is proclaimed in Sunday lectionaries.

'When the Advocate comes' (John 15.26)

In the context of persecution and alienation, for the third time so far in his farewell discourse Jesus assures the disciples of the coming of the Holy Spirit, the Advocate, the Spirit of truth whom he will send to them (15.26–27). In this Gospel, there is a long line of those who bear witness or testify to Jesus: John (1.7; 15, 32, 34; 3.32; 5.33), the woman of Samaria (4.39), the Father (5.32, 37; 8.18), the works of Jesus (5.36; 10.25); the Scriptures (5.39); and the crowd (12.17). Now, Jesus assures the disciples that through the presence of the Advocate who testifies on his behalf (15.26), they as the followers of Jesus will also testify because they have been with him from the beginning (15.27).

Oratio (Prayer) → *Contemplatio* (Contemplation) → *Actio* (Action) →

- The function of the new commandment is to sustain and to encourage the disciples during the hard times they will experience when, guided by the Holy Spirit, they will complete the works of God. How does this new commandment of loving one another *as* Jesus had loved them (13.34) extend to sustain and encourage disciples to respond *to both the cry of the earth and the cry of the marginalized*? A way forward is to see that these cries are interconnected, as shown by Wangari Maathai (1940–2011), the founder of the Green Belt Movement (GBM). Her motivation came from thinking about how 'to solve problems on the ground'.[11] Rural women in Kenya said they did not have clean drinking water, adequate and nutritious food, income and sufficient energy for cooking and heating. GBM began with little steps. The women were encouraged to work together to grow seedlings and plant trees to bind the soil, store rainwater, provide food and firewood, and receive a small monetary token for their work. For Wangari Maathai, their efforts were not only about planting trees but about 'sowing seeds of a different sort – the ones necessary to heal the wounds inflicted on communities that robbed them of their self-confidence and self-knowledge'.[12] Within communities, individuals had to 'rediscover their authentic voice' in order to speak on behalf of their rights (human, environmental, civic and political). The key to self-empowerment and conservation is in traditional spiritual values: love for the environment, self-betterment, gratitude and respect, and a commitment to serve others, which includes non-humans.[13] Such universal values define our humanity. When ignored, their place is taken by vices such as selfishness, corruption, exploitation and greed.

- What does the image of the vine and branches mean for our relationship with God and with each other? How might this be lived in our faith community? What are the implications of abiding in Jesus? What are the implications of the image of the pruning of the vine, which evokes a language of love and fullness that is a different language from that of self-sacrifice and self-denial suggested by the carrying of the cross?

Notes

1 Margaret Daly-Denton, 2017, *John: An Earth Bible Commentary: Supposing Him to be the Gardener*, London: Bloomsbury T&T Clark, p. 189. The Greek word usually translated as 'vine' is *ampelos* and the one usually translated as 'branches' is *lēmata*.

2 On translating John 19.30 as he 'handed over the Spirit' rather than 'gave up his spirit', see that section on John 19.30 in this book.

3 Dorothy Lee, 1997, 'Abiding in the Fourth Gospel: A Case-Study in Feminist Biblical Theology', *Pacifica* 10.2, p. 136.

4 Gisela H. Kreglinger, 2016, *The Spirituality of Wine*, Grand Rapids MI: Eerdmans, p. 211.

5 Daly-Denton, *John*, p. 191. This paragraph draws on her work.

6 Daly-Denton, *John*, p. 191.

7 In the Greek Old Testament, Wisdom 'abides', as in, 'Among all these [every people and nation] I sought a resting place; in whose territory should I abide (*meneō*)?' (Ecclus. 24.7).

8 Mary Sullivan RSM, 2019, Keynote Address (via videoconference, 7 June), Ngā Kaiarataki o te Atawhia Hui Taumata Mercy Leaders Summit, Auckland.

9 Gail R. O'Day, 2004, 'Jesus as Friend in the Gospel of John', *Interpretation: A Journal of Bible and Theology* 58.2, p. 146.

10 LCL translation of Plato, *Symposium* (*Symp*.179B) and Aristotle, *Nicomachean Ethics* (*Eth. Nic.* 9.8.9), quoted in O'Day, 'Jesus as Friend', pp. 146 and 156.

11 Wangari Maathai, 2010, *Replenishing the Earth: Spiritual Values for Healing Ourselves and the World*, New York: Doubleday Image, p. 13. On the Green Belt Movement, see www.greenbeltmovement.org (accessed 1.10.19).

12 Maathai, 2010, *Replenishing the Earth*, p. 14.

13 Maathai, 2010, *Replenishing the Earth*, pp. 14–15.

Jerusalem
Third Part of the Last Supper Discourse – John 16.4b–15

'So that your joy may be complete' (John 16.24c)

Pentecost Sunday Vigil of Year B (RL Option B)
John 15.26–27 (see John 15); 16.12–15
Day of Pentecost of Year B (RCL)
John 15.26–27 (see John 15); 16.4b–15
Sunday after Pentecost: Holy Trinity of Year C (RL)
Trinity Sunday of Year C (RCL)
John 16.12–15

Jesus' long discourse, which we have divided into three parts, now flows into the last part (Third Part, 16.4b–33), which is similar to the first (First Part, 13.31—14.31) though less positive in tone (see structure above). The scene is still the Last Supper, where after the footwashing (13.1–30), Jesus gives a farewell discourse (13.31—16.33) and then prays (17.1–26). Two passages from John 16 are in the lectionaries: 4b–15 and 12–15. In what follows, the reader is encouraged to consider these passages in the context of the whole of John 16. Two reflections are offered. In the *Meditatio*/Meditation section on John 16.4b–15, both these passages are placed in the context of the whole of John 16.4a–33. In the second reflection we focus specifically on 16.12–15 because these verses give us significant insights into how Jesus remains with us through the work of the Holy Spirit as we complete the works of God.

Lectio/Reading of John 16.4b–15

The reader is encouraged when reading and rereading John 16.4b–15 to place this passage in the context of the whole of John 16.1–33, mindful that it is part of Jesus' farewell discourse.

Meditatio/Meditation

In John 16, we find talk about the future, questions about moving beyond the known, confusion, notions of time and a new vision of life possible for all who follow Jesus. Just before his arrest, trial and death, Jesus prepares the disciples for his departure and for their life in his absence. This future is the reality for those who read this Gospel today because the present-day Church lives without the physical presence of Jesus and is sustained by his words in the new questions of our times. One such question concerns science, which demonstrates beyond all doubt that our universe is unfinished. John Haught asks what 'faith might mean if we take fully into account the fact that our universe is on the move'. He continues:

> What if ... theologians and teachers began to take more seriously the evolutionary understanding of life and the ongoing pilgrimage of the whole natural world? ... that the cosmos, the earth, and humanity, rather than having wandered away from an original plenitude, are now and always invited toward the horizon of fuller being up ahead?[1]

The Second Vatican Council, Haught recalls, encourages Christians 'to become more evolutionary in their understanding of the world and more biblical in their spirituality'.[2]

In the light of these two prongs of becoming – more evolutionary in our understanding of the world and more biblical in our spirituality – and in the light of other questions about the future, the reader is invited to reflect on John 16.4a–33, from which two passages are proclaimed during Year C. Let us place 16.4b–15 (Day of Pentecost of Year B, RCL) and 16.12–15 (Trinity Sunday) in the context of a conversation between Jesus and unnamed disciples in three parts (16.4b–15; 16.15–24; 16.25–33). The focus is again on Jesus' presence (16.4b), departure (16.5; cf. 13.36; 14.4) and absence in the painful times of hostility, suffering and persecution (16.2–4). A pattern recurs. Three named disciples interrupted the John 14 part of his discourse (14.5, 8, 22). Now, unnamed disciples discussing among themselves misunderstand and ask questions (16.17–19; 29–31). Jesus speaks of how the disciples will abandon him (16.32) but also of how he will never abandon them. They are to take courage because he has overcome the world (16.30).

Written by believers for believers

A Gospel is an interpretative narrative of the appearance, ministry and death-resurrection of Jesus and tells of the significance of that story for those who hear or read it. It was told by believers for believers in particular situations. Their social context involved more than Jewish–Christian tensions. In Palestine at the time of Jesus and in Ephesus where John's Gospel was probably written, believers were subjects of the Roman Empire. All religious, social and economic life was lived under imperial domination. The book of Revelation shows this tension.[3] One of the theological concerns of the writer is to expose the Roman Empire for what it is – a threat to the reign of God in the world – and to encourage Christians to resist its values. This Gospel was shaped by resistance and witness.

Religious interactions need to be set against this background in which readers/hearers face difficult choices because Jesus breaks into their lives. They could remain in their local synagogue as members of a religious group with official recognition in the empire and avoid the scrutiny of its officials. They could stay with the synagogue while at the same time also worshipping secretly as Christians. They could break away from the synagogue, worship openly as Christians and risk the consequences. John encourages the latter choice. We find the expression 'put out of the synagogue' (16.2), which has been used in 9.21–22 and 12.42.[4] In the whole of Greek literature this word is found only in John.[5] After a process of decades, their belief in Jesus led to a parting of the ways. The brave Johannine church left the familiar world they loved and began to tell the old story of Jesus in new and often unique ways, as seen in the prologue and the farewell discourses.

Gathering of present and future communities

In his barrier-crossing ministry, Jesus has moved among representatives of groups in conflict with each other: the nationalist Nathanael (1.47), Nicodemus, a 'ruler of the Jews' and 'the teacher of Israel' (3.1–21), the woman of Samaria (4.4–42), the royal official (4.46–54), those marginalized by ignorance of the Torah (7.49) and those with physical disabilities (5.2–9; 9.1–41). The reader learns from the latter stages of the ministry of Jesus that his death is connected with the gathering of present and future communities. He will bring other sheep into the fold (10.15–16); he will gather the dispersed children of God (11.50–52); many will believe in him (12.11); Greeks will come to him (12.20–23); and when he is lifted up, he will draw all people to himself (12.32).

The future and the present merge together in one narrative moment in ways that contest the usual understandings of time. God and Jesus are present now and their interactions are not confined by the past, present and future. Jesus' words concern his future, which, he implies, is connected with the future of the disciples and with that of the reader. The transformation and the merging of the times are conveyed by the mysterious word 'hour', which is used in various ways with the verb 'come' (16.2, 4, 21, 25, 32). 'My/the hour' is an image for Jesus' death-resurrection. It draws others also into this mystery. For these times, there are words of promise and assurance (16.12–15, 33). The discourse is interlaced with grief and joy related to the absence and presence of Jesus in his death-resurrection as well as the suffering that faces disciples. This is evoked in the often-overlooked parable of 16.21 and its explanation (16.22). This image is one of several that hold the tension of Jesus' death-resurrection.

'I have said these things to you' (John 16.1)

This discourse moves between the present and future, indicating that a new age has begun. Jesus' words containing the expression 'put out of the synagogue' (16.2) are framed by his saying, 'I have said these things to you to keep you from stumbling' (16.1, 4). He states that his disciples are to remember his words when the hard times come. 'I have said these things/ this to you' is repeated three more times (16.6, 25, 33). In John 16.12–15, we find a change of tense: 'I still have many things to say to you.' Here Jesus links his departure with the coming of the Spirit of truth. He has already told the disciples that his going is to their advantage. Otherwise the Advocate will not come (16.7). Jesus then describes the twofold role of the Spirit: to expose (16.8–11) and to guide (16.12–15).

'But I will tell you plainly' (John 16.25)

In 16.29–33 the disciples say to Jesus, 'now you are speaking plainly'. Speaking 'frankly' or 'plainly', as we have seen, was a characteristic of the ancient ideal of friendship. The biblical figure of Wisdom-Sophia also gathered her friends. The earthly Jesus gathers his friends. Later, the risen Jesus gathers the Johannine community and communities throughout the ages to be 'friends of God and prophets' (Wisd. 7.27). At the street corners, Wisdom-Sophia cried out for justice. Likewise, the words and actions of Jesus show that his ministry is lived in public, speaking frankly, often in Jerusalem, the centre of religious and political power (John 7.4, 13, 26; 10.24; 11.14, 54; 16.25, 29; 18.20). Jesus had said, 'No one has greater love than this, to lay down one's life for one's friends' (15.13). In his barrier-crossing ministry of creating a new community, Jesus' life is the incarnation of this teaching (15.12–13).

Oratio (Prayer) → *Contemplatio* (Contemplation) → *Actio* (Action) →

- John Haught encourages Christians 'to become more evolutionary in their understanding of the world and more biblical in their spirituality'.[6] Jesus' barrier-crossing ministry began in the prologue. The Word made flesh is inserted into God's interconnected and evolving story. That insertion evokes not only biblical creation accounts. For those immersed in the ancient Hellenistic world, terms such as 'in the beginning', 'the Word' and 'all things' evoke contemporary cosmological and philosophical understandings. The Evangelist was informed about the best science of the time and drew on it in the prologue, which is the framework through which to read the Gospel that follows. My experience is that this is not so in the Church today as a whole and it is not often the case in preaching and worship. Internally and outwardly, many Christian Churches, including the one I know best (Catholicism), are in crisis. Although ecclesial disfunction may be deep, John Haught is convinced that 'At bottom ... the problem is both cosmological and metaphysical.' The Church is anchored in a 'worldview that lacks sufficient hope for the world's future, it clings to a sense of being that has yet to face the fact of the world's becoming'. Teachers, theologians and preachers are out of touch with science and other significant developments in the world of thought. Those in the pews 'become too comfortable with a spirituality out of touch with evolutionary biology and contemporary cosmology'.[7] In 1919, Teilhard de Chardin wrote, 'God is as *vast* and as mysterious as the Cosmos.' He continues that any God who seems smaller than the world revealed by science is unworthy of our worship.[8] The discourse of John 16 moves between the present and the future to indicate that a new age has begun. The future and the present merge together in one narrative moment in ways that contest the usual understandings of time. The works of God unfold in the unfinished universe stretching ahead of us, as we learn in evolutionary biology and contemporary cosmology.

Lectio/Reading of John 16.12–15

In reading and rereading John 16.12–15, place this passage in the context of the whole of John 16.1–33, mindful that it is part of Jesus' farewell discourse. Be attentive to how Jesus remains with us *through the work of the Holy Spirit* to enable us to complete the works of God.

Meditatio/Meditation

'But you cannot bear them now' (16.12)

John Haught writes of creating a 'spiritual space for a fresh throb of hope' and of living a biblical spirituality of 'Abrahamic adventure'.[9] In our context, this might mean we tell the old story in a bold new way by becoming more evolutionary in our understanding of the world and more biblical in our spirituality. We may need to ask questions such as: what is the empire of Rome in our situation? What choices do we face to be open to respond *to both the cry of the earth and the cry of the marginalized*? About what are we called to speak 'frankly or plainly'? The words of Jesus proclaimed on Trinity Sunday (John 16.13–15) show how he remains with us through the work of the Holy Spirit, enabling us to complete the works of God.

Jesus repeats the verb 'declare' (NRSV) or 'tell' (JB) three times in John 16.13–15. We find clues to its significance in the Greek Old Testament, where this verb has the sense of re-announcing what has been heard previously – mysteries already communicated are described.[10] So Jesus is encouraging the disciples to face the hard times ahead by seeking deeper meaning in what has already happened. Raymond Brown explains:

> The declaration of the things to come consists in interpreting in relation to each coming generation the contemporary significance of what Jesus has said and done. The best Christian preparation is not an exact knowledge of the future but a deep understanding of what Jesus means for one's own time.[11]

In other words, the ministry and trial of Jesus are over. But the implications of his death-resurrection for disciples of all generations and for all creation need to be worked out in every generation, in every time and in every place. Jesus knew the hearts of those earliest disciples were troubled; he knows our hearts are troubled too (14.1, 27). He says, 'I still have many things to say to you, but you cannot bear them now' (16.12). When they, and we today, can bear it, the Spirit will re-announce, re-proclaim, what has been received from Jesus who was sent by God (16.14).

God, Jesus and the Spirit

Jesus' identity and his relationship with God are central issues. Jesus is 'the way' because he is 'the word made flesh' who reveals who God is ('truth'). When people come to believe *into* him, they share in eternal 'life'. In the work of guiding disciples, Jesus and the Spirit share similar titles. Jesus is 'the truth' (14.6) and the Paraclete is the Spirit of truth (14.17; 15.26; 16.13), who will 'guide you into all truth'. The Greek word for Spirit (*pneuma*) is used throughout the Scriptures for the Hebrew *ruah*, meaning the 'wind'. Sometimes it is translated as 'breath', which is necessary for life. Wind and breath are beautiful images for the Spirit as an unseen wonder, known by what it does, the effect it has and how it feels. The Spirit flows through all creation, bringing life and love.

Just as Jesus teaches and guides (6.59; 7.14; 8.20), so does the Paraclete (16.13; 14.26). The Paraclete's teaching glorifies Jesus (16.14) and Jesus glorifies God (14.13; 17.4). As Raymond Brown says, 'the one whom John calls "another Paraclete" is really another Jesus. Since the Paraclete can only come when Jesus departs, the Paraclete is the presence of Jesus when Jesus is absent.'[12] Jesus names the Spirit as his successor who is a bridge between the past of his historical life and the post-Easter life of the Church in this world God so loves (3.16).

Oratio (Prayer) → *Contemplatio* (Contemplation) → *Actio* (Action) →

- What does the Spirit re-announce to us in our generation and place about the contemporary significance of the truth of God *already communicated* in what Jesus has said and done? Surely the Spirit was present when, on 25 April 2019, the World Council of Churches released the practical resource, *Roadmap for Congregations, Communities and Churches for an Economy of Life and Ecological Justice*, saying, 'We need a STRONG MOVEMENT OF TRANSFORMATIVE FAITH.' Their practical resource continues: 'We invite congregations, communities and churches to join a pilgrimage for an Economy of Life and climate, to commit to make changes in the way we live, to share successful ideas and to encourage one another.'[13] A few days later, on 6 May 2019, the United Nations released the document *The Intergovernmental Science-Policy Platform on Biodiversity and Ecosystem Services* (IPBES), which is the most comprehensive report on the global state of biodiversity to date. One million species are threatened with extinction. This report documents the extent of our predicament. The IPBES Chair, Sir Robert Watson, summarizes: 'The health of ecosystems on which we and all other species depend is deteriorating more rapidly than ever. We are eroding the very foundations of our economies, livelihoods, food security, health and quality of life worldwide.'[14] The report also states that it is not too late to make a difference if we start now at every level from local to global. Through 'transformative change', nature can still be conserved, restored and used sustainably. We could say that it was a coincidence that these two reports were released so close to each other. But God acts through incidences not coincidences. The words of Jesus echo through the generations: 'I still have many things to say to you, but you cannot bear them now' (16.12). The ecumenical Christian Church is one of the largest groups of people in the world. It is time to 'bear', to hear the truth and, enabled by the Spirit, transform our faith into action. *Laudato Si'* encourages us: 'The Spirit, infinite bond of love, is intimately present at the very heart of the universe, inspiring and bringing new pathways' (§238).

Notes

1 John E. Haught, 2015, *Resting on the Future: Catholic Theology for an Unfinished Universe*, New York: Bloomsbury Academic, p. 1.
2 Haught, *Resting on the Future*, p. 15.
3 Kathleen P. Rushton, 2014, 'The Book of Revelation – A Call to "Consistent Resistance"', in Neil Darragh (ed.), *But Is It Fair? Faith Communities and Social Justice*, Auckland: Accent Publication, pp. 50–1.
4 The Greek word for 'put out of the synagogue' (16.2; 9.21–22; 12.42) is *aposunagōgos*.
5 Francis Moloney, 2013, 'Understanding the World and Message of John's Gospel', in *Gospel of St. John: The Love of God Made Visible*, 9th National eConference, The Broken Bay Institute, DVD.
6 Haught, *Resting on the Future*, p. 15.
7 Haught, *Resting on the Future*, p. 12.
8 Pierre Teilhard de Chardin, 1978, *The Heart of the Matter*, René Hague (trans.), New York: Harcourt Brace Jovanovich, p. 212.
9 Haught, *Resting on the Future*, pp. 1–2.
10 Brendan Byrne SJ, 2014, *Life Abounding: A Reading of John's Gospel*, Collegeville MN: Liturgical Press, pp. 271–2.
11 Raymond E. Brown, 1966–1970, *The Gospel According to John*, 2 vols, The Anchor Bible 29–29A, Garden City NY: Doubleday, p. 716.
12 Brown, *Gospel According to John*, p. 1141.
13 World Council of Churches, 2019, *Roadmap for Congregations, Communities and Churches for an Economy of Life and Ecological Justice* (25 April), pp. 2–3 (upper case theirs), www.oikoumene.org/en/resources (accessed 16.09.19).
14 United Nations, 'The Intergovernmental Science-Policy Platform on Biodiversity and Ecosystem Services' (IPBES), 6 May 2019, www.ipbes.net/news/Media-Release-Global-Assessment (accessed 16.09.19).

Jerusalem
Jesus Prays – John 17.1–26

'By finishing the work you gave me to do' (John 17.4)

Seventh Sunday of Easter of Year A
John 17.1–11
Seventh Sunday of Easter of Year B (RL)
John 17.11–19
Seventh Sunday of Easter of Year B (RCL)
John 17.6–19

'That they may be completely one' (John 17.23)

Seventh Sunday of Easter of Year C
John 17.20–26

Lectio/Reading of John 17.1–26

In reading and rereading a passage selected from John 17, place it in the cultural context of the prayer or blessing that Jesus prays as a departing leader for those who will be left behind. He knows his time for completing the works of God is drawing near and prays for disciples who 'will do greater works than these' (14.12). We are included in Jesus' prayer. Be aware of his praying for us as we complete the works of God by responding to *both the cry of the earth and the cry of the marginalized.*

Meditatio/Meditation

'For those who believe in me through their word' (John 17.20)

The long farewell discourse (John 13.31—16.33) following the foot washing (13.1–30) leads into the prayer of Jesus (17.1–26) that forms the last unit of the supper (John 13—17). This long and beautiful prayer needs to be considered within this context and also within the cultural context of a farewell address that often included prayer or a blessing for those the speaker is leaving behind. Earlier, we reviewed elements found in this way of speaking in which a well-known person approaching death expressed deep concern for the well-being of followers. That person gave a review of their life to set the record straight, asserted that relationships were to be continued, revealed beneficial things that were to happen, and gave predictions about future hard times ahead. Aspects of these elements are found in the prayer of Jesus.

The Johannine Jesus does not teach his disciples to pray. In John, 'the Word made flesh' acts. He gives flesh to action. Jesus does not talk about prayer. He prays. He models prayer. The tense of the verbs moves backwards and forwards. Some are in the future tense. Others are in the past tense. Some verses are prayers of petition – Jesus prays for himself, for his disciples present with him and for future disciples. In some verses, he focuses on himself – speaking with the 'I' of *'first-person speech'* ('I have kept your word') and *'celebrating the record'* of the past works of God.[1] That kind of prayer may be understood as the risen One looking back over his own ministry and also looking forward to the coming generations of believers, including twenty-first-century believers. In the first five verses Jesus prays for himself (17.1–5), then for the disciples (17.6–19) and finally for future believers (17.20–26).

'The hour has come' (John 17.1)

Jesus prays for himself in John 17.1–5. He enters bodily into a posture of prayer – literally 'lifting the eyes of him to heaven' (17.1; 11.41). Prayer is an activity involving one's whole being. And to what was Jesus looking up? It was evening. It was dark. Maybe through an opening in the house, or even while outside, he looks up to the starlit sky made bright by the full moon of the Passover.

The ground of Jesus' prayer is his relationship with God (17.1, 'your son', 'the son'). Images, used for his death-resurrection enter his prayer ('the hour' and 'glorification'). Jesus surrenders to God, for 'the hour has come' (17.1), and not as in Mark, 'remove this cup from me' (14.36). 'Glory' and its related terms of 'glorify' and 'glorification' are found five times in John 17.1–5 and portray Jesus as the abundant, visible human presence of the unseen God. The core concerns of this Gospel are found here. Before God and in the hearing of his disciples, Jesus prays in the first person, using 'I', celebrating faithfulness and constancy because, 'I glorified you on earth by finishing the work that you gave me to do' (17.4).

Once again, finishing the works of God (4.34; 5.36) is found and will be heard again in the last words of Jesus on the cross (19.28, 30).

Jesus prays, 'you gave him authority over all *flesh*, to give eternal life to all whom you have given him' (17.2). A link to the prologue is obscured and rendered human-centred in translations. The NRSV uses 'people' and the JB 'mankind', whereas the Greek tells us Jesus was given 'authority over all *flesh*' (17.2). Earlier, we saw how the term for 'flesh', which Jesus became, linked him to humanity and to all living creatures. Jesus prays to be restored to the glory 'that I had in your presence before the world existed' (17.5). So his prayer evokes yet again the prologue and his existence from the beginning with God (1.1–3; 8.58). Jesus is given authority over all living flesh to give eternal life, which is fullness of life, to all God had given to him. Eternal life is knowing God and Jesus, the one whom God sent.

'That they may be one as we are one' (John 17.11)

In 17.6–19, Jesus prays for his disciples. In many ways this section and the other two in John 17 are best read reflectively, imagining and entering into the prayer of Jesus. He prays for the disciples whom God had given him and not for 'the world' (17.9). Here, as elsewhere, we need to distinguish three senses of 'the world' (*kosmos*) in this Gospel. John 1.10 illustrates all three: 'He came into the world' – a geographical space or place; 'and the world came into being through him' – the reality God loved and made, as in 'God so loved the world' (3.16); and 'yet the world did not accept him' – those who reject Jesus.

Jesus continues speaking in the 'I' of first-person speech ('I have kept your word') and celebrating the record of his having finished the works of God. He celebrates because, 'I have made your name known' (17.6, 26); 'the words that you gave me I have given to them' (17.8, 14); 'I protected them in your name' (17.12); 'I have guarded them' (17.12); 'I send them into the world' (17.18); and 'I sanctify [consecrate] myself' (17.19). We shall look more closely at some of these.

The disciples are to be in a new situation following the departure of Jesus (17.12–13). Keeping them together is crucial. Jesus' prayer for these disciples with him is summed up in the word 'protect', which is found three times (17.11, 12, 15).[2] Below the surface is the sense of Jesus as Good Shepherd. The role of shepherds is to protect the sheep under their care – to keep them united, from being scattered or lost, and free from theft or attack.

Jesus addresses God as 'holy' (17.11), which recalls the characteristic that sets God apart (Isa. 5.16; 6.3). Likewise, those who worship God are to be holy as God is holy (Lev. 11.44; 19.2; 20.7). Jesus prays for his disciples in the world that they may be one as he and the Father are one, united in holiness with all creation. Jesus asks the Father to 'sanctify' (consecrate) the disciples 'in the truth' (17.17–19). In the biblical tradition, 'sanctify' or 'sanctification' evoke being set apart for sacred works, as in the case of Aaron and companions (Exod. 28.41). Jesus stands in this tradition of being set apart and sent (John 17.18) by God to finish the works of God. Jesus, who had earlier said he was 'the one whom the Father had sanctified and sent into the world' (10.36), celebrates in prayer that 'for their sakes I sanctify [consecrate] myself, so that they also may be sanctified in truth' (17.19).

Jesus does not request that they be taken out of the world (17.15), and by extension neither should the Church desire to be taken out of the world. The tension is to be in the world but not to compromise with the world or to escape from it. Alan Culpepper summarizes the concerns of 17.6–19 as follows: that Jesus' identity and work (often called Christology), the nature of the believing community (often called ecclesiology), and the mission of the Church in the world (often called missiology) are unified in a deep reflection on the death-resurrection of Jesus.[3]

'Those who will believe in me through their word' (John 17.20)

Finally, in his prayer of 17.20–26, Jesus prays for the next generation of believers, who are those for whom this Gospel was first written, and by extension for all generations of future believers. The essential point here is not about distinctions between the first disciples and later ones. What is at stake is that all disciples of whatever generation have a sense of mission, a sense of being sent, as Jesus had, to pass on and witness to what they have seen and believed. This is highlighted by the word 'send'. In John 17, Jesus mentions five times that 'you have sent me' (17.3, 18, 21, 23, 25) and 'so I have sent them into the world' (17.18). In particular, Jesus prays 'on behalf of those who will believe in me through their word' (17.20). The Greek here means, literally, 'the ones *believing in me through the word of* them'. This echoes the pattern of what is said of a second-generation disciple, the woman of Samaria, that many Samaritans 'believed in him because of the woman's testimony' (4.39 means literally, '*believed in him through the words of* the woman bearing witness'). Believers are not only to believe but to take into the world the divine life in which they participate.

The oneness and unity for which Jesus prays for all believers is a gift from above flowing from the oneness and unity that exists between God and Jesus. Disciples participate in this in a vertical sense in that they are drawn into that divine communion of love. This evokes the Gospel's language of indwelling, 'that they may all be one. As you, Father, are in me and I am in you, may they also be in us' (17.21, 23). The purpose is that all may believe (17.21; cf. 20.31). Near the end of his prayer, we find Jesus expressing desire: 'Father, I desire ... (17.24).[4] He desires that those who have been given to him 'may be with me where I am', that they may see the glory that God has given him 'because you [God] loved me before the foundation of the world' (17.24). Jesus returns yet again to the prologue, which sets out that he was with God from the beginning (1.1-2, 18). We disciples of later generations are drawn into the cosmic interrelationship of God and all creation expressed in divine communion.

'That they may become completely one' (John 17.23)

On the evening of his suffering and death, Jesus prays 'that they may all be one. As you, Father, are in me and I am in you, may they also be in us, so that the world may believe that you have sent me' (17.21). In *A Handbook of Spiritual Ecumenism*, Walter Kasper writes, 'It is significant that Jesus did not primarily express his desire for unity in a teaching or in a commandment ... but in a prayer ... Unity is a gift from above ...'[5] In praying for this gift that has its origins in the loving communion of the Trinity, Christians share in the prayer of Jesus. According to Vatican II, 'public and private prayer for the unity of Christians, should be regarded as the soul of the whole ecumenical movement, and can rightly be called "spiritual ecumenism".'[6] The Scriptures are a fundamental source for public and private prayer, and a bond of unity for all Christians.

Oratio (Prayer) → *Contemplatio* (Contemplation) → *Actio* (Action) →

- The three-year lectionary cycle is a shared treasure for liturgical and personal prayer. Ecumenical work is essentially a spiritual task because it is participation in the prayer of Jesus, 'that they may all be one' (17.21). Learning to understand this prayer of Jesus is a spiritual process, a work and a gift of the Holy Spirit. At the heart of ecumenism is spiritual ecumenism, which, according to Walter Kasper and Rowan Williams, is about mission and prayer.[7] Personal and communal prayer together, such as is prayed during the Week of Prayer for Christian Unity, has its origins in the loving communion of the Trinity. The Spirit can create a space for the exchange of gifts for mission. Writing in the World Council of Churches publication, *Economy of Life*, Rogate Mshana and Athena Peralta stress, 'The mission of the ecumenical movement today is about transforming the world into a place of justice and peace for all God's creation ... [in a] participatory search for alternatives that are centred on the people and the Earth.'[8] Likewise, in *Laudato Si'*, for Pope Francis, 'we have to realize that a true ecological approach *always* becomes a social approach; it must integrate questions of justice in debates on the environment, so as to hear *both the cry of the earth and the cry of the poor*' (§49, italics his).

Notes

1 On the types of prayer in John 17, see Jerome H. Neyrey, 2007, *The Gospel of John*, New York: Cambridge University Press, pp. 278–81 (italics his).

2 On John 17, see Brendan Byrne SJ, 2014, *Life Abounding: A Reading of John's Gospel*, Collegeville MN: Liturgical Press, pp. 280–91. On 'protect' (*tērēson*), which is found three times (17.11, 12, 15), see p. 284.

3 R. Alan Culpepper, 1998, *The Gospel and Letters of John*, Nashville TN: Abingdon Press, p. 220.

4 The Greek for 'desire' is *thelō* (17.24).

5 Walter Kasper, 2007, *A Handbook of Spiritual Ecumenism*, New York: New City Press, p. 10.

6 Vatican II, 1964, *Decree on Ecumenism* (*Unitatis Redintegratio*) §8, www.vatican.va/archive/hist_councils/ii_vatican_council/documents/vat-ii_decree_19641121_unitatis-redintegratio_en.html (accessed 10.08.19).

7 Kasper, *Handbook*, p. 10; Rowan Williams, 2003, 'Keynote Address', in *May They All Be One ... But How?: Proceedings of the Conference Held in St Albans Cathedral on 17 May 2003*, St Albans: St Albans Centre for Christian Studies.

8 Rogate R. Mshana and Athena Peralta (eds), 2015, *Economy of Life: Linking Poverty, Wealth and Ecology*, Geneva: WCC Publications, pp. vii, ix–x.

Jerusalem
The Passion and Death of Jesus
– John 18.1—19.42

'He bowed his head and handed over the Spirit' (John 19.30)

Good Friday of Years ABC
John 18.1—19.42
Holy Saturday (Alternative) of Years ABC (RCL Alternative)
John 19.38–42
Thirty-Fourth Sunday in Ordinary Time of Year B: Christ the King (RL)
Reign of Christ (RCL)
John 18.33–37

Lectio/Reading of John 18.1—19.42

Jesus' barrier-crossing ministry in Roman-occupied Galilee and Judea that led to his arrest, trial and crucifixion are foreshadowed in the prologue (1.10–11). The presence of the Spirit is also evoked as Jesus is inserted into God's ongoing work of creation and re-creation (1.1–5). In reading and rereading John 18.1—19.42, be aware of those clues and of the consequences for Jesus that continue to unfold in the Gospel narrative because of his commitment to complete the works of God.

Meditatio/Meditation

Re-creation – Jesus 'handed over the Spirit' (John 18.1—19.42)

The often talked about 'hour' of Jesus (John 3.14; 8.28; 12.32–33; 13.1) arrives when he would be 'lifted up'. This is the glorification of Jesus. He seems hardly to suffer. There is no agony in the garden – no man of sorrows. His freedom to lay down his life has been stressed (10.18) and continues to be. Parallels are found with the Synoptic accounts: the arrest in the garden, his appearances before the Jewish authorities and before

Pilate, the crucifixion and burial of Jesus and later the discovery of the empty tomb. Features unique to John play a very significant part in the liturgy and spirituality of the Church and in art. Jesus as king is accentuated. We find the following: the seamless garment; the cry of Jesus, 'I am thirsty'; the presence of the mother of Jesus, the women and the Beloved Disciple near the cross; the piercing of the side of Jesus, with blood and water flowing; and his giving of his mother into the care of the Beloved Disciple. There are many scriptural quotations and allusions. Imagery and symbolism, irony and double meanings are everywhere. This is, therefore, a particular interpretation of the death-resurrection of Jesus refracted through the prism of John's particular theological concerns.

In what follows, we shall divide John 18—19 into two main sections, and our discussion will focus on some areas that are often obscured or overlooked. In the first main section of 18.1—19.16, we shall consider the betrayal and arrest of Jesus (18.12) and his time before Pilate (18.12-16a) against the background of Roman power, which leads to his public trial and execution.[1] Then, in the second main section of 19.16b-40, we shall consider the crucifixion of Jesus, and his burial, through three interconnected theological strands critical to hearing *both the cry of the earth and the cry of the marginalized*: creation and re-creation, the last words of Jesus, and the handing over of the Spirit.

'Search the scriptures' (John 5.39)

The earliest Christians of Jewish origin knew their Scriptures. They turned to them to understand and make sense of the death of Jesus. To have the shameful event of crucifixion, a form of capital punishment imposed by the Roman Empire on a conquered people, at the centre of their faith was incomprehensible in cultural terms. Raymond Brown explains:

> How was Jesus' death on the cross meaningful in the divine plans for God's people? The only language in which they could answer that question was scriptural, i.e., the descriptions of the suffering one in the psalms and the prophets. Too often we tend to speak of the early Christians 'turning to' Scripture, implying that they turned to the Bible to look up relevant passages as we do. Rather their minds were imbued with biblical images and phrases, so that scriptural motifs naturally oriented their interest and understanding. The first followers of Jesus would have known many things about crucifixion in general and almost surely some of the details about Jesus' crucifixion ... Nevertheless, what is preserved in the narrative is mostly what echoes Scripture.[2]

So with 'their minds imbued with biblical images and phrases', the Johannine Christians 'search[ed] the scriptures' (John 5.39) to make meaning of the life and death-resurrection of Jesus in the Roman-occupied world.

'Jesus replied, "I am"' (John 18.8)

Only in John are a Roman cohort (600 soldiers, one-tenth of a Roman legion) and its tribune, a high-ranking officer, involved alongside Judas and 'police from the chief priests and the Pharisees' in the arrest of Jesus in an unnamed garden (18.3–12). Whether or not it is a whole cohort or a section of it is not the issue. The fact is that right from the beginning of Jesus' arrest there is official Roman interest. In the face of this, what is described is not so much an arrest but a confrontation in which Jesus is very much in control and takes the initiative. He speaks the first (18.4) and last words (18.11). He is conscious of what lies ahead of him (18.4). Coming forward, Jesus asks, 'Whom are you looking for?' (18.7; cf. 1.38; 20.15). The reply of those who approach him, 'Jesus of Nazareth', brings to mind Nathanael's first response to the human origins of Jesus (1.46). In contrast to those lowly origins, Jesus replies, 'I am'. Armed soldiers behave in an unusual way before an unarmed man – they fall to the ground (18.3–8). English translations insert 'he' (not in Greek), thereby obscuring that while at one level Jesus is simply saying who he is, there are other echoes that include the 'I AM' of Exodus 3.14 and other recurring biblical revelations of the divine name. There are echoes here of the 'I am' statements of Jesus (John 6.35, 41, 48, 51; 8.12; 10.11, 15; 11.25; 14.6; 15.1, 5). With no need to assert further who he is because he is the one they are looking for, Jesus acts as the Good Shepherd laying down his life for his sheep (10.11, 17–18) by instructing those who intend to arrest him to 'let these men go' (18.8). None have been lost who have been entrusted to him (17.12). The disciples' escape is not desertion as in the Synoptics. Rather, it highlights his loving concern for 'his own'. While Jesus rebuking Peter for drawing his sword and cutting off the ear of the slave of the high priest (18.10–11) may be about non-violence, it is also about his 'drinking the cup', the consequence of his completing the works of God.

In 18.3–11, the recurring pattern of discipleship takes another turn. Here, Judas brings others to Jesus who are set on destroying him. This departs from what has happened previously, where a disciple speaks to another, or others, to invite them to 'come and see' Jesus, who then confirms the relationship: the first disciples (1.35–50); the woman of Samaria and her villagers (4.27–30); Martha to Mary (11.28–33); Mary Magdalene and the Beloved Disciple (20.1–10); and the disciples and Thomas (20.24–25).

THE 'HOUR' OF JESUS

'I have spoken openly to the world' (John 18.20)

In a somewhat confusing movement between Annas and Caiaphas, the high priest for that year, Jesus is interrogated rather than put formally on trial (18.13–14; 19–24). Greater prominence is given to Peter's three denials (18.15–18, 25–27) rather than to the high priest's interrogation. This non-trial highlights for the reader that, in this gospel story, Jesus has been on trial ever since he heals the man in John 5 and aligns himself openly and in public with marginalized outcasts.[3] He is accused of breaking the Sabbath and of blasphemy (5.16–18). More trials take place at the Feast of Booths (7.10–52; 8.12–59). The Pharisees investigate Jesus in his absence after he has healed the poor beggar born blind (9.13–34). Yet again, Jesus is interrogated and charged with blasphemy at the Feast of Dedication (10.22–39). After the raising of Lazarus, he is tried in his absence, convicted and sentenced to death. Caiaphas pronounces a verdict (11.45–52). In 18.19–24, Jesus is subjected to the high priest's questions and scrutiny. Throughout this ongoing trial, two other significant features of Jesus' ministry recur – testifying, and the quality of speaking or acting 'openly' or 'boldly'.

This confrontation is the last occasion on which Jesus models for his disciples bold, open testimony to his participation in finishing the works of God. In broad strokes, in the first 11 chapters of John, the healings and actions of Jesus for and among the marginalized usually take place in public. When questioned about his disciples and his teachings, Jesus answers, 'I have spoken openly to the world.' He teaches in synagogues where Jews gather and in the temple. He 'said nothing in secret' (18.20). Jesus, imaged as Wisdom-Sophia who cried out for justice at street corners, shows boldness of speech and action by speaking 'openly' or 'frankly' (7.4, 13, 26; 10.24; 11.14, 54; 16.25, 29; 18.20), as well as embodying a quality of ancient Hellenistic friendship.

No Jewish court ever charges Jesus formally or condemns him. No Jews beat him or mock him (beyond a single slap in 18.22). Even though the Jewish leadership instigates his trial and execution, the omission of the Sanhedrin trial means that the formal responsibility for the humiliation and condemnation of Jesus is entirely with the Roman prefect Pilate. No attempt is made to free the Romans of blame or load guilt on the Jews. More emphasis is given to the political nature of the charges against Jesus than anywhere else in the New Testament.[4]

The depictions of the adversaries of Jesus as 'the Jews' contain strong language and negative imagery. So who are Jesus' adversaries in John's Gospel? And what is the nature of Jesus' conflict with them? The following groups and entities are depicted as being hostile towards Jesus: the Pharisees, the chief priests, Annas, Caiaphas, the authorities, the Jews, the

Council (Sanhedrin), Judas, Satan and the world. Once this Gospel's complex use of the term 'the Jews' is closely examined, all these persons and entities form a single allied group portrayed as strongly rejecting Jesus and consciously seeking to bring about his end.[5] To emphasize this significant point, it will be restated. The group demanding that Pilate put Jesus to death is essentially an alliance of Pharisees and chief priests whose conflict with Jesus reaches back into the previous events of the gospel story and arises because of Jesus' claims about his identity and relationship with God. This alliance is distinct from the Jewish population of Jerusalem. No crowd demands the death of Jesus.

'I came into the world to testify to the truth' (John 18.37)

The imperial authorities are not mentioned until rather late, when the Roman governor also becomes involved in the controversy (18.28). Cassidy points out that this Gospel describes 'a careful portrayal of how a Roman governor, at once powerful and threatened, finally acceded to the pressure of Jesus' intransigent adversaries for his death'.[6] While Pontius Pilate did acquiesce to the demands of the chief priests, he exacts a price of his own from them. By his words and questions Pilate extracts from them the self-debasing protest, 'We have no king but the emperor' (19.15). While the chief priests may well have achieved their aim of obtaining Jesus' death by pressuring Pilate, the governor still exercises the prerogatives of his office and later refuses to grant their request to alter the inscription on Jesus' cross (19.22).

The Roman trial of Jesus is dramatic, highly symbolic and structured carefully in seven brief scenes (18.29–32, 33–38a, 38b–40; 19.1–3, 4–7, 8–11, 12–16a). The key person in each scene is Pilate, who moves back and forth between where Jesus is held inside the Roman praetorium and 'the Jews' in the outer courtyard. Two trials are taking place. On the narrative level is the seemingly obvious trial of Jesus. On the symbolic level is the trial of 'the Jews', Pilate and all humanity. They could choose the reign of God as revealed by Jesus in the world or choose the world. Pilate is caught between these two worlds and pulled between them: the world Jesus represented is that of God or the world of Caesar. Usually Pilate's weakness and insecurities are stressed when speaking of his role in the death of Jesus. This happens for three reasons.[7]

First, the trial is read from the perspective of blaming 'the Jews' for the death of Jesus. The context is treated as a religious dispute. Second, this leads to the obscuring of the imperial and political background of negotiation in which the Jerusalem leaders as the allies of Rome are those who seek to get rid of Jesus. This is seen in an ethnic framework rather than in its imperial and political realities. The Jerusalem elites gathered around the temple were leaders in their society who wielded power as allies of Rome and were dependent and subordinate to Rome. This alliance was distinct from the Jewish population of Jerusalem who, in John, did not demand that Jesus be crucified. Third, no consideration is given to how governors functioned in the Roman hierarchal, imperial system, which had at its core small allied elites. Pilate was identified with the praetorium (18.28), which was derived from a title of a Roman official (praetor) who had military and judicial duties. Men who had been appointed governors came from the Roman aristocracy. Their families usually had wealth based in land, as well as being well connected with other civilian and military elites. Pilate would have most likely come from this ruling elite class.

The roles of governors included the following: settling disputes and keeping order, collecting taxes, being responsible for fiscal administration, engaging in public and building projects, commanding troops and administering justice, including power to put people to death.[8] Pilate seized money from the temple treasury to build an aqueduct. Ancient writers like Philo and Josephus record that he ruled with an iron fist and was removed from office by the Roman authorities because of his cruelty. In writing about governors, Josephus used the image of governors as bloodsucking flies and attributed this image also to Tiberius, who was emperor when Pilate was governor of Judea.[9]

Jesus as king

Against the background of the powerful role of the Roman governor, the portrayal of Jesus as a different kind of king is accentuated in the trial (13 times). Jesus is addressed as king (1.49; 6.15; 12.13, 15) more often than in any other Gospel. In the trial scenes, Pilate is the first to use the word 'king'. The word for 'king' (*basileus*) was used of the Roman emperor, so Jesus is presented in an opposing relationship to the emperor (*basileus*) and his representative, Pilate. Jesus is not silent before Pilate (as in the other three Gospels). When Jesus asserts twice that his *basileia* (empire) 'is not from this world', again he is set in opposition to Rome, for the same term was used for the *basileia* of Rome. The issue is about power and sovereignty and *how* this is expressed. Jesus is a real political threat to *how* Rome and Jerusalem order the world.

Central to the threat that Jesus poses was the origin of his *basileia*. For Jesus, the world is created and loved by God (1.10; 3.16). Jesus' *basileia* is from God (3.31; 8.23, 42; 16.28). Jesus reveals God's claim over all human lives and structures. It is a political claim to assert that God's *basileia* prevails over all, including Pilate's *basileia*. There is no armed resistance from Jesus' followers (18.36). The word Jesus used for his followers is also used of those (usually translated as 'police') sent by the temple elite to arrest him (18.3, 12, 18, 22; 19.6). The sense of this word means one who works with another as the instrument of that person's will. The world of Pilate's empire and his Jerusalem allies is based on coercive power and domination, while the role of Jesus in God's mission is to testify to the truth.

Truth – God's faithful saving action

Truth, a key word in John, needs to be defined carefully.[10] Jesus describes himself as 'truth' (8.32; 14.6). Although the term 'truth' can mean 'genuine' or 'real', in the biblical tradition, however, it often means 'faithfulness' or 'loyalty'. It has the sense of being faithful to one's obligations and commitments (Gen. 24.49). The Hebrew term for 'truth' or 'true' (*'emet*) is often translated as 'faithfulness' (Gen. 32.10; Exod. 34.6). God acts 'truthfully' or 'in truth' when God is faithful to God's covenantal promises by showing *hesed* to save God's people. *Hesed* is a word for 'mercy' (often translated as steadfast love or loving kindness). In Exodus 34.6, for example, God is described as 'abounding in steadfast love (*hesed*) and faithfulness (*'emet*). God's 'truthfulness' means God acts powerfully and truthfully to save the people (Ps. 40.11–12; 108.4).

When Jesus declares that his mission is to testify to 'the truth' (John 18.37), he is telling Pilate that he is witnessing to God's faithfulness in saving the people. Jesus witnesses to the truth (3.33), declares he is the truth (14.6) and reveals that God is acting faithfully to save the world God so loves (3.16–17; 8.14–18). Truth, then, refers to God's faithful saving action. Jesus also explains to Pilate that the characteristic of those who 'belong to the truth' is that they listen to his voice, as do the sheep in the Good Shepherd parable (10.4–6, 16, 27) and Mary of Bethany (11.28–29). Pilate does not listen. He does not 'see' who Jesus is or his origin or his work of completing the works of God. Rensberger understands that this Gospel:

> confronts the issue of Israel's freedom in the late first-century Roman Empire with an alternative to both zealotry and collaboration, by calling for adherence to the king who is not of this world, whose servants do not fight but remain in the world bearing witness to the truth before the rulers of both synagogue and Empire.[11]

THE 'HOUR' OF JESUS

'So must the Son of Humanity be lifted up' (John 3.14)

Having considered the arrest and trial of Jesus against the background of the Roman Empire, we shall look at the account of his crucifixion, death and burial (John 19.16b–42) by giving attention to four interconnected theological strands: creation and re-creation, the last words of Jesus, the handing over of the spirit, and the blood and water flowing from his side.

The actual crucifixion of Jesus is told very sparsely (19.16b–18). Three details are provided that are also found in the Synoptics but which have Johannine nuances. Jesus carries his own cross 'by himself' – unaided by Simon of Cyrene (unlike Mark 15.21 and parallels). He is crucified with two others, who are called neither thieves nor evildoers and who are not said to curse him. The inscription on the cross is in three languages: Hebrew, the language of the Scriptures; Latin, the language of the Roman Empire; and Greek, the language of Hellenistic culture. These were languages of religion, state and culture. The Johannine nuances relate to the 'lifting up' sayings of Jesus (John 3.14; 8.28; 12.32), which understand his death as part of his glorification. The 'lifting up' is the first stage of Jesus' exaltation and glorification; that is, his death-resurrection. The emphasis is on Jesus as king, the one whose death would be significant for all peoples. John expands the scene of dividing the garments. Here, as the tunic was seamless, the soldiers cast lots (19.24; cf. Ps. 22.18). This underscores the unity that is found in the one vine, one flock and one shepherd images.

'There was a garden' (John 18.1; 19.41)

Strands of creation and re-creation, which in the prologue speak of the incarnation of Jesus, continue in his death-resurrection, his absence and presence in the Spirit. The account of his passion, death and burial begins and ends in a 'place' where 'there was a garden' (John 18.1; 19.41), which evokes creation and the garden of Genesis, as did the first words of this Gospel (1.1). God 'planted a garden in Eden, in the East' (Gen. 2.8). Like a gardener, God cultivated it (2.9) and walked in it (3.8). As God is central to biblical creation, so too is Jesus inserted in God's creation. In the prologue, Jesus is portrayed as Wisdom-Sophia who was with God at the beginning of the various works of creation (Prov. 8.22–36).

'It is finished' (John 19.30)

Features such as his loud cry of abandonment, darkness, earthquakes and the rending of the temple veil are absent. As his death approaches, we hear about how the works of God come to completion in Jesus. We are told, 'Jesus knew that all was finished' (John 19.28), and then that he exclaims, 'I thirst' (19.28; cf. Ps. 69.21). He is given sour wine on a branch of hyssop, the herb used to smear the blood over the lintels before the Passover (Exod. 12.21–23). His last words on the cross, 'It is finished' (NRSV; 'accomplished' in JB, John 19.30), have the sense of accomplishing or completing. Earlier, Jesus had explained his own work in relation to God's work. His food is to complete the works of God (4.34). God gave him works to complete (5.36). Jesus speaks of God doing works through him (14.10), and those who believe in Jesus 'will do the works that I do and, in fact, greater works than I do' (14.12). These references echo Genesis, where 'God rested from all the work that God had done in creation' (Gen. 2.2). A completed creation was sealed by Sabbath rest on the seventh day (Gen. 2.3), yet God's work is incomplete. Jesus has continued God's work. He has healed and has re-created even on the Sabbath.

'And handed over the Spirit' (John 19.30)

Jesus' death is usually expressed as he 'gave up his spirit'. Nowhere else in the ancient world was this expression used to describe someone's death.[12] The verb used in the Greek text means to 'hand over', and is used of the action of Judas, in the Synoptics, when he 'handed over' Jesus after he betrays him.[13] So a more accurate translation would be, he 'handed over the spirit' – the Greek has no 'his'. In the light of this, James Swetnam observes that, 'at the deeper level the climax of the Passion of the Jesus of the Fourth Gospel is not the death of Jesus, but a bestowal of the Spirit.'[14] The Spirit has been promised previously (John 7.39; 14.16–17). Underlying the words of Jesus in John 14 is the assurance that when he is absent, he is present through the Spirit. So in continuity with that assurance, the climax of the passion is not a death but a leave-taking. Jesus 'handed over the Spirit' to the disciples at the foot of the cross.

All four Gospels record the presence of women at the cross. After Jesus dies, the other Gospels have them watching at a distance (cf. Ps. 38.11). John records that not only are the women, including his mother, 'standing near the cross' before and after his death but that Jesus 'saw' her and the disciple whom he loved and spoke to them (John 19.26–27). Raymond Brown points out, 'it would be unusual for the Romans to permit family and friends such proximity.'[15] Luise Schottroff argues that the women were at risk as followers of a crucified person and that their presence was part of their resistance to Roman oppression.[16] Previously we discussed seeing Jesus' life and death within the ancient understanding of friendship and noble death – as such, women and friends were usually present or nearby.[17]

So Jesus handed over the Spirit to the disciples at the foot of the cross to continue the works of God. And those disciples are the mother of Jesus, the women and the Beloved Disciple.[18] As his mother is present at the beginning of Jesus' public ministry (2.1), she is there at the end. The prominence of women continues with two or three other women present (the Greek is ambiguous). The identity of the Beloved Disciple has been much debated, as that person's identity cannot be discovered from the evidence of the Gospel itself. While tradition links that person to the apostle John, and even to the author of the Gospel, there have been many candidates for the identity of this character over the centuries.[19] Some suggest that the Beloved Disciple is, in fact, the reader, who is to insert herself or himself into the place of the Beloved Disciple in order to become a Beloved Disciple.[20]

'One of the soldiers pierced his side with a spear' (John 19.34)

A proper burial for crucified criminals was not usual because the Romans left crucified bodies exposed on the cross for days for scavenging birds or disposed of them on rubbish heaps. This Roman practice horrified Jews. According to Jewish custom, the bodies could not be left on the cross (cf. Deut. 21.22–23) because the next day was the Sabbath and that year it was also the Passover. Therefore, a request is made to Pilate to have the legs of the crucified broken in order to hasten death. As Jesus is found to be already dead his legs are not broken. Instead his side is pierced with a lance. This incident evokes several biblical traditions. Jesus dies at the time when lambs are being slaughtered in the temple, recalling the bones of the Passover lamb, which must not be broken.

Often overlooked is how John's attention to creation and re-creation, which is laid out in the prologue, comes again to the fore. The Greek word for 'side' in John 19.34 suggests the order of creation and of God's work, for it appears in the creation account of Genesis 2.21–22 in the Greek Old Testament.[21] Through the body of Jesus, God creates the new humanity, the new community of the Church, just as God chose to create Eve to perfect and complete the world.[22] The Spirit was present at creation. The blood and water that flows from the side of his crucified body suggests that Jesus dies so that the Spirit can now be given. This life-giving stream is the Spirit given to all who believe in him (John 7.38–39). The living water means one is never thirsty again (4.14). Jesus has said, 'my blood is true drink' (6.55).[23] This is an allusion to 'strike the rock, and water will come out of it for the people to drink' (Exod. 17.6; cf. Num. 20.11 and 1 Cor. 10.4).

'And in the garden there was a new tomb' (John 19.41)

All four canonical Gospels have Joseph of Arimathea ask Pilate for the body of Jesus. Only in John is he called a secret believer, 'because of his fear of the Jews' (19.38; cf. 12.42). Only in John is he assisted by Nicodemus (3.1–21; 7.45–52) to bury Jesus. In their actions of requesting the body and burying a publicly executed criminal, both of these men risk life and reputation. We are told explicitly, 'there was a garden in the place where he was crucified' (19.41). The burial details, as well as his being buried 'in a new tomb in which no one had ever been laid', show that Jesus is given a proper burial according to Jewish custom (19.40). He is anointed with a lavish quantity of spices. While many see Nicodemus' gesture of anointing the body of Jesus as an act of unbelief and inadequate faith in his resurrection, there is another possible way of interpreting what is happening here. Nicodemus brings 'a mixture of myrrh and aloes, weighing about a hundred pounds' (19.39). According to John 12.1–8, Mary of Bethany anointed Jesus with a pound of pure nard, which was valued at 300 days' wages. The huge and expensive amount – about eight gallons of spice in liquid measure – brought by Nicodemus indicates that he is a very rich man.[24] This is no ordinary burial but suggests some of the trappings of a royal burial. The first-century Jewish historian Josephus tells of massive amounts of spices at the funeral of King Herod the Great.[25] Maybe the one who comes to Jesus in secret by night comes to faith. In John, the women do not, therefore, come to the tomb to anoint the body, as that has been attended to with a copious amount of myrrh and aloes. In addition, Jesus has already been anointed for burial by his friend Mary of Bethany (12.3–8). Jesus has affirmed that her anointing of him both anticipated and was performed for his burial (12.7).

Oratio (Prayer) → *Contemplatio* (Contemplation) → *Actio* (Action) →

- Jesus was a not generic person. There are only concrete persons in particular places and times. Jesus was Jewish, living in a complex Jewish society. He lived in, and this Gospel was written in, turbulent historical conditions under Roman occupation, which affected both the land and the people. The time was dangerous. Jesus witnessed to the truth (18.37). He had been on trial not only before Pilate but throughout the gospel story. He is arrested, convicted unjustly on dubious charges and is executed. Through the body of Jesus the Spirit is handed over to disciples. God creates the new humanity, the new community of the Church, to perfect and complete the works of God. The link between the people and the earth is at the core of the advocacy and the commitment of many people despite the dangers. We can recall Dietrich Bonhoeffer in Nazi Germany; Dorothy Stang in rainforests of the Amazon; Martin Luther King Jr in the United States of America; Steve Biko in South Africa; Oscar Romero and many companions in El Salvador; and Doctors without Borders in Syria. With and alongside such leaders are multitudes of Indigenous people and people at the grass roots. The World Council of Churches reminds us that in the Philippines, people of faith, Christians, Muslims and Indigenous leaders have given their lives 'to maintain their connection to and to continue to sustain themselves from the lands to which they belong'.[26]

- How do we reframe the Feast of Christ the King or the Reign of Christ, titles with which today we may be a bit uncomfortable? What is the empire today? How is it opposed to the *basileia* of Jesus? Pope Francis is calling on the world to rethink fundamentally the definition of economic and social progress to develop one that is in harmony with creation. He speaks of it being 'easy to accept the idea of infinite or unlimited growth which proves so attractive' (*LS* §106) and of the dangers of 'compulsive consumerism' (*LS* §203). If truth refers to God's faithful saving action then, as disciples today, we are called to be faithful to our obligations and commitments, which include completing the works of God. How do we participate in completing the works of God by caring for the earth and the marginalized?

Notes

1 Brendan Byrne SJ, 2014, *Life Abounding: A Reading of John's Gospel*, Collegeville MN: Liturgical Press, pp. 292–314.

2 Raymond E. Brown, 1994, *The Death of the Messiah: From Gethsemane to the Grave. A Commentary on the Passion Narratives in the Four Gospels*, 2 vols, London: Geoffrey Chapman, p. 15.

3 Jerome H. Neyrey, 2007, *The Gospel of John*, New York: Cambridge University Press; on the Judean trial of Jesus, see pp. 292–6.

4 David Rensberger, 1998, *Johannine Faith and Liberating Community*, Philadelphia PA: Westminster, p. 87.

5 Richard Cassidy, 2015, *John's Gospel in New Perspective: Christology and the Realities of Roman Power, With the New Essay, 'Johannine Footwashing and Roman Slavery'*, first published 1992, Eugene OR: Wipf & Stock, pp. 40–1.

6 Cassidy, *John's Gospel*; on 'The Roman Trial of Jesus', see pp. 40–53, especially pp. 40–1 and 46–7.

7 Warren Carter, 2008, *John and Empire: Initial Explorations*, New York: T&T Clark, pp. 289–90.

8 Carter, *John and Empire*, pp. 291–2.

9 Carter, *John and Empire*, p. 296.

10 Carter, *John and Empire*; on Pilate and the role of the Roman governor, see pp. 289–314, especially pp. 289–90 and 296. On 'truth' in John and its biblical background, I draw on p. 303.

11 Rensberger, *Johannine Faith*; on the Roman trial, see pp. 86–106, especially p. 100.

12 James Swetnam, 1993, 'Bestowal of the Spirit in the Fourth Gospel', *Biblica* 74.4, pp. 564 and 566.

13 The Greek verb *paradidōmi*, which is usually translated as 'he gave up' in John 19.30, is the same verb used of the act of Judas several times in this Gospel and at other times for the handing over of Jesus to Pilate (18.30, 35).

14 Swetnam, 'Bestowal of the Spirit', p. 566.

15 Brown, *Death of the Messiah*, p. 1194.

16 Luise Schottroff, 1995, *Lydia's Impatient Sisters: A Feminist Social History of Early Christianity*, Barbara and Martin Rumscheidt (trans.), Louisville KY: Westminster John Knox Press, pp. 104–5.

17 Kathleen Corley, 1995, 'He was Buried, On the Third Day He was Raised: Women and the Crucifixion and Burial of Jesus', paper presented to the Jesus Seminar, Fall, p. 36.

18 On various views about the presence of family and friends near the cross, see Kathleen P. Rushton, 2011, *The Parable of the Woman in Childbirth of John 16:21: A Metaphor for the Death and Glorification of Jesus*, Lewiston NY: The Edwin Mellen Press, pp. 259–60.

19 James H. Charlesworth, 1995, *The Beloved Disciples: Whose Witness Validates the Gospel of John?* Valley Forge PA: Trinity Press International.

20 Sandra M. Schneiders, 1999, 'Because of the Woman's Testimony', in *Written that You May Believe: Encountering Jesus in the Fourth Gospel*, New York: Crossroad, pp. 224–8.

21 The Greek for 'side' (*pleura*) in John 19.34 is in the creation account of Genesis 2.21–22.

22 On how interpretations of 19.34 as birth have contributed not only to the subjection of women but also to the subjection of earth, see Deborah Sawyer, 2003, 'John 19.34: From Crucifixion to Birth, or Creation?', in Amy-Jill Levine (ed.), *A Feminist Companion to John, Vol. II*, Cleveland OH: The Pilgrim Press, pp. 131–8. See my article, Kathleen P. Rushton, 2014, 'On the Crossroads between Life and Death: Reading Birth Imagery in John in the Earthquake Changed Regions of Otautahi Christchurch', in Jione Havea, David Neville and Elaine Wainwright (eds), *Bible, Borders, Belonging(s): Engaging Readings from Oceania*, Atlanta GA: Society of Biblical Literature, pp. 57–72.

23 Charles H. Dodd, 1963, *Historical Tradition in the Fourth Gospel*, Cambridge: Cambridge University Press, p. 428.

24 Robert J. Karris, 1990, *Jesus and the Marginalized in John's Gospel*, Collegeville MN: Liturgical Press, p. 98.

25 Karris, *Jesus and the Marginalized*, p. 98.

26 WCC, 'Economy of Life', §19, in Rogate R. Mshana and Athena Peralta (eds), 2015, *Economy of Life: Linking Poverty, Wealth and Ecology*, Geneva: WCC Publications.

Jerusalem Appearances of the Risen Jesus – John 20.1–31

'Supposing him to be the gardener' (John 20.15)

Easter Sunday: Resurrection of the Lord – Option 1 of Years ABC (RL)
John 20.1–9
Resurrection of the Lord – Alternative of Years ABC (RCL Alternative)
John 20.1–18

'He breathed on them and said to them, "Receive the Holy Spirit"'
(John 20.22)

Pentecost Sunday of Years ABC (RL)
Day of Pentecost of Year A (RCL)
John 20.19–23
Second Sunday of Easter of Years ABC
John 20.19–31

Jesus' work of completing the works of God is over. He has told us himself in his last words on the cross, 'It is finished' (19.28, 30). The works of God are to be continued through the work of the disciples (14.12; 17.20–21) and through the Holy Spirit (14.25–29). In his farewell discourse, Jesus says, 'I still have many things to say to you, but you cannot bear them now' (16.12). He has assured his disciples that the Spirit will guide them and re-announce to them the significance of the truth God has already communicated to them through the words and works of Jesus (16.14). In his post-resurrection appearances, first in Jerusalem and then in Galilee, Jesus assures his disciples of his ongoing presence.

In Jerusalem, the risen Jesus continues to assure his disciples in three scenes followed by a conclusion (20.30–31). The first scene is on the morning of Jesus' resurrection when Mary Magdalene, Peter and the Beloved Disciple go to the tomb (20.1–18). The second scene takes place that evening when Jesus appears to the male disciples in the absence of Thomas (20.19–23). Both these scenes evoked creation and re-creation. In the third scene, eight days later Jesus appears to male disciples when Thomas is present (20.24–29).

Lectio/Reading of John 20.1–18

In reading and reading John 20.1–18 (the first appearance scene), recall the framework of the prologue, where Jesus is inserted in God's ongoing work of creation and re-creation. Jesus is arrested in a garden (18.1), crucified and buried in a garden (19.41). This calls us to be attentive to how ongoing creation continues in this unfolding story.

Meditatio/Meditation

'Supposing him to be the gardener' (John 20.15)

Time and again, we hear about how, in John's resurrection story, Mary Magdalene is confused when, 'weeping outside the tomb', she turns, sees Jesus and thinks he is the gardener (John 20.11–15).[1] It may be that Mary is confused. It may be that Mary is not confused at all – Jesus is the gardener. How could this be so? Only this Gospel states that Jesus is buried and raised in a garden – the graciousness of God in creation is linked with our re-creation in the death-resurrection of Jesus in whose flesh is seen God. Creation and ongoing creation interweave. In the Scriptures, creation is the garden of God. God is the gardener who 'planted a garden in Eden, in the East' (Gen. 2.8). Like a gardener, God cultivated the garden (2.9) and walked in it (3.8). John begins by evoking the garden of Genesis, 'In the beginning' (John 1.1), and ends with, 'Now there was a garden in the place where he was crucified, and in the garden there was a new tomb' (19.41). Ongoing creation is evoked when Jesus is raised on the first day of the week (20.1) and appears to his disciples, also on the first day of the week (20.19). Incarnation and death-resurrection are linked with ongoing creation. Jesus is the Gardener! As God is central to biblical creation, so too is Jesus inserted in God's ongoing evolving creation. In the prologue, Jesus is portrayed as Wisdom-Sophia who was with God at the beginning of the work of creation (Prov. 8.22–36).

'Let there be light' (Gen. 1.3)

In the Genesis creation narrative, the first specific creative act of God deals with the darkness that covered the earth. God acts by the creative word, 'Let there be light' (Gen. 1.3). Darkness is not dispelled by the creation of light but ordered in relation to light. In the incarnation narrative, the Word is the life that is 'the light of all people' (John 1.4). The One later named as Jesus is 'The light [that] shines in the darkness, and the darkness does not overcome it' (1.5). The resurrection narrative also begins with darkness evoking re-creation: 'Early on the first day of the week ... while it was still dark', Mary Magdalene comes to the tomb (20.1). She comes in darkness, in the night of suffering, grief and loss. At this time, when the pain and suffering of our world seems overwhelming, Mary, like us, does not immediately recognize Jesus, her light in the darkness. He asks, 'Who are you looking for?' (20.15). The verb 'to look for' echoes throughout this Gospel, beginning with Jesus' question to Andrew and another disciple, 'Who are you looking for?' (1.38).

'Saw and believed' (John 20.8)

For Jews, the tomb with its sealing stone was the final sign of being cut off from life. Imagine Mary Magdalene as she discovers that the stone has been removed. The open and empty tomb is a sign that Jesus is not in the power of death but is alive with God. Imagine Mary running to Simon Peter and the other disciple. Run with them to the tomb. The other disciple waits for Peter to enter. The Evangelist tells us, 'the cloth that had been on Jesus' head [was] not lying with the linen wrappings but rolled up in a place by itself' (20.7). The other disciple 'saw and believed' (20.8). What did he believe? The next verse states, 'as yet they did not understand the scripture that he must rise from the dead' (20.9). It was possibly the face veil that led the other disciple to believe.[2] It is not a normal burial cloth. The Greek text uses the same word for 'the cloth' as is used for the face veil worn by Moses to protect the people of Israel from the glorification of his face by his encounter with God on Sinai (Exod. 34.29–35). Jesus, the new Moses, leaves his earthly flesh to return to God. In John, Jesus' death is the victorious culmination of his life. 'Exalt' or 'lift up' evokes the lifting up of Jesus on the cross (John 3.14; 8.28; 12.32). The word 'glorify' describes the effect on Jesus of his 'lifting up' in crucifixion (7.39; 12.16–23; 13.31–32).

Those who use the Roman lectionary will notice that the reading ends at 20.9. John 20.10 tells us, 'The [two] disciples returned to their homes', while one stays at the tomb (20.11). Here, and in the other three Gospels, this disciple is the first witness to the resurrection. John's account reveals what is now possible in the relationship between God and disciples. This change is found in two overlooked aspects that obscure Mary Magdalene's significance as a disciple. First, much is made of Jesus' words to Mary, 'Do not hold on to me' (20.17, NRSV) and of his invitation to Thomas to touch him (20.27). This prohibition and encouragement are overplayed because in each case there are different Greek words for 'hold' or 'place'. Attempts to link these words – both often rendered 'touch' in English – are misplaced.[3] In contrast, we find the same word for 'touch' when the woman told the serpent that they were not to touch the fruit of the tree in the middle of the garden (Gen. 3.3) and in the words of Jesus (John 19.17). A link is made here between the woman who did not obey and Mary who does obey by telling the disciples that Jesus had been raised. The materiality of the body is acknowledged by the use of the verb 'touch'.

Second, generations of artists depict Jesus with hands raised towards Mary in a 'stop-do-not-come-near-me' gesture. Often those paintings are called, *Noli me tangere!* ('Don't touch me!'). While much attention is given to the first half of 20.17, the commission of Jesus to Mary in the second half is obscured, 'But go to my brothers and sisters and say to them, "I am ascending to my Father and your Father, to my God and your God".' Likewise overshadowed is the statement, 'Mary Magdalene went and announced to the disciples, "I have seen the Lord", and she told them that he had said these things to her' (20.18). Mary is commissioned by Jesus to announce his resurrection *and* by implication to announce that the relationship between God and human persons has been transformed.[4] To this point, Jesus has spoken of the Father as 'my Father' or 'the Father' but never as '*your* Father'. In John's Gospel, we are never instructed to say, '*Our* Father'. We are never instructed to address God as 'my God'. After his death-resurrection, Jesus announces a change. Now disciples have become children of God as promised (1.12). God becomes, in the words of Jesus, '*your* Father' and '*your* God'. Mary is entrusted with this climatic announcement. Now, with Thomas, we may exclaim, '*My* Lord and *my* God' (20.28). A distinction is still made between the unique relationship that Jesus has with God and that which is now possible for disciples.

The early Church recognized the significance of the commission of Jesus to Mary by calling her 'apostle of the apostles' (*apostola apostolorum*). Medieval art depicts Mary in this role. Interestingly, for the early centuries of the Church the symbol of the resurrection was the empty tomb with Mary and the women pointing to it. In later art, their role as the first witnesses to the resurrection is replaced with depictions of them carrying spices to the tomb. The traditional role of women in mourning customs included anointing a body for burial.

THE 'HOUR' OF JESUS

'We do not know where they have laid him' (John 20.2)

The story of John 20 is shaped around a theological answer to the spiritual question, 'Where is the Lord?' Although this question is posed by Mary Magdalene, it is not presented as a personal problem but a community problem, for she answers in the plural, *'we* do not know where they have laid him' (20.2). Mary represents those who have not understood the meaning of 'the hour' of Jesus. She is seeking Jesus, whom she associates with his corpse. Equating the person with the body and body with flesh is precisely what Easter faith must transcend. Personified in Mary is the theological problem of how the earthly Jesus (the Word made flesh) relates to the glorified and risen Jesus. Later, the scene with Thomas suggests this is precisely the problem for disciples for all time. Sandra Schneiders sums up this concern as, 'We are dealing with the historical experience (that of the disciples) of the nonhistorical reality (the glorified Jesus) somehow mediated by the body (which is what we mean by the risen Jesus).'[5] This leads us to consider the significance of the body and what body means.

Body as a symbol of the self

The body is a symbol of the self in four ways.[6] First, the body grounds *identity through change* – every cell is replaced every seven years. The same person, the same individual is revealed through photos at ages 10, 20 and 60. The human body holds both change and identity. Second, the body makes 'a person one in herself [himself] and distinct from all others' (personal consistence). The embodied self is marked off inwardly and outwardly from everyone else and all creation. Third, the body is the ground of interaction with others. We need to be aware of the wider-than-human creation and extend the ground of interaction to all of creation. The body allows one to be present, to speak and hear, to touch and be touched, to interact with people and all creation physically and spiritually. Fourth, the body enables each person to be part of a network of relations among others and all creation. This means that all who relate to an individual in some way relate to each other and to all creation.

We turn to the post-Easter Jesus. All differing biblical accounts of the resurrection of Jesus attest to the fact and significance of how Jesus is present among his disciples. The risen Jesus is recognized as being the same person whom the disciples knew pre-Easter in his earthly life. In the appearances of the risen Jesus, his disciples encounter someone who is really present, able to be seen as a distinct person. The disciples could interact with Jesus – they could see him, talk to him and touch him. The disciples found themselves sharing in common their relationship with

Jesus in the present. As they talk about their experience with each other, they know they are talking about the same person.

The resurrection brings a new way of embodied life, not a return to life as it was. Yet a theology of resurrection means facing squarely the reality of death. John's Gospel affirms that people find life in Jesus by relating to him in the present. This Gospel also states clearly that people of faith will die (11.3; 16.2; 21.19, 23). What then is the significance of the resurrection for those who face the coming of their own death? Jesus is able to say '*I am* the resurrection' because he undergoes death-resurrection and comes to embody resurrection hope. Underpinning resurrection is a wholistic understanding about what it means to be a human person. The whole person is affected by death.

Resurrection's wholistic sense of life and death differs from the idea that a person can be divided neatly into a body (*sōma*) and a soul (*psychē*).[7] Both of these terms, 'body' and 'soul', are used of Jesus as a whole person and of his death-resurrection. When he drives the sellers out of the temple, he says, 'Destroy this temple and in three days I will raise it up.' The Evangelist explains he is talking about the temple of his 'body' (*sōma*, 2.21). As an embodied person, Jesus dies and is raised up again. Later, Jesus uses the term *psychē* to express his 'life' or 'self': 'I lay down my life (*psychē*) in order to take it up again ... I have power to lay it down, and I have power to take it up again' (10.17–18). Again, the whole person of Jesus, body and soul, is involved in death-resurrection. The resurrection of the body means transformation into another form of existence. The Word became flesh (*sarx*, 1.14). Jesus indicates he would give his flesh for the life of the world (6.51). The Gospel does not tell us that Jesus' 'flesh' is resurrected. Jesus is not brought back to normal life. The more flexible terms, 'body' (*sōma*) and 'life' or 'self' (*psychē*), are used for Jesus. As a whole person, he goes through death and is resurrected to a life that is no longer under the threat of death. There is a contrast between the resurrection of Jesus and the raising of Lazarus. When Lazarus is called out of his tomb by Jesus, he comes forth wrapped in burial cloths. He must be unbound and let go (11.44). Jesus leaves his grave cloths behind. This suggests that he is freed from death and will not die again, while Lazarus will.

Oratio (Prayer) → *Contemplatio* (Contemplation) → *Actio* (Action) →

- In his 2005 Easter Vigil homily, Benedict XVI stated that Jesus' resurrection:

was like an explosion of light, an explosion of love ... It ushered in a new dimension of being, a new dimension of life in which, in a transformed way, matter too was integrated and through which a new world emerges ... It is a qualitative leap in the history of 'evolution' and of life in general towards a new future life, towards a new world which, starting from Christ, already continuously permeates this world of ours, transforms it and draws it to itself.[8]

This linking of the resurrection to evolution offers an illuminating context for our thinking about the resurrection today as we respond to *both the cry of the earth and the cry of the marginalized*. The prologue set the cosmic context. There we find 'all things' (1.3), which was a term for 'the universe' – nothing is excluded. Jesus the Word made flesh (1.14) joins all living creatures (Gen. 6.13–22). This does not solve the problem of suffering, but God 'is present in the midst of anguish, bearing every creature and all creation forward with an unimaginable promise'.[9] *Laudato Si'* speaks about how in the days of his flesh 'the gaze of Jesus' was attentive to the beauty of creation and lived in harmony with it (§96–§100). Now the risen and glorious Jesus is 'mysteriously holding' the creatures of earth 'to themselves and directing them towards fullness as their end ... The very flowers and the birds which his human eyes contemplated and admired are now imbued with his radiant presence' (§100). The World Council of Churches' 'Economy of Life' states that ultimately 'our hope springs from Christ's resurrection and the promise of life for all.'[10] Pope Francis points out that 'The earth, our home, is beginning to look more and more like an immense pile of filth' (*LS* §66). We are to be gardeners in the work of re-creation: 'Let us sing as we go. May our struggles and our concern for this planet never take away the joy of our hope' (*LS* §244).

- 'Who are you looking for?' (20.15). Do we hear Jesus' question that frames this Gospel (1.28) echo in our lives? Do we come in the darkness and do we stay at the tomb, the place of grief and suffering, as Mary does? When have I 'turned around and seen Jesus there', eventually recognizing light in darkness (20.14)? How do I respond to the risen One?

Lectio/Reading of John 20.19–29

Attention has been drawn in this book to the presence of the Spirit in John. The works of God will be completed through the Spirit and the works of disciples. In reading and rereading John 20.19–29, be aware of this.

Meditatio/Meditation

For the earliest Christian communities, the story of the Spirit began long before Pentecost. To their listening of John's Gospel they brought their rich traditions of the Spirit/Wind/Breath of God, which was a way of speaking about the powerful presence of the God of Israel. The Spirit expresses the creative, prophetic and renewing presence of God not only to the people of Israel but to the wider world. The word *pneuma* is used in the Scriptures for the Greek translation of the Hebrew word *ruah* meaning 'wind' or 'breath' or 'spirit'. These images describe the Spirit as an unseen wonder known by what it does, the effect it has and how it is experienced. The Spirit flows through all creation bringing life and love. And for people today, the coming of the Spirit begins before the biblical creation story. The Creator Spirit is the dynamic, energizing presence who enabled the universe to come into being some 14 billion years ago and is creatively at work enabling the ongoing emergence of the universe and the evolution of all life on earth.

'Breathed on them' (John 20.22)

Against this background, let us consider the risen Jesus. The resurrection story enters its second phase in 20.19–29, not at the garden tomb but on the evening of the first day of the week 'where the disciples were gathered' as a community. The focus now is a new question: 'How can the Risen Jesus be experienced?'[11] Above, we have recalled the significance of there being a 'garden in the place where he was crucified and in the garden there was a new tomb' (19.41). Now suddenly, Jesus 'stood in midst of' the community. This evokes the tree of life, which stood 'in the midst of the garden' (Gen. 2.9). Jesus on the cross was in the middle of two others who were crucified with him (John 19.18).

Two actions initiated by Jesus unfold. First, his 'Peace be with you' fulfils his promise to give a peace the world cannot give (cf. 14.27; 16.33). He shows his disciples his hands and his side. Even though glorified, his bodyself wears the marks of his paschal mystery. There is continuity and discontinuity with his pre-Easter body, his taking on the flesh of all living creatures. After repeating his gift of peace, Jesus then commissions the new People of God as he had been commissioned by God. Second, he 'breathed on' those present, saying 'Receive the Holy Spirit' (20.22). This recalls the Spirit sweeping over the waters (Gen. 1.2) and the Breath of God breathing life into the dust of the earth to create the earth creature (*ādām*) from the earth (*hā-adāma*) – earthling from the earth, groundling from the ground (Gen. 2.7; cf. Wisd. 15.11).[12] The verb 'breathed on', found only here in the New Testament, is used in the Greek Old Testament to refer directly to creation. The prophet Ezekiel is told to breathe on the dry bones so that the House of Israel might be re-created. Human persons would stay alive only if they have the Divine Breath abiding in them (Gen. 6.3). This applies to all creatures. God warns that the flood would 'destroy from under heaven all flesh in which there is the breath of life' (Gen. 6.17) and 'everything on dry land in whose nostrils was the breath of life died' (Gen. 7.22). The interconnected images of the Breath of God and the Word of God are linked together explicitly in the creation of the universe: 'By the word of the Lord the heavens were made and, and all their host [i.e. sun, moon and stars] by the breath of God's mouth' (Ps. 33.6).

This is the baptism with the Holy Spirit that Jesus brings. John, known as the Baptizer, speaks also about this outpouring of the Spirit, testifying that Jesus is the one on whom he sees the Spirit abiding (John 1.32–33) and who gives God's Spirit 'without measure' (3.34). Understood in the light of the death-resurrection, the Spirit is life-giver (6.63). Jesus is led by the Spirit in his preaching, healing, compassion for the marginalized, in his passion and death. His death is a leave-taking in which he hands over the Spirit to the women and the Beloved Disciple at the cross (19.30). The Spirit is with Jesus at every stage of his life. Jesus and the Spirit are interrelated and in communion with all life. The Evangelist sees this same Spirit being given to his friends as their Advocate or Paraclete (*paraklētos*) (14.16, 26; 15.26; 16.7). *Paraklētos* means 'one called alongside of'. Under this title, many meanings come together in a rich all-embracing picture of the Spirit as presence, teacher, comforter, guide, helper, friend, advocate, one who intercedes, consoler, spokesperson, witness, one who goes with, supports and stands beside another.

New pathways

Fruitfulness, beauty and co-operation are part of the long history of life on earth, as are predation, competition, death and extinction. In a finite, limited and bodily world, death is part of the way things are and central to the shape of biological life. In the face of this, Christian theology has no theories about why this is so except to bear witness to the death-resurrection of Jesus. Through the life and death of Jesus, God enters into the pain of the world, suffering with all creation. At the same time, in the resurrection and in the outpouring of the Spirit, new life is promised and given.[13]

While Jesus is the human face of God made flesh in our midst, the Spirit is revealed mysteriously as the Breath of God who breathes through all creation and through the hearts, minds and lives of human persons and all biological life. More often than not, the Spirit is described not in human terms (anthropomorphic) but in images taken from the natural world – as breath, wind, water, fire, oil and anointing. These images from nature remind us of 'the otherness' of the Spirit and resist human tendencies to domesticate the Spirit who is experienced in the depths of human relationships and in the wilderness and beauty of the natural world.

'I will not believe' (20.25)

Eight days later Jesus appeared to the male disciples with Thomas present (20.24–29). There is nothing to suggest that anyone is missing on Easter night. Thomas, however, is 'not with' the gathered disciples and is one of generations who would know the resurrection not through the experience of Easter but through the testimony of the Church: 'We have seen the Lord.' Thomas refuses this new structure of faith.[14] He does not doubt. At that point, he refuses: 'I will not believe' (20.25). Believing or not believing and its implications are always a choice in this Gospel. John 20 concludes by referring to the believers of all times (20.30–31).

Oratio (Prayer) → *Contemplatio* (Contemplation) → *Actio* (Action) →

- In our living into the ever-new question of how the risen Jesus is to be experienced we are called to enter into God's ongoing creative process, for in 'the Christian understanding of the world the destiny of all creation is bound up with the mystery of Christ' (*LS* §99). We hear constantly that we are saved by the death and resurrection of Jesus. This is often thought of as being an 'up there' and 'back there' belief that happened in the heavens in the death-resurrection of Jesus rather than as an experience in our own life. 'The way we are saved by the death and the resurrection of Jesus', Richard Rohr explains, 'is by walking through our own death and resurrection. The important word here is *and*.' Much emphasis is given to the death, while 'We were not taught much about how to hold the resurrection nor even how to go there.'[15] The death part is over-glorified and not the resurrection. Resurrection is all around us. We see it in spring, the beauty of people, animals, the sky. Rohr continues:

  > Yet resurrection is always tempered by the fact it does not last. Not everyone is enjoying the resurrection all the time. We all have to walk

through the valley of death, and through solidarity we are with others in their pain as they do so. We are there with others as we watch the evening news, as we see Syria, as we view the refugee camps – or more accurately said, the death camps.

Solidarity by its very nature provokes action, including at times confrontation, but it does so always on the basis of a vision of community and of being called to live with dignity and respect in the human community and the whole earth community. As Rohr so aptly says, 'We have to stay in both the dance of death and the dance of resurrection.' On any one day or through any one period of our life, we can hope and pray that God might leads us to both the resurrection and to the valley, for there is no other path.

Notes

1 This is an expanded version of Kathleen Rushton, 2016, 'Jesus the Resurrected Gardener (John 20:1-9)', *Tui Motu InterIslands*, Dunedin, New Zealand, Issue 203, April, pp. 24-5.

2 On the face veil, I draw on Sandra M. Schneiders, 2013, *Jesus Risen in Our Midst: Essays on the Resurrection of Jesus in the Fourth Gospel*, Collegeville MN: Liturgical Press, p. 85.

3 Francis J. Moloney, 1998, *The Gospel of John*, Sacra Pagina Series 4, Collegeville MN: Liturgical Press, pp. 529-30.

4 Teresa Okure, 1992, 'The Significance Today of Jesus' Commission to Mary Magdalene', *International Review of Mission* 81.321, pp. 177-88.

5 Schneiders, *Jesus Risen*, p. 14.

6 Schneiders, *Jesus Risen*, pp. 21-2 (italics hers).

7 Schneiders, *Jesus Risen*, pp. 41-3, 66-8.

8 Benedict XVI, 2006, Easter Vigil Homily, 15 April, http://w2.vatican.va/content/benedict-xvi/en/homilies/2006/documents/hf_ben-xvi_hom_20060415_veglia-pasquale.html (accessed 15.04.19).

9 Elizabeth Johnson, 2018, *Creation and the Cross: The Mercy of God for a Planet in Peril*, Maryknoll NY: Orbis, p. 189.

10 WCC, 'Economy of Life', §18, in Rogate R. Mshana and Athena Peralta (eds), 2015, *Economy of Life: Linking Poverty, Wealth and Ecology*, Geneva: WCC Publications

11 Schneiders, *Jesus Risen*, p. 41.

12 Phyllis Trible, 1992, *God and the Rhetoric of Sexuality*, London: SCM Press, pp. 76-8.

13 Denis Edwards, 2004, *Breath of Life: A Theology of the Creator Spirit*, Maryknoll NY: Orbis, p. 106.

14 Schneiders, *Jesus Risen*, p. 51.

15 Richard Rohr OFM, 2017, 'An Interview with Richard Rohr, OFM: Living with Paradox, Uncertainty and Mystery', in Annmarie Sanders IHM (ed.), *The Occasional Papers: Leadership Conference of Women Religious*, 46.2. The quotations in this paragraph are from p. 13 (italics his).

Galilee
Appearance of the Risen Jesus to Seven Disciples – John 21.1–25

'Come and have breakfast' (John 21.12)

Third Sunday of Easter of Year C
John 21.1–19

Some biblical scholars consider that the original Gospel ended with John 20 and that 21.1–25 was added by another author. The ending of the Gospel in 20.30–31 supports this conclusion. Even if John 21 was written later, and by a different author, it is found in all early manuscripts of the Gospel. Most, therefore, regard this chapter as integral to the Gospel. As we have seen, the post-Easter Gospel readings for Year C show two ways in which Jesus is present and through which people came into the family of faith after his resurrection. The first is through the Holy Spirit (e.g. 20.21–22; 14.23–29). The second way is through the work of the disciples. Most of John 21 is concerned with ordinary human situations such as fishing, catching nothing, working hard all night, recognizing someone on the shore, having breakfast, being young and growing old. Into these ordinary human situations, the symbolism, special words and concerns of the Gospel are interwoven.

Lectio/Reading of John 21.1–19

In your reading and rereading of John 21.1–19, note how the disciples returned to their home place and to their ordinary lives of work and struggle. There Jesus reveals himself to them (21.1).

Meditatio/Meditation

'Jesus revealed himself to the disciples' (John 21.1)

The first words of this extended scene at the Sea of Tiberias in Galilee, when Jesus 'revealed' himself to the disciples (21.1; NRSV has 'showed'), take us back to the first scene of his public ministry at Cana, when 'he revealed his glory, and his disciples believed *into* him' (2.11).[1] We are told that Nathanael came from Cana of Galilee (21.2). So far, all the post-resurrection appearances of Jesus have been in Jerusalem. In Galilee, the inner circle of disciples is named as being present, 'Simon Peter, Thomas called the Twin, Nathanael of Cana in Galilee, the sons of Zebedee, and two others of his disciples' (21.2). This adds up to a total of seven disciples. Seven is a number of symbolic completeness.[2] Surely, we see here a group who represent the future church community through the ages.

In John, there is no prior mention of any of the disciples being fishers. Fishing, however, was well known in the tradition as a symbol of mission. A further interplay occurs between the day and night, light and darkness symbolism. Led by Peter, the disciples go fishing and 'that night they caught nothing' (21.3). Then, 'just after daybreak', Jesus stands unrecognized on the shore (21.4). Like the disciples on the road to Emmaus (Luke 24.13-35) and Mary Magdalene (John 20.15), no one in the boat recognizes Jesus. Then, the disciple whom Jesus loved declares, 'It is the Lord' (21.7). Peter, with his characteristic enthusiasm, adds a comical twist to the scene by donning some clothes before leaping into the sea to swim towards Jesus, who is on the shore.

Jesus has addressed the disciples as 'children' (21.5), which recalls the promise that believers will become 'children of God' (1.12). After his death-resurrection their new intimacy of relationship is now possible. Jesus makes this explicit when he inserts 'your' to describe the communion that is now possible between the disciples and the divine in his commission to Mary Magdalene to tell the disciples that he is ascending 'to my Father and *your* Father ... my God and *your* God' (20.17).

Jesus has told the disciples to continue fishing. They are not able to 'draw' in the net because of the huge catch of fish (21.6). When Jesus asked for some fish, Peter returned to the boat and 'drew' the net ashore. Their work is fruitful through the presence of the risen Jesus. The significance of Peter 'drawing' (21.6, 11) in the net becomes clear in the light of earlier passages.[3] Note that another Greek word is used for the boat 'dragging' the net behind it (21.8). After feeding the crowd by the sea, Jesus has explained that no one could come to him unless 'drawn' by God (6.44). Near the end of his public ministry, he has said, 'And I, when I am lifted up from the earth, will draw all people to myself' (12.32). How would the crucified and risen Jesus 'draw' people? The story of the huge catch of fish shows that he does this 'drawing in' through his disciples. Yet the disciples cannot draw in a catch of fish without Jesus. Likewise, people cannot come to faith by themselves. Through the risen Jesus, the disciples 'draw' many and will bring them to Jesus. Underlying this scene may be Jesus' words that 'apart from me you can do nothing' (15.4–5).

'Come and have breakfast' (John 21.12)

When the disciples go ashore for breakfast on the beach, they see a charcoal fire (21.9). This links the scene back to Peter's denials, the only other time a charcoal fire has been mentioned (18.18). The abundance of the fish echoes the abundance in other meal situations – the abundance of the wine at Cana (2.1–11) and the abundance of bread and fish (6.1–13). Here, 'Jesus came and took the bread and gave it to them and did the same with the fish' (21.13). This echoes so closely his earlier meal story of the loaves and fishes, which also happened in Galilee (6.11). Eucharistic overtones are present. All eat and recognize Jesus.

In Luke, the catch is so large that nets were breaking. For John, the 'net [which] was not torn' (John 21.11) is part of the imagery of unity and oneness. Jesus has said that there will be 'one flock and one shepherd' (10.16). He has prayed that the disciples might be one (17.21–23). His seamless garment was not to be torn or divided (19.23). The focus moves from Peter the fisherman and provider of food to Peter as shepherd.

'Feed my sheep' (John 21.17)

The prominence given to Peter when he recruited some disciples to go fishing (21.2–3, 7, 11) now intensifies. The scene focuses on him. A charcoal fire on the shore (21.9) is one of several details that take us back to the scene of Peter's denial of Jesus, where there is a charcoal fire (18.17–18). His failure must be lived through.[4] The threefold questioning of Peter, 'Do you love me?' and his triple 'yes' to the triple, 'Feed ... feed ... feed ...' (21.15–18) contrast with his earlier threefold denial of Jesus (13.38; 18.15–18). This triple command of Jesus, 'feed my lambs', 'tend my sheep' and 'feed my sheep', evokes the Good Shepherd who would lay down his life for his sheep (10.1–6, 11–18). Using the language Jesus has applied to himself (10.11–15), Peter has declared and boasted, 'I will lay down my life for you' (13.37). He had turned out to be more like the 'hireling' (18.15–18).

Much earlier, Andrew finds his brother Simon and brings him to Jesus, who says, 'You are to be called Cephas', which means 'Rock' (Greek *petros*, and Aramaic *cephas*; 1.40–42). Peter had been with Jesus and was tested (6.7–71). His denial had been foretold (13.36–38). He went to the court of the high priest and denied Jesus (18.15–17, 25–27). In this scene, Jesus addresses him as 'Simon, son of John' (21.15) rather than by 'Cephas' because he has not lived up to his name of 'Peter' meaning 'rock' (1.42). Jesus commissions Peter, 'Follow me' (21.19). This recalls how earlier at the supper, Peter has both questioned and declared, 'Why can I not follow you now? I will lay down my life for you' (13.37). There is irony in this scene. Those early communities who first heard or read John 21 knew that by then Peter had probably given his life. Underlying the story is the story of the good shepherd who lays down his life, and the love commandment (13.14–15; 14.15, 21, 23–25; 15.12–14). Recalled also is that the greatest expression of friendship is the willingness to die for friends (15.13; 10.11).

'The third time that Jesus appeared' (John 21.14)

John 21.1 notes that 'Jesus showed himself again to the disciples', who we have seen numbered seven (21.2). Then, John 21.14 states that this is the third time Jesus has appeared to them. Interestingly, three appearances have already been described in John 20. The first of these was to Mary Magdalene (20.11–18), second to the male disciples without Thomas (20.19–23), and then to the male disciples with Thomas (20.24–29). This leaves the possibility that it is the appearance to Mary Magdalene that has not been included. In nearly all cases this numerical discrepancy can be explained by attributing a diminished role to Mary Magdalene by claiming that she was not a disciple.

It is important to look at that claim. For Dorothy Lee, Mary Magdalene was 'a woman of faith whose credentials have been established at the foot of the cross' (19.25).[5] She was the first to receive a resurrection appearance (20.1–18) and the first to announce, 'I have seen the Lord' (20.18; cf. 20.25). Further, Jesus' commission gave her a unique role in this Gospel as witness to the resurrection (20.17). In the light of all this, Mary Magdalene is surely a disciple. Both John and the Beloved Disciple go to the tomb (20.3–10) but neither see the risen Jesus nor are given a commission. The author of John 20 portrays a woman in the role of witness. She gives testimony to Jesus' disciples, which in the portrayal of disciples in John 1—20 includes both women and men. There is no listing of the Twelve. Now in John 21, not only do women disappear from the scene but the reader is led to believe that the women are not really disciples. Instead, the image of Peter, in John 21, undergoes a dramatic change from the presentation of Peter in John 1—20.[6] This leads some to understand that while the

'Great Church' placed its focus on Peter and the Twelve, the Johannine community had a different emphasis with a tradition of a wider group of male and female disciples. However, it would seem that the addition of John 21 affirms the role of Peter in line with what is held in the traditions of the Synoptic Gospels.

It is important to remember that what is written in this Gospel most probably reflects what is happening in the life of the community from which it arose. Clearly, in 21.20–23 we find a situation of rivalry between Peter and the Beloved Disciple. As was suggested above, Peter has probably already laid down his life for his friends. The early Christian communities expected that the Parousia, the second or final coming of Jesus, was imminent. They had to face the fact that Jesus was already present among them as a 'yet' and 'yet not' presence. Culpepper suggests that John 21 overviews several roles for the followers of Jesus: fishing (the mission task), shepherding (the pastoral task), and faithful witness (through life or death).[7] The final ending advises the reader that the story just read does not exhaust all that could be said about Jesus. A selection has been made (21.24–25).

Oratio (Prayer) → *Contemplatio* (Contemplation) → *Actio* (Action) →

- The hope of ongoing creation and human dysfunction intermingle. The place where 'Jesus revealed himself again' (21.1) is named as the 'sea' of the Roman occupier rather than by its local name. The located-ness of the disciples is affirmed. They return to the place of the crowd (6.2) and engage in ordinary everyday things. Exclusion looms in the male bias of the text that discounts Jesus' appearance to Mary Magdalene, and her discipleship is disregarded. Women disappear entirely in John 21. Despite this, the 'net was not torn' (21.11; cf. 10.16; 19.23). Jesus has prayed that the disciples might be one (17.21–23). He is already present among them as a 'yet' and 'yet not' presence. John has used the language of being with, of accompanying, as in Jesus' statement, 'I am with you.' Redemption means God is walking with the people and being with the earth in solidarity with pain and suffering unto death. Elizabeth Johnson observes that there is a double solidarity: the solidarity of the actual Jesus who walked in sandals on the earth (1.27) and 'lived with all who live, suffer and die'; and the solidarity of 'the resurrecting God of life with the ministering and crucified Jesus'.[8] The symbolism of the seven named disciples suggests a group who represent the future church community through the ages, who are to 'believe *into*' the Cosmic Christ in order to complete the works of God. The urgent call for action of the WCC's Poverty, Wealth and Ecology (PWE) Programme 'is born of our profound hope and belief: An Economy of Life is not only possible, it is in the making.'[9] The work of transformation does not end with critique. Churches 'have a vital role to play in fostering the moral courage essential for witnessing to a spirituality of justice and care for all creation and building synergies for a political movement advocating for an Economy of Life'.[10] In coming together to care for our common home, *Laudato Si'* exhorts us, 'Let us sing as we go. May our struggles and our concern for this planet never take away the joy of our hope' (§244). Because our reflection on *hearing both the cry of the earth and the cry of the marginalized* 'has been both joyful and troubling' (*LS* §246), a prayer is proposed that we can share with all who believe in God:

A Prayer for Our Earth

All-powerful God
you are present in the whole universe
and in the smallest of your creatures.
You embrace with your tenderness all that exists.
Pour out upon us the power of your love,
that we may protect life and beauty.
Fill us with peace, that we may live
as brothers and sisters, harming no one.
O God of the poor,
help us to rescue the abandoned
and forgotten of this earth,
so precious in your eyes.
Bring healing to our lives,
that we may protect the world and not prey on it,
that we may sow beauty,
not pollution and destruction.
Touch the hearts
of those who look only for gain
at the expense of the poor and the earth.
Teach us to discover the worth of each thing,
to be filled with awe and contemplation,
to recognize that we are profoundly
united with every creature
as we journey towards your infinite light.
We thank you for being with us each day.
Encourage us, we pray, in our struggle
for justice, love and peace.[11]

Notes

1 The Greek word translated as 'showed' (NRSV) is *ephanerōsen*, which means 'revealed' (21.1). For an overview of John 21, see Brendan Byrne SJ, 2014, *Life Abounding: A Reading of John's Gospel*, Collegeville MN: Liturgical Press, pp. 341–54.

2 Rudolf Schnackenburg, 1990, *The Gospel According to St. John*, David Smith and G. A. Kon (trans.), Herders theologischer Kommentar zum Neuen Testament IV, vol. 3, New York: Crossroad, p. 352.

3 The same Greek verb, *helkein*, is used for Peter 'drawing' (21.6, 11) in the net and by Jesus (6.44; 12.32). Another Greek verb, *surein*, which has 'the sense pulling with exhausting effort', is used for the boat 'dragging' the net behind it (21.8). See Schnackenburg, *Gospel According to St. John*, p. 356.

4 David Fleer and Dave Bland (eds), 2008, *Preaching John's Gospel: The World It Imagines*, St Louis MO: Chalice, p. 15.

5 Dorothy Lee, 1995, 'Partnership in Easter Faith: The Role of Mary Magdalene and Thomas in John 20', *Journal for the Study of the New Testament* 17.58, p. 41.

6 On speculations that this chapter is about the papacy, Moloney observes: 'Discussions of the Petrine office in the Roman tradition of Christianity are out of place in an exegesis of this passage.' Francis J. Moloney, 1998, *The Gospel of John*, Sacra Pagina Series 4, Collegeville MN: Liturgical Press, p. 555.

7 R. Alan Culpepper, 1998, *The Gospel and Letters of John*, Nashville TN: Abingdon Press, p. 249.

8 Elizabeth Johnson, *Creation and the Cross: The Mercy of God for a Planet in Peril*, Maryknoll NY: Orbis, p. 106.

9 WCC, 'Economy of Life', §1, in Rogate R. Mshana and Athena Peralta (eds), 2015, *Economy of Life: Linking Poverty, Wealth and Ecology*, Geneva: WCC Publications.

10 Mshana and Peralta, *Economy of Life*, p. 69.

11 Francis, 2015, *Laudato Si': An Encyclical Letter on Ecology and Climate Change*, Strathfield NSW: St Paul's Publications.

Appendix 1

Gospel of John: Sunday and Main Feasts Liturgical Year Readings

Roman Lectionary			Page	Revised Common Lectionary		
John	Year	Sunday/Feast		John	Year	Sunday/Feast
1.1–18 or 1.1–5, 9–14	ABC	Christmas Day	3	1.1–14	ABC	Nativity of the Lord
1.1–18 or 1.1–5, 9–14	ABC	2nd Sunday after Christmas	3	1.(1–9) 10–18	ABC	2nd Sunday after Christmas Day
1.6–8, 19–28	B	3rd Sunday of Advent	19	1.6–8, 19–28	B	3rd Sunday of Advent
1.29–34	A	2nd Sunday in Ordinary Time	23	1.29–42	A	2nd Sunday after Epiphany
1.35–42	B	2nd Sunday in Ordinary Time	26			
			29	1.43–51	B	2nd Sunday after Epiphany
2.1–11	C	2nd Sunday in Ordinary Time	33	2.1–11	C	2nd Sunday after Epiphany
2.13–25	B	3rd Sunday of Lent	41	2.13–22	B	3rd Sunday in Lent
			46	3.1–17	A	2nd Sunday in Lent (*alt.*)
			46		B	Trinity Sunday
3.14–21	B	4th Sunday of Lent	51	3.14–21	B	4th Sunday in Lent
3.16–18	A	Sunday after Pentecost: Holy Trinity	51			

207

Roman Lectionary			Page	Revised Common Lectionary		
John	Year	Sunday/Feast		John	Year	Sunday/Feast
4.5–42 or 4.5–15, 19b–26, 39a, 40–42	ABC	3rd Sunday of Lent	56	4.5–42	A	3rd Sunday of Lent
			65	5.1–9	C	6th Sunday of Easter (*alt.* 14.23–29)
6.1–15	B	17th Sunday in Ordinary Time	72	6.1–21	B	9th Sunday after Pentecost
6.24–35	B	18th Sunday in Ordinary Time	77	6.24–35	B	10th Sunday after Pentecost
6.41–51	B	19th Sunday in Ordinary Time	79	6.35, 41–51	B	11th Sunday after Pentecost
6.51–58	B A	20th Sunday in Ordinary Time Sunday after Trinity Sunday: Body and Blood of Christ	81	6.51–58	B	12th Sunday after Pentecost
6.60–69	B	21st Sunday in Ordinary Time	81	6.56–69	B	13th Sunday after Pentecost
7.37–39	ABC	Pentecost Sunday: Vigil Mass	85	7.37–39	A	Day of Pentecost (*alt.* 20.19–23)
8.1–11	C	5th Sunday of Lent	90			
9.1–41 or 9.1, 6–9, 13–17, 34–38	ABC	4th Sunday of Lent	95	9.1–41	A	4th Sunday in Lent
10.1–10	A	4th Sunday of Easter	102	10.1–10	A	4th Sunday of Easter
10.11–18	B	4th Sunday of Easter	105	10.11–18	B	4th Sunday of Easter
			106	10.22–30	C	4th Sunday of Easter

APPENDIX I

Roman Lectionary				Revised Common Lectionary		
John	Year	Sunday/Feast	Page	John	Year	Sunday/Feast
10.27–30	C	4th Sunday of Easter	106			
11.1–45 or 11.3–7, 17, 20–27, 33b–45	ABC	5th Sunday of Lent	109	11.1–45	A	5th Sunday in Lent
			115	12.1–8	C	5th Sunday in Lent
12.12–16	B	Palm Sunday: Procession Palms (*opt.* 2)	121	12.12–16	B	Liturgy of the Palms (*alt.*)
12.20–33	B	5th Sunday of Lent	124	12.20–33	B	5th Sunday in Lent
13.1–15	ABC	Holy Thursday: Mass of the Lord's Supper	131 140	13.1–17, 31b–35	ABC	Maundy Thursday
13.31–33a, 34–35	C	5th Sunday of Easter	140	13.31–35	C	5th Sunday of Easter
14.1–12	A	5th Sunday of Easter	144	14.1–14	A	5th Sunday of Easter
14.15–16, 23b–26	C	Pentecost Sunday (*opt.* C)	144	14.8–17 (25–27)	C	Day of Pentecost
14.15–21	A	6th Sunday of Easter	144	14.15–21	A	6th Sunday of Easter
14.23–29	C	6th Sunday of Easter	144	14.23–29	C	6th Sunday of Easter (*alt.* 5.1–9)
15.1–8	B	5th Sunday of Easter	152	15.1–8	B	5th Sunday of Easter
15.9–17	B	6th Sunday of Easter	156	15.9–17	B	6th Sunday of Easter
15.26–27; 16.12–15	B	Pentecost Sunday (*opt.* B)	156 162	15.26–27; 16.4b–15	B	Day of Pentecost
16.12–15	C	Sunday after Pentecost: Holy Trinity	162	16.12–15	C	Trinity Sunday

Roman Lectionary				Revised Common Lectionary		
John	Year	Sunday/Feast	Page	John	Year	Sunday/Feast
17.1–11a	A	7th Sunday of Easter	170	17.1–11	A	7th Sunday of Easter
17.11b–19	B	7th Sunday of Easter	170	17.6–19	B	7th Sunday of Easter
17.20–26	C	7th Sunday of Easter	173	17.20–26	C	7th Sunday of Easter
18.1—19.42	ABC	Good Friday of the Lord's Passion	176	18.1—19.42	ABC	Good Friday
18.33b–37	B	34th Sunday in Ordinary Time: Christ the King	180	John 18.33–37	B	Reign of Christ
			186	19.38–42	ABC	Holy Saturday (*alt.*)
20.1–9	ABC	Easter Sunday: Resurrection of the Lord (*opt. 1*)	189	20.1–18	ABC	Resurrection of the Lord (*alt.*)
20.19–23	ABC	Pentecost Sunday	195	20.19–23	A	Day of Pentecost (*alt.* 7.37–39)
20.19–31	ABC	2nd Sunday of Easter	195	20.19–31	ABC	2nd Sunday of Easter
21.1–19 or 21.1–14	C	3rd Sunday of Easter	200	21.1–19	C	3rd Sunday of Easter
Approx. Times per Liturgical Year (John is sometimes alternative to Gospel reading of Year: A Matthew, B Mark, C Luke) A = 17 B = 25 C = 19				Approx. Times per Liturgical Year (John is sometimes alternative to Gospel reading of Year: A Matthew, B Mark, C Luke) A = 18 B = 22 C = 16		

APPENDIX I

Roman Lectionary

Felix Just SJ, 'Scripture Index of Lectionary Readings Used for Sundays and Major Feasts', http://catholic-resources.org/Lectionary/Index-Sundays.htm (accessed 15.06.19).
(*Revision mandated by the Second Vatican Council, 1963*. Latin edition, 1969)

Bible Translations used in the Roman Lectionaries of English-Speaking Countries

- JB: Jerusalem Bible – Australia, England/Scotland/Wales, Ireland, India (option), New Zealand, Pakistan, South Africa
- RSV: Revised Standard Version – India (option)
- RSV–CE: Revised Standard Version, 2nd Catholic edition – Antilles
- NRSV: New Revised Standard Version – Canada; under consideration for Australia, England/ Scotland/Wales, Ireland
- NAB: New American Bible (2nd edn) – United States, Philippines

Revised Common Lectionary

http://lectionary.library.vanderbilt.edu/ (accessed 15.06.19)
The Revised Common Lectionary, first published in 1992, derives from The Common Lectionary of 1983, both based on the Ordo Lectionem Missae of 1969, a post-Vatican II ground-breaking revision of the Roman Lectionary. 'The post-Vatican II Roman Lectionary represented a profound break with the past. Not only were the readings organized according to a plan whereby a richer fare of scripture was read in liturgical celebrations, in contrast to the medieval lectionary where the choice of readings was simply helter-skelter, but for the first time in history the Sunday lectionary covered a period of three years, each year being dedicated to a particular synoptic author – Matthew, Mark, or Luke. A fourth year was not dedicated to the gospel of John because readings from this gospel permeate the sacred seasons, especially the latter part of Lent and most of Easter' (Frank C. Quinn, 1994, 'The Roman Lectionary and the Scriptures Read in Church', *National Catholic Reporter* 31.5 (November 2018), p. 6), http://lectionary.library.vanderbilt.edu/faq2.php (accessed: 15.06.19). The Revised Common Lectionary uses the New Revised Standard Version of the Bible.

Appendix 2

Key Words in the Gospel of John

José Comblin observes, 'In a sense the entire substance of the Fourth Gospel consists of fifteen words, and Jesus' discourse in the Fourth Gospel concerns all the possible connections among these fifteen words' (1979, *Sent from the Father: Meditations on the Fourth Gospel*, Carl Kabat (trans.), Dublin: Gill & MacMillan, 1979, p. vii). Below, 14 of these words, which comprise some of those most frequently used by the author, are compared with the number of times they are used in Matthew and Luke to highlight the distinctive quality of John.

Greek key word	English equivalent	John	Matt.	Luke
agapan, agapē	to love, love	43	9	13
alētheia	truth	25	1	3
doxazein, doxa	to glorify, glory	41	11	22
zēn, zōē	to live, life	53	13	14
Iēsous	Jesus	237	150	89
Ioudaios	Jew	71	5	5
kosmos	world	78	8	3
martyrein, martyria	to testify, testimony	47	1	2
menein+	to remain, to abide	40	3	7
patēr (used of God)	the Father	118	45	17
pempein	to send	32	4	10
pisteuein	to believe	98*	11	9
phōs	light	23	7	7
*zētein***	to seek	34	14	25

(List above adapted from: Brian Grenier, *St John's Gospel: A Self-Directed Retreat*, Homebush NSW: St Pauls Publications, 1991, p. 34.)

+ Also translated as 'stay', 'remain', 'dwell' or 'live'.

* Included in this total are the 34 times the expression, 'believing *into*' (*pisteuein eis*), which is unique to John, is used rather than 'believing *in*'. 'Believing *into* Jesus' is a work of God required of all who seek to follow him.

** Also translated as 'look for', 'want'.

APPENDIX 2

Other words

'Openly' or 'frankly'. Nine times in John, Jesus is described as speaking 'openly' or 'frankly' (*parrēsia*) in public places (7.4, 13, 26; 10.24; 11.14, 54; 16.25, 29; 18.20). *Parrēsia* is found 31 times in the New Testament – a third are in Johannine literature (9 times in John and 4 times in 1 John; 8 times in the epistles) and only once in the other Gospels (Mark 8.32).

Works/working. This book gives attention to our part in finishing 'the works of God:
completing/finishing (*teleō/teleioō*) the works (*ergon*) of God (John 4.34; 5.36; 17.4 *teleō* and 19.28, 30 *teleioō*). I have chosen to use the words 'complete' or 'finish' the works of God as this suggests that Jesus' entire being is involved in carrying out the ongoing, evolving works of God; that is, completing/finishing what was begun by God. The NRSV uses 'complete' (4.34; 5.36) and 'finish' (17.4; 19.28, 30).

Jesus sends disciples to participate in completing 'the works of God'. There are 28 references:

to the work (*ergon*) or works of God and Jesus or
to God or Jesus working works or to working or
to disciples/we working with God

John 4.34	sent me to complete his work.
John 5.17	But Jesus answered them, 'My Father is still working, and
John 5.17	I also am working.
John 5.20	is doing; and he will show him greater works than these,
John 5.36	But I have a testimony greater than John's. The works that
John 5.36	the Father has given me to complete, the very works that
John 6.27	Do not work for the food that perishes, but for the food
John 6.28	Then they said to him, 'What must we do to perform the works
John 6.29	Jesus answered them, 'This is the work of God, that you
John 6.30	then, so that we may see it and believe you? What work are
John 7.3	so that your disciples also may see the works you are doing;
John 7.7	against it that its works are evil.
John 7.21	Jesus answered them, 'I performed one work, and all of you
John 9.3	he was born blind so that God's works might be revealed
John 9.4	We must work the works of him who sent me while it is day;
John 9.4	We must work the works of him who sent me while it is day;
John 9.4	night is coming when no one can work.
John 10.25	The works that I do in my Father's name testify to me;
John 10.32	Jesus replied, 'I have shown you many good works from the

John 10.33 The Jews answered, 'It is not for a good work that we are
John 10.37 If I am not doing the works of my Father, then do not believe
John 10.38 the works, so that you may know and understand that the
John 14.10 my own; but the Father who dwells in me does his works.
John 14.11 me; but if you do not, then believe me because of the works
John 14.12 also do the works that I do and, in fact, will do greater
John 14.12 works than these, because I am going to the Father.
John 15.24 If I had not done among them the works that no one else
John 17.4 I glorified you on earth by finishing the work that you

Parable of the father/son-apprentice 5.17, 19–20.

Glossary

Cosmology: understanding of the nature and origin of the universe, which influences a person's world view.

Encyclical: letter from the pope to bishops and local churches offering guiding principles.

Eschatology: has come to be associated with 'the last things' (heaven, hell, death, judgement) that will happen in the future at the end of history or at the end of time in another world. Biblical eschatology concerns promises for a future in this world.

Genre: a type or style of writing, such as a prologue or Gospel or farewell discourse.

Gospel/gospel: 'good news' referring to the saving message preached about Jesus by his followers (gospel) and also used of the interpretative narratives of his life, ministry and death-resurrection.

Greek: the common language of the Mediterranean region after the conquest of Alexander the Great. It is the language of both the Septuagint and the New Testament.

Johannine: used to name the literature, community and theology found in the books in the New Testament attributed to John.

Lectio divina: (Latin: 'reading with God') an ancient form of praying with Scripture used by individuals or groups. It has several steps: *lectio* (reading), *meditatio* (reflection/meditation), *oratio* (prayer), *contemplatio* (rest/contemplation) and *actio* (action).

Lectionary: a collection of readings selected from the Scriptures, arranged in an orderly sequence by a particular faith community for proclamation of the Word of God in public worship.

Lectionary, Revised Common: first published in 1992, derives from The Common Lectionary of 1983, both based on the Ordo Lectionem Missae of 1969, a post-Vatican II ground-breaking revision of the Roman Lectionary.

Lectionary, Roman: the Ordo Lectionem Missae of 1969, post-Vatican II Roman Lectionary. For the first time in history, the Sunday lectionary had a three-year cycle with each year dedicated to a particular synoptic author Matthew (Year A), Mark (Year B) or Luke (Year C). Readings from the Gospel of John permeate the sacred seasons, especially in the latter part of Lent and most of Easter.

Narrative: a spoken or written account of connected events; a story.

Prologue: an introduction to a work of literature that calls attention to the theme, enhances the plot, introduces characters, gives background information, indicates the wider context, sets the tone, language and style of the story that follows.

Representative characters: in John's Gospel, characters speaking alone with Jesus, are not just individuals but are representative of groups or communities. Woven into each of the stories of these representative characters are the language and symbolism of this Gospel.

Roman Empire: the political, military and legislative entity that emerged from the Roman Republic and commenced with the establishment of the first emperor Octavian in 27 BCE.

Scripture: from the Latin for 'writings' (*scriptura*) referring to the sacred writing of Judaism and Christianity.

Septuagint (LXX): the name given to the oldest Greek translation of the Old Testament, which probably came from Alexandria, Egypt, in the third century BCE. This version was known to the evangelists and quoted in the Gospels.

Sign: describes what the other Gospels call the 'mighty wonders' (miracles) of Jesus; John has seven 'signs' (*semeia*; 2.1–11; 4.46–54; 5.1–15; 6.1–15; 6.16–21; 9.1–41; 11.1–44).

Synoptic Gospels: also called the 'Synoptics', are the three canonical Gospels of Matthew, Mark and Luke, which are said to share a similar perspective (synoptic: 'seeing together') of the life and teaching of Jesus.

GLOSSARY

Torah: Hebrew for the 'tradition', which is the term for the first five books of the Bible.

Version: a translation of the Bible. The following are some versions listed under the two approaches to translating the original Hebrew or Greek:

Word-for-word translations (Literal or formal correspondence)
RSV   Revised Standard Version (1952)
NAB   New American Bible (1970)
NRSV New Revised Standard Version (1991)

Meaning-for-meaning translations (literary or dynamic equivalence)
JB   Jerusalem Bible (1996)
NJB   New Jerusalem Bible (1985)
GNB   Good New Bible (NT 1966; Complete Bible 1976)
CCB   Christian Community Bible (1994)

Bibliography

Allen, Ronald J. and Clark M. Williamson, 2015 [2004], *Preaching the Gospels without Blaming the Jews: A Lectionary Commentary*, Louisville KY: Westminster John Knox Press.
Armstrong, Karen, 2014, *Fields of Blood: Religion and the History of Violence*, London: The Bodley Head.
Armstrong, Karen, 2019, *The Lost Art of Scripture: Rescuing the Sacred Texts*, London: The Bodley Head.
Armstrong, Neil, quoted in www.azquotes.com/quote/10823 (accessed 18.07.19).
Augustine, *In Iohannis Evangelium* 33.5 CCSL XXXVI, 309: *Reliciti sunt duo, misera et misericordia*.
Bales, Kevin, 2016, *Blood and Earth: Modern Slavery, Ecocide, and the Secret to Saving the World*, New York: Spiegel & Grau.
Ball, Philip, 2001, *Life's Matrix: A Biography of Water*, Berkeley CA: University of California Press.
Bauckham, Richard, 2010, *The Bible and Ecology: Rediscovering the Community of Creation*, Waco TX: Baylor University Press.
Belleville, Linda, 1980, 'Born of Water and the Spirit: John 3:5', *Trinity Journal* 1.2, pp. 125-40.
Benedict XVI, 2006, Easter Vigil Homily, 15 April, http://w2.vatican.va/content/benedict-xvi/en/homilies/2006/documents/hf_ben-xvi_hom_20060415_veglia-pasquale.html (accessed 15.04.19).
Boff, Leonardo, *Cry of the Earth, Cry of the Poor*, Maryknoll NY: Orbis, 1997.
Brackley, Dean, 2004, *The Call to Discernment in Troubled Times: New Perspectives on the Transformative Wisdom of Ignatius of Loyola*, New York: Crossroad.
Brague, Rémi, 2003, *The Wisdom of the World: The Human Experience of the Universe in Western Thought*, Teresa Lavender Fagan (trans.), Chicago IL: University of Chicago Press.
Braudis, Ann, 2016, '*Laudato Si*' and Evolutionary Consciousness', in *Maryknoll Office for Global Concerns NewsNotes*, May-June, p. 3, https://maryknollogc.org/sites/default/files/newsnotes/attachments/MayJune2016_NewsNotes.pdf (accessed 10.10.19).
Brodie, Thomas L., 1993, *The Gospel According to John: A Literary and Theological Commentary*, Oxford: Oxford University Press.
Brooks, Geraldine, 2015, *The Secret Chord*, Sydney: Hachette Australia.
Brown, Jeannine K., 2010, 'Creation's Renewal in the Gospel of John', *Catholic Biblical Quarterly* 72.2, pp. 275-91.
Brown, Raymond E., 1966-1970, *The Gospel According to John*, 2 vols, The Anchor Bible 29-29A, Garden City NY: Doubleday.
Brown, Raymond E., 1979, *The Community of the Beloved Disciple: The Life,*

Loves, Hates of an Individual Church in New Testament Times, Mahwah NJ: Paulist Press.

Brown, Raymond E., 1994, *The Death of the Messiah: From Gethsemane to the Grave. A Commentary on the Passion Narratives in the Four Gospels*, 2 vols, London: Geoffrey Chapman.

Brown, Raymond E., 1997, 'The Death of Jesus and Anti-Semitism: Seeking Interfaith Understanding', *Catholic Update*, March (no pages given).

Byrne SJ, Brendan, 2014, *Life Abounding: A Reading of John's Gospel*, Collegeville MN: Liturgical Press.

Byrne SJ, Brendan, 2016, *Freedom in the Spirit: An Ignatian Retreat with Saint Paul*, Mahwah NJ: Paulist Press.

Cadwallader, Alan, 2011, '"Give the Girl a Drink": Reading John 4 from a Dry, Parched Land', in Norman Habel and Peter Trudinger (eds), *Water: A Matter of Life and Death*, Interface 14.1, pp. 97–100.

Carter, Warren, 2008, *John and Empire: Initial Explorations*, New York: T&T Clark.

Cassidy, Richard J., 2015, *John's Gospel in New Perspective: Christology and the Realities of Roman Power, With the New Essay, 'Johannine Footwashing and Roman Slavery'*, first published 1992, Eugene OR: Wipf & Stock.

The Catholic Comparative New Testament, Oxford: Oxford University Press, 2006.

Charbit, Yves, 2018, 'Woman as Actors in Addressing Climate Change', in Nancy E. Riley and Jan Branson (eds), *International Handbook on Gender and Demographic Processes*, International Handbook of Population Series, No. 8, Dordrecht: Springer, pp. 317–28.

Charlesworth, James H., 1995, *The Beloved Disciples: Whose Witness Validates the Gospel of John?* Valley Forge PA: Trinity Press International.

Collins, Raymond F., 1990, 'Representative Figures', in Raymond F. Collins, *These Things Have Been Written: Studies on the Fourth Gospel*, Louvain Theological & Pastoral Monographs 2, Louvain: Peeters, pp. 1–43.

Collins, Raymond F., 1990, 'Discipleship in John's Gospel', in Raymond F. Collins, *These Things Have Been Written: Studies on the Fourth Gospel*, Louvain Theological & Pastoral Monographs 2, Louvain: Peeters, pp. 46–55.

Coloe, Mary, 2001, *God Dwells with Us: Temple Symbolism in the Fourth Gospel*, Collegeville MN: Liturgical Press.

Comblin, José, *Sent from the Father: Meditations on the Fourth Gospel*, Carl Kabat (trans.), Dublin: Gill & MacMillan, 1979.

Corley, Kathleen, 1995, 'He Was Buried, On the Third Day He Was Raised: Women and the Crucifixion and Burial of Jesus', Paper Presented to the Jesus Seminar, Fall.

Culpepper, R. Alan, 1998, *The Gospel and Letters of John*, Nashville TN: Abingdon Press.

Daly-Denton, Margaret, 2017, *John: An Earth Bible Commentary: Supposing Him to be the Gardener*, London: Bloomsbury T&T Clark.

Dalziel, Paul, Caroline Saunders and Joe Saunders, 2018, *Wellbeing Economics: The Capabilities Approach to Prosperity*, Basingstoke: Palgrave MacMillan. Open Access EBook: www.palgrave.com/gp/book/9783319931937.

Department of State, United States of America, 2018, *Trafficking in Persons Report (TIP)*, 2018, www.state.gov/trafficking-in-persons-report-2018/ (accessed 21.07.19).

Department of State, United States of America, 2019, *Trafficking in Persons Report*

(TIP), www.state.gov/wp-content/uploads/2019/06/2019-Trafficking-in-Persons-Report.pdf (accessed 21.07.19).

Dodd, Charles H., 1963, *Historical Tradition in the Fourth Gospel*, Cambridge: Cambridge University Press.

Dodd, Charles H., 1968, 'A Hidden Parable in the Fourth Gospel', in Charles H. Dodd (ed.), *More New Testament Studies*, Manchester: Manchester University Press, pp. 30–40.

du Bourguet, Pierre, 1971, *Early Christian Art*, Thomas Burton (trans.), New York: William Morrow and Company.

Dunn, James D. G., 1983, 'Let John be John: A Gospel for Its Time', in Peter Stuhlmacher (ed.), *Das Evangelium und die Evangelien*, WUNT 28. Tübingen: Mohr Siebeck, pp. 309–39.

Dysinger OSB, Luke, 1989, 'Accepting the Embrace of God: The Ancient Art of Lectio Divina', pp. 1–12. For a downloadable copy, see www.valyermo.com/ld-art.html.

Edwards, Denis, 2004, *Breath of Life: A Theology of the Creator Spirit*, Maryknoll NY: Orbis.

Edwards, Denis, 2017, 'Eucharist and Ecology: Keeping Memorial of Creation', first published 2008, in Denis Edwards, *The Natural World and God: Theological Explorations*, Scholars Collection, Hindmarsh SA: ATF Press, pp. 137–56.

Edwards, Denis, 2017, 'Celebrating Eucharist in a Time of Global Climate Change', in Denis Edwards, *The Natural World and God: Theological Explorations*, Scholars Collection, Hindmarsh SA: ATF Press, pp. 157–85.

Elvey, Anne F., 2011, *The Matter of the Text: Material Engagements between Luke and the Five Senses*, The Bible in the Modern World 37, Sheffield: Sheffield Phoenix Press.

Ensor, Peter W., 2002, 'The Authenticity of John 12:24', *The Evangelical Quarterly* 74.2, pp. 99–107.

Ferrara, Pasquale, 2019, 'Sustainable International Relations: Pope Francis' Encyclical *Laudato Si*' and the Planetary Implications of "Integral Ecology"', *Religions* 10.466, pp. 1–20, www.mdpi.com/2077-1444/10/8/466/htm (accessed 10.10.19).

Fitzmyer, Joseph, 1981, *The Gospel According to Luke (I–IX)*, Anchor Bible 28, Garden City NY: Doubleday.

Fleer, David and Dave Bland (eds), 2008, *Preaching John's Gospel: The World It Imagines*, St Louis MO: Chalice Press.

Food and Agriculture Organization of the United Nations, 2015, 'Soils and Diversity'. International Year of Soils, www.fao.org/documents/card/en/c/43b565e7-57c2-43c6-b4f0-812091486ed3/ (accessed 16.04.19).

Francis, 2015, *Laudato Si': An Encyclical Letter on Ecology and Climate Change*, Strathfield NSW: St Paul's Publications.

Francis, 2015, *Misericordiae Vultus: Bull of Indiction of the Extraordinary Jubilee of Mercy*, Strathfield NSW: St Paul's Publications.

Freyne, Sean, 2004, *Jesus, a Jewish Galilean: A New Reading of the Jesus-Story*, London: T&T Clark International.

Gagarin, Yuri, quoted in www.nmspacemuseum.org/halloffame/detail.php?id=8 (accessed 18.07.19).

Gibler, Linda, 2010, *From the Beginning to Baptism: Scientific and Sacred Stories of Water, Oil, and Fire*, Collegeville MN: Liturgical Press.

Gown, Donald E., 2000, *Eschatology in the Old Testament*, 2nd edn, Edinburgh: T&T Clark.

BIBLIOGRAPHY

Hardin, Garrett, 1968, 'The Tragedy of the Commons', *Science*, 162.3859, pp. 1243–8.

Harris, W. V., 1999, 'Demography, Geography and the Source of Roman Slaves', *Journal of Roman Studies* 89, pp. 62–75.

Haugh, John E., 2015, *Resting on the Future: Catholic Theology for an Unfinished Universe*, New York: Bloomsbury Academic.

Hill, Craig C., 2002, *In God's Time: The Bible and the Future*, Grand Rapids MI: Eerdmans.

Intergovernmental Science-Policy Platform on Biodiversity and Ecosystem Services (IPBES), www.ipbes.net/deliverables/1c-ilk (accessed 12.10.19).

John Paul II, 1988, *Encyclical Letter Sollicitudo Rei Socialis (On Social Concerns)*, Homebush NSW: St Paul Publications.

Johnson, Elizabeth, 2018, *Creation and the Cross: The Mercy of God for a Planet in Peril*, Maryknoll NY: Orbis.

Karris, Robert J., 1990, *Jesus and the Marginalized in John's Gospel*, Collegeville MN: Liturgical Press.

Kasper, Walter, 2004, *That They May All Be One: The Call to Unity Today*, London: Burns & Oates.

Kasper, Walter, 2007, *A Handbook of Spiritual Ecumenism*, New York: New City Press.

Keener, Craig S., 2003, *The Gospel of John: A Commentary*, 2 vols, Peabody MA: Hendrickson Publishers.

Koester, Craig K., 2003, *Symbolism in the Fourth Gospel: Meaning, Mystery, Community*, 2nd edn, Minneapolis MN: Augsburg Fortress.

Kreglinger, Gisela H., 2016, *The Spirituality of Wine*, Grand Rapids MI: Eerdmans.

Lacugna, Catherine Mowry, 1992, *God for Us: The Trinity and Christian Life*, New York: HarperCollins.

Lee, Dorothy, 1995, 'Partnership in Easter Faith: The Role of Mary Magdalene and Thomas in John 20', *Journal for the Study of the New Testament* 17.58, pp. 37–49.

Lee, Dorothy, 1997, 'Abiding in the Fourth Gospel: A Case-Study in Feminist Biblical Theology', *Pacifica* 10.2, pp. 123–36.

Lledo Gomez, Cristina, 2015, 'The Motherhood of the Church: Mary, the Quotidian and the People of God', in Catholic Women Speak Network (eds), *Catholic Women Speak*, Mahwah NJ: Paulist Press, pp. 32–6.

Lund, Patricia, 2011, *Massively Networked: How the Convergence of Social Media and Technology is Changing Your Life*, San Francisco CA: PLI Media.

Maathai, Wangari, 2010, *Replenishing the Earth: Spiritual Values for Healing Ourselves and the World*, New York: Doubleday Image.

Malina, Bruce J., 1989, 'Christ and Time: Swiss or Mediterranean?' *Catholic Biblical Quarterly* 51.1, pp. 1–31.

Malina, Bruce J. and Richard L. Rohrbaugh, 1998, *Social-Science Commentary on the Gospel of John*, Minneapolis MN: Augsburg Fortress Press.

McDonald, J. I. H., 1995, 'The So-Called *Pericope de Adultera*', *New Testament Studies* 41.3, pp. 415–27.

Menken, Maarten J. J., 1993, 'John 6,51c–58: Eucharist or Christology?' *Biblica* 74.1, pp. 1–26.

Merton, Thomas, 1968, *Faith and Violence*, Notre Dame IN: University of Notre Dame Press.

Miranda, José Porfirio, 1997, *Being and the Messiah: The Message of St. John*, John Eagleson (trans.), Maryknoll NY: Orbis.

Mitchell, Edgar, quoted in www.nmspacemuseum.org/halloffame/detail.php?id=45 (accessed 18.07.19).
Moloney, Francis J., 1998, *The Gospel of John*, Sacra Pagina Series 4, Collegeville MN: Liturgical Press.
Moloney, Francis, 2005, 'Christ in the Eucharist', Address at Lay Centre, Rome, in John R. Allen, 2005, 'The Word from Rome', *National Catholic Reporter*, 21 October, http://nationalcatholicreporter.org/word/word102105.htm (accessed 6.04.19).
Moloney, Francis, 2013, 'Understanding the World and Message of John's Gospel', in 'Gospel of St. John: The Love of God Made Visible', 9th National eConference, The Broken Bay Institute, DVD.
Moltmann, Jürgen, 1973, *Theology and Joy*, London: SCM Press.
Morisada Rietz, Henry W., 2009, 'Time,' in *The New Interpreter's Dictionary of the Bible*, Vol. 5. Katharine Doob Sakenfield (ed.), Nashville TN: Abingdon, pp. 595–600.
Motyer, Stephen, 1995, 'Jesus and the Marginalised in the Fourth Gospel', in *Mission and Meaning: Essays Presented to Peter Cotterell*, Antony Billington, Tony Lane and Max Turner (eds), Carlisle: Paternoster Press, pp. 70–89.
Moxnes, Halvor, 2003, *Putting Jesus in His Place: A Radical Vision of Household and Kingdom*, Louisville KY: Westminster John Knox Press.
Mshana, Rogate R. and Athena Peralta (eds), 2015, *Economy of Life: Linking Poverty, Wealth and Ecology*, Geneva: WCC Publications.
Müller, Peter and Angel Fernández de Aránguiz SCA, 2010, *Every Pilgrim's Guide to Walking to Santiago de Compostela*, Laurie Dennett (trans.), Norwich: Canterbury Press.
Murphy-O'Connor, Jerome, 1998, *The Holy Land: An Oxford Archaeological Guide from Earliest Times to 1700*, 4th edn, Oxford: Oxford University Press.
Murray, Paul D. (ed.), 2008, *Receptive Ecumenism and the Call to Catholic Learning: Exploring a Way for Contemporary Ecumenism*, Oxford: Oxford University Press.
Okure, Teresa, 1992, 'The Significance Today of Jesus' Commission to Mary Magdalene', *International Review of Mission* 81.321, pp. 177–88.
Neyrey, Jerome H., 1979, 'Jacob Traditions and the Interpretation of John 4.10–26', *Catholic Biblical Quarterly* 41.3, pp. 419–37.
Neyrey, Jerome H., 2007, *The Gospel of John*, New York: Cambridge University Press.
Nolan, Albert, 2006, *Jesus Today: A Spirituality of Radical Freedom*, Maryknoll NY: Orbis.
O'Day, Gail R., 1995, 'The Gospel of John', in *The New Interpreters Bible*, vol. 9, Nashville TN: Abingdon, pp. 493–865.
O'Day, Gail R., 2002, *The Word Disclosed: Preaching the Gospel of John*, St Louis MO: Chalice Press.
O'Day, Gail R., 2004, 'Jesus as Friend in the Gospel of John', *Interpretation: A Journal of Bible and Theology* 58.2, pp. 144–57.
O'Loughlin, Frank, 2012, *This Time of the Church*, Mulgrave, Vic.: Garratt.
Painter, John, 1977, 'Christ and Church in John 1, 45–51', in M. De Jonge (ed.), *L'Évangile de Jean: Sources, Rédaction, Théologie, BETL* 44, Leuven: Leuven University Press, pp. 359–63.
Peng, Junhua H., Dongfa Sun and Eviatar Nevo, 2011, 'Domestication, Evolution, Genetics and Genomics in Wheat', *Molecular Breeding* 28.3, pp. 281–301.

Peppard, Christiana Z., 2014, *Just Water: Theology, Ethics, and the Global Water Crisis*, Maryknoll NY: Orbis.
Pilch, John J., 1996, *The Cultural World of Jesus: Sunday by Sunday, Cycle B*, Collegeville MN: Liturgical Press.
Plaskow, Judith, 1993, 'Anti-Judaism in Christian Feminist Interpretation', in Elisabeth Schüssler Fiorenza (ed.), *Searching the Scriptures. Volume 1: A Feminist Introduction*, New York: Crossroad, pp. 117–29.
Plato, *Symposium*, in *Plato in Twelve Volumes: With an English Translation*, W. R. M. Lamb (trans.), Loeb Classical Library, vol. 5, London: Heinemann, 1914, pp. 457–505.
Rayan, Samuel, 1993, 'Jesus and the Poor in the Fourth Gospel', in Rasiah S. Sugirtharajah and Cecil Hargreaves (eds), *Readings in Indian Christian Theology Vol. 1*, London: SPCK, pp. 213–28.
Reinhartz, Adele, 1994, 'The Gospel of John', in Elisabeth Schüssler Fiorenza (ed.), *Searching the Scriptures. Volume 2: A Feminist Commentary*, New York: Crossroad, pp. 561–600.
Rensberger, David, 1998, *Johannine Faith and Liberating Community*, Philadelphia PA: Westminster.
Ringe, Sharon H., 1999, *Wisdom's Friends: Community and Christology in the Fourth Gospel*, Louisville KY: Westminster John Knox Press.
Robbins, Jim, 2018, 'Native Knowledge: What Ecologists are Learning from Indigenous People', *Yale Environment 360*, 26 April, https://e360.yale.edu/features/native-knowledge-what-ecologists-are-learning-from-indigenous-people (accessed 12.10.19).
Robinson, Mary, 2018, *Climate Justice: Hope, Resilience and the Fight for a Sustainable Future*, London: Bloomsbury.
Rohr OFM, Richard, 2017, 'An Interview with Richard Rohr, OFM: Living with Paradox, Uncertainty and Mystery', in Annmarie Sanders IHM (ed.), *The Occasional Papers: Leadership Conference of Women Religious* 46.2, pp. 11–14.
Rushton, Kathleen P., 2006, 'Eucharistic Wisdom and Friendship in the Gospel according to John', in Helen Bergen and Susan Smith (eds), *Whangaia ki te Taro o te Ora. Nourished by the Eucharist: New Thoughts on an Ancient Theme*, Auckland: Accent Publications, pp. 45–53.
Rushton, Kathleen P., 2011, *The Parable of the Woman in Childbirth of John 16:21: A Metaphor for the Death and Glorification of Jesus*, Lewiston NY: The Edwin Mellen Press.
Rushton, Kathleen P., 2013, 'The Cosmology of John 1.1–14 and Its Implications for Ethical Action in this Ecological Age', *Colloquium* 45.2, pp. 137–53.
Rushton, Kathleen P., 2013, 'Rediscovering Forgotten Features: Scripture, Tradition and Whose Feet May be Washed on Holy Thursday Night', in Anne Elvey, Carol Hogan, Kim Power and Claire Renkin (eds), *Reinterpreting the Eucharist: Explorations in Feminist Theology and Ethics*, Sheffield: Equinox Publishing, pp. 91–112.
Rushton, Kathleen P., 2014, 'The Book of Revelation – A Call to 'Consistent Resistance', in Neil Darragh (ed.), *But Is It Fair? Faith Communities and Social Justice*, Auckland: Accent Publication, pp. 47–53.
Rushton, Kathleen P., 2014, 'On the Crossroads between Life and Death: Reading Birth Imagery in John in the Earthquake Changed Regions of Otautahi Christchurch', in Jione Havea, David Neville and Elaine Wainwright (eds), *Bible, Borders, Belonging(s): Engaging Readings from Oceania*, Atlanta GA: Society of Biblical Literature, 2014, pp. 57–72.

Rushton, Kathleen P., 2015, 'The Implications of the Cosmology of the Prologue for Johannine Eschatology', *Interface Theology* 1.1, pp. 37–54.

Rushton, Kathleen P., 2015, 'The Implications of an Eschatological, Cosmological Reading of the Prologue for Johannine Harvest Imagery', unpublished paper given at Australian Catholic Biblical Association Conference, Sydney (2–5 July).

Rushton, Kathleen, 2016, 'Jesus the Resurrected Gardener (John 20:1–9)', *Tui Motu InterIslands*, Dunedin, New Zealand, Issue 203, April, pp. 24–5.

Rushton, Kathleen P., 2018, 'Atonement', in Tamar Kamionkowski, *Leviticus. Wisdom Commentary Vol. 3*, Collegeville MN: Liturgical Press, pp. 154–5.

Rushton, Kathleen, 2018, 'Jesus Washed Feet: John 13.1–17', *Tui Motu InterIslands*, Dunedin, New Zealand, Issue 224, March, pp. 22–3.

Rushton, Kathleen P., 2018, 'Waterlings from Water: Exploring a Cosmological Reading of "Living Water" in John 4.4–42 amidst the Braided Rivers of Canterbury, Aotearoa New Zealand', in Nicola Hoggard Creegan and Andrew Shepherd (eds), *Creation and Hope: Reflections on Ecological Anticipation and Action from Aotearoa New Zealand*, Eugene OR: Pickwick Publications, pp. 90–108.

Savary, Louis M., 2010, *The New Spiritual Exercises: In the Spirit of Pierre Teilhard de Chardin*, Mahwah NJ: Paulist Press.

Sawyer, Deborah, 2003, 'John 19.34: From Crucifixion to Birth, or Creation?', in Amy-Jill Levine (ed.), *A Feminist Companion to John, Vol. II*, Cleveland OH: The Pilgrim Press, pp. 131–8.

Schnackenburg, Rudolf, 1990, *The Gospel According to St. John*, David Smith and G. Kon (trans.), Herders theologischer Kommentar zum Neuen Testament IV, vol. 3, New York: Crossroad.

Schneiders, Sandra M., 1999, 'Women in the Fourth Gospel', in *Written that You May Believe: Encountering Jesus in the Fourth Gospel*, New York: Crossroad, pp. 93–114.

Schneiders, Sandra M., 1999, 'The Community of Eternal Life (John 11:1–53)', in *Written that You May Believe: Encountering Jesus in the Fourth Gospel*, New York: Crossroad, pp. 149–61.

Schneiders, Sandra M., 1999, 'A Community of Friends (John 13:1–20)', in *Written that You May Believe: Encountering Jesus in the Fourth Gospel*, New York: Crossroad, pp. 162–79.

Schneiders, Sandra M., 1999, 'Because of the Woman's Testimony', in *Written that You May Believe: Encountering Jesus in the Fourth Gospel*, New York: Crossroad, pp. 211–32.

Schneiders, Sandra M., 2013, *Buying the Field: Catholic Religious Life in the Mission to the World*, Mahwah NJ: Paulist Press.

Schneiders, Sandra M., 2013, *Jesus Risen in Our Midst: Essays on the Resurrection of Jesus in the Fourth Gospel*, Collegeville MN: Liturgical Press.

Schottroff, Luise, 1995, *Lydia's Impatient Sisters: A Feminist Social History of Early Christianity*, Barbara and Martin Rumscheidt (trans.), Louisville KY: Westminster John Knox Press.

Schottroff, Luise, 1998, 'The Samaritan Woman and the Notions of Sexuality in the Fourth Gospel', in F. F. Segovia (ed.), *'What is John?' Volume II: Literary and Social Readings of the Fourth Gospel*, Atlanta GA: Scholars Press, pp. 157–81.

Senior, Donald, 1998, 'The Eloquent Meaning of the Jesus' Death in the Gospel of John', *Chicago Studies* 37.1, pp. 37–46.

Shepard, Alan, quoted in www.nmspacemuseum.org/halloffame/detail.php?id=55 (accessed 18.07.19).

Sullivan RSM, Mary, 2019, Keynote Address (via videoconference, 7 June), Ngā Kaiarataki o te Atawhia Hui Taumata Mercy Leaders Summit, Auckland.
Swetnam, James, 1993, 'Bestowal of the Spirit in the Fourth Gospel', *Biblica* 74.4, pp. 556–76.
Teilhard de Chardin, Pierre, 1978, *The Heart of the Matter*, René Hague (trans.), New York: Harcourt Brace Jovanovich.
Thompson, Leonard L., 1990, *The Book of Revelation: Apocalypse and Empire*, New York: Oxford University Press.
Trible, Phyllis, 1992, *God and the Rhetoric of Sexuality*, London: SCM Press.
van Tilborg, Sjef, 1996, *Reading John in Ephesus*, Supplements to Novum Testamentum Series, Leiden: Brill.
United Nations, 2019, The Intergovernmental Science-Policy Platform on Biodiversity and Ecosystem Services (IPBES), 6 May, www.ipbes.net/news/Media-Release-Global-Assessment (accessed 23.05.19).
Vatican II, 1964, *Decree on Ecumenism* (*Unitatis Redintegratio*), www.vatican.va/archive/hist_councils/ii_vatican_council/documents/vat-ii_decree_19641121_unitatis-redintegratio_en.html (accessed 10.10.19).
WHO/UNICEF, Joint Monitoring Programme (JMP) Report 2019, www.wateraid.org/facts-and-statistics (accessed 10.10.19).
Westcott, B. F., 1903, *The Gospel According to St. John*, London: John Murray.
Williams, Ritva H., 1997, 'The Mother of Jesus at Cana: A Social-Science Interpretation of John 2:1–12', *Catholic Biblical Quarterly* 59.4, pp. 679–92.
Williams, Rowan, 2003, 'Keynote Address', in *May They All Be One ... But How?: Proceedings of the Conference Held in St Albans Cathedral on 17 May 2003*, St Albans: St Albans Centre for Christian Studies.
Williamson Jr, Lamar, 2004, *Preaching the Gospel of John: Proclaiming the Living Word*, Louisville KY: Westminster John Knox Press.
World Council of Churches, 2019, *Roadmap for Congregations, Communities and Churches for an Economy of Life and Ecological Justice*, 25 April, www.oikoumene.org/en/resources (accessed 23.05.19).
Yamaguchi, Satoko, 2002, *Mary and Martha: Women in the World of Jesus*, Maryknoll NY: Orbis.

Index of Bible References

Genesis
1.1	5, 183
1.1–2.4	6
1.2	196
1.3	191
1.3–26	7
2.1–3	67, 70
2.2	150, 184
2.3	184
2.7	97, 149, 196
2.8	183, 190
2.9	190, 196
2.21–22	185
2.24–25	11
3.3	192
3.8	183, 190
3.18–19	33
6.3	197
6.13–22	11, 195
6.17	197
7.15–16	11
7.22	197
8.11	24
9.4	81
9.8–11	11
9.20	33
17.11	11
24.49	182
27.35	31
29.7	58
32.10	182
32.28–29	31
48.22	58
49	141

Exodus
3.14	178
12	23
12.1–18	42
12.21–23	184
15.17	156
16.2	80
16.7–8	80
16.4	78
17.6	87, 185
28.41	173
30.11–16	43
34.6	182
34.29–35	191

Leviticus
11.44	173
17.10	81
19.2	173
19.18	143
20.7	173
20.10	92
21.17–23	96
22.17–23	66

Numbers
20.11	185
27.16–17	104

Deuteronomy
2.14	68
8.6–10	29
8.7–15	122
16.16	42
21.22–23	185
22.22	92
31–33	141
32.46–47	7

1 Kings
8.2	86

2 Kings
4.42–44	76
17.13–34	58
17.24	61

Nehemiah
3.1	66

Job
29.12–17	66

Psalms
22.18	183
23.1	76–7
31.10	66
33.6	7, 25, 197
38.11	184
40.11–12	182
42.1–2	87
63.1	87
69.21	184
76.17	66
77.16	66
77.20	66
79.2–3	82
80.8–16	153
104.15	33, 34
104.29	122
105.41	87
107.20	7
108.4	182
119.1	147
119.14	147
119.27	147
119.32	147
119.33	147
119.105	7
119.128	147
136.25	11
145.21	11

Proverbs		32.14–15	7	Zechariah	
1.20	87	35.6	66	9.9	31
1.20–23	10, 148	40.3	21	9.9–10	122
1.20–28	27	43.3, 11	61	14.6–11	87
4.11	147	44.3	7		
8	xxvi	45.15	61	**Wisdom**	
8.2–3	87	45.21	61	7.27	xxvi
8.22–25	7	45.21–22	61		
8.22–36	183, 190	54.13	80	**Baruch**	
8.23	7	55.11	7	3.9–4.4	10
8.32	147	58.6–7	53	3.9–24	148
8.35	27	65.17	69	3.37	11
9.1–6	78	66.22	69		
9.5	72, 74, 75			**1 Maccabees**	
21.13	66	**Jeremiah**		4.52–59	106
22.22	66	2.12	153	7.17	82
23.19	147	3.15	105	13.51	121
31.5	66	14.2–7	xiv		
31.6–7	33	23.1–8	104	**2 Maccabees**	
31.9	66			10.7	121
		Ezekiel			
Wisdom		11.17–19	7	**4 Maccabees**	
6.12–13	27	19.10–11	156	6.6	82
6.16	27	32.5–6	82		
7.3	119	34.11–16	105	**Matthew**	
7.15–22	8	34.12	103	5.38–48	53
7.24	8	34.23–24	105	6.1–4	117
7.26–27	157	36.26–27	7	9.9	60
7.27	8, 24, 82, 158, 165	37.1–14	48	9.36	104
		37.15–23	47, 48	10.6	104
8.1	8	37.23	50	16.16	111
8.4–5	8	37.24	105	16.24	154
8.13	7	39.29	7	18.10–14	104
8.26	7	47.1–12	87	23.2	75
9.1–2	8			25.31–46	53
10.17–18	147	**Hosea**		26.7	117
15.11	196	1.1	7	26.8	117
		2.2	58		
Ecclesiasticus		14.7	155	**Mark**	
17.1–2	122			1.11	20
24.7	157	**Joel**		1.18	60
24.8	11	1.1	7	3.4	53
24.17	155	2.21	125	8.29	29
		2.28–29	7	8.34	154
Isaiah				14.3	117
3.14–15	155	**Micah**		14.4	117
5.16	172	4.3–4	155	15.21	183
6.3	172	4.4	34		
27.2–3	153	5.4	105	**Luke**	
27.2–6	155	6.8	53	1.5–8	21
27.12–13	124			9.23	154

INDEX OF BIBLE REFERENCES

10.38–42	115–16	1.17	147	2.13–23	109		
15.3–7	104	1.19	23	2.13–25	41–4		
24.13–15	201	1.19–28	19–21	2.14–22	xxvii, 47		
		1.19–34	26	2.17	44		
John		1.19–37	20	2.18	38		
1–11	xxvi	1.22	28	2.18, 20	43		
1–20	203	1.23	30, 147	2.19	43		
1.1	6–7, 107,	1.26–28	22	2.20	68		
	146, 190	1.27	23, 103,	2.20–22	105		
1.1–2	174		204	2.21	43		
1.1–3	4, 122, 172	1.28	195	2.22	44		
1.1–5	xix, 5, 20,	1.29	25, 44	2.22–36	47		
	176	1.29–34	23–5	2.23	38		
1.1–18	3–13, 38,	1.29–42	36	2.23–24	131		
	79	1.32	20, 24, 25,	2.23–25	xxvii, 47		
1.3	8, 125, 148,		28, 160	3.1	68		
	195	1.32–33	49, 157,	3.1–12	48		
1.4	20, 78, 148		197	3.1–15	46, 47		
1.4–5	56	1.34	20, 160	3.1–21	xxvii,		
1.4	191	1.35–39	26		46–54, 56,		
1.5	191	1.35–50	178		164, 186		
1.4	7	1.35–51	26–31	3.2	38, 46,		
1.5	8, 7, 10	1.37	107		47–8, 49		
1.6	24	1.38	178, 191	3.3	48, 124,		
1.6–8	19–21	1.38–39	24, 157		126		
1.7	20, 160	1.38–42	27–9	3.5	48, 100		
1.9	4, 7, 52	1.38	27, 28	3.7	48		
1.9–10	xxviii, 5	1.47	xxvii	3.8	48–9, 49,		
1.9–18	xix	1.48	27, 28		50, 107,		
1.10	172, 181	1.39	124		148		
1.10–11	52, 61, 148,	1.40–2	26	3.10	99		
	176	1.40–42	124, 203	3.11–12	48		
1.11	xxvii, 10,	1.41	27, 107	3.12	56		
	131	1.42	203	3.13–14	105		
1.12	11–12, 20,	1.43	107	3.14	176, 183,		
	38, 146,	1.43–45	27		191		
	192, 201	1.43–51	26, 29–31,	3.15	48		
1.13	xxvii		36	3.15–16	107		
1.14	4, 5	1.46	178	3.16	51–2, 52,		
1.15	20, 160	1.47	46, 56, 164		107, 148,		
1.18	174	1.49	111, 181		168, 172,		
1.9–10	8–10, 53	2–12	150		181		
1.12–13	49	2.1	185	3.16–17	9, 182		
1.13	xxvii, 131	2.1–11	66, 68, 202	3.16–18	46		
1.14	11, 12, 20,	2.1–12	33–40	3.17	52, 61		
	37, 43, 81,	2.2–3	34–5	3.17–19	53		
	125, 134,	2.4	124	3.18–21	xxvii		
	147, 194,	2.7	37	3.19	52, 54		
	195	2.11	12, 68, 201	3.19–21	10		
1.15	20, 23	2.13	42, 115	3.21	53, 54		
1.16	37	2.13–22	xxvi, 122	3.22–36	xxvii, 20		

3.29	20, 37, 107, 110, 116	5.1–15	66, 80, 96	5.45–47	69
3.29–30	37	5.1–18	xxvii, xxviii, 65, 95	6	81
3.31	48, 181			6.1	75
3.32	20, 160	5.1–47	65–70	6.1–13	202
3.33	182	5.2	67	6.1–15	67, 72, 74
3.34	49, 197	5.2–9	164	6.1–21	73
3.35	125	5.3	66	6.1, 23	78
3.36	107	5.5	67, 68	6.1–69	71–83
4.1–42	47	5.6	66, 70	6.2	38, 67, 204
4.4	58	5.7	66, 112, 146	6.3	75, 77
4.4–42	xxviii, 57, 80, 164			6.4	65, 75, 115
		5.9	66, 67	6.4–14	42, 109
4.5	58	5.10–13	67	6.5	75
4.5–42	56–61, 85	5.11	66	6.5–6	76
4.6	60	5.12–15	135	6.7–71	203
4.7–26	xxvii, 46, 50	5.13	75	6.8	113
		5.14	66, 67	6.9	76–7
4.10	62	5.15	66, 68	6.11	76, 79, 112, 202
4.13–14	87	5.16	68		
4.14	59, 62, 107, 185	5.16–18	105, 179	6.11–12	74
		5.17	65, 67, 69, 150	6.12	76, 107
4.18	58, 61			6.12–13	37
4.19–22	61	5.18	68, 106	6.14	38, 52
4.21	44, 124, 146	5.19	68–9	6.14–15	78, 121
		5.19–20a	69	6.14–40	78
4.23	60, 124	5.19–30	65	6.15	77, 181
4.27–30	178	5.19–47	67, 68	6.16	38
4.29	61	5.20b–30	69	6.16–21	67, 72, 74
4.29–30	124	5.24	107	6.20	77
4.34	xxiv, xxvii, 56, 60, 144, 172, 184	5.24–26	148	6.22–24	73
		5.28	107	6.22–59	68, 74
		5.31–47	20, 65, 68	6.23–34	77–8
4.35–38	124	5.32	20, 160	6.24–25	113
4.36	107	5.33	20, 23, 160	6.25	78
4.39	20, 60, 160, 173	5.33–35	69	6.25–34	73
		5.34	144	6.25–59	78
4.39–42	xxvii	5.35	20, 60	6.26	37, 38
4.42	60, 61–2, 107, 111	5.36	xvii, xxiv, xxvii, 20, 69, 137, 160, 172, 184	6.26–71	72
				6.27	76, 105, 107
4.43	137			6.28	xxvii
4.43–46	164			6.28–29	79
4.43–54	xxvii, xxviii			6.29	78–9
4.46	29	5.37	20, 160	6.30	78
4.46–54	66, 67, 68, 80	5.37–38	69	6.31	143
		5.39	xxv, xxv–xxvi, 20, 69, 107, 160, 177–8, 178	6.32	78
4.53	68			6.34	78, 79
4.54	38			6.35	104, 147, 178
5	100				
5–10	42			6.35–50	73, 79–80
5.1–8	98	5.43	148	6.35–71	79–80

INDEX OF BIBLE REFERENCES

6.38	80	7.38	154	9.1–4	67		
6.39	107	7.38–39	185	9.1–5	97		
6.40	107	7.39	184, 191	9.1–41	xxvii,		
6.41	104, 147, 178	7.40	96		xxviii, 65, 67, 95–100,		
6.41–59	78	7.40–41	105		103, 164		
6.42	36, 78	7.40–44	98	9.4	95, 100		
6.44	125, 201	7.43	96	9.5	97–8, 104		
6.45	107	7.45–52	186	9.6–7	97–8		
6.46	20	7.48	99	9.7	67		
6.47	107	7.48–49	95–6	9.8	96		
6.48	104, 147, 178	7.49	xxviii, 80, 99, 164	9.8–9	105		
				9.8–12	97, 98		
6.51	104, 105, 178, 194	7.50	49–50	9.8–34	98		
		7.50–51	98	9.9–41	67, 68		
		7.52	29	9.10	96		
6.51–59	73, 79, 80–2, 81	8	75	9.11	99		
		8.1–11	xxvii, 90–4	9.13–17	99		
6.52	78	8.3	92	9.13–34	179		
6.53–57	105	8.5	91	9.14	96		
6.54	107	8.7	92	9.16	38, 99, 105		
6.55	185	8.9	92–3	9.17	96, 99		
6.56	28	8.10	92–3	9.18–23	97, 98		
6.59	168	8.11	92–3	9.21	96, 98–9		
6.60–66	78	8.12	8, 28, 58, 86, 97, 104, 107, 147, 178	9.21–22	164		
6.60–71	73, 74			9.22	98, 145, 148		
6.63	197						
6.66	131						
6.67	82	8.12–59	179	9.24	99		
6.67–71	78	8.14	48	9.24–34	97, 99		
6.68	107	8.14–18	182	9.29	48, 99		
6.69	111	8.15	53	9.30	96		
7.1	106	8.18	20, 160	9.30–33	49		
7.1–9	xxvii, 36	8.20	86, 105, 106, 124, 168	9.31–33	106		
7.2	65, 86, 106			9.32	96		
7.3	119			9.33	20, 99		
7.4	165, 179	8.23, 42	181	9.34	99		
7.10	121	8.24	106, 124, 126, 191	9.35	67, 103		
7.10–52	179			9.35–38	97, 99		
7.12	105	8.28	176, 183	9.38	99, 111		
7.13	165, 179	8.31	28	9.39	52		
7.14	103, 168	8.32	147, 182	9.39–41	97, 99		
7.19	148	8.35	134	9.40–41	99		
7.23	66	8.37	106, 148	10.1	107, 157		
7.25–27	105	8.38	107	10.1–4	66		
7.26	107, 165, 179	8.40	106	10.1–5	103		
		8.43	107	10.1–6	202		
7.27–29	48	8.58	172	10.1–21	103		
7.29	20	8.59	86, 106, 107	10.1–30	102		
7.30	105, 124			10.3	107		
7.37	87	9	66, 100	10.4	102, 107		
7.37–39	85–8	9.1	67	10.4–5	28, 107		

10.4–6	182	11.25	148	12.17	20, 112, 160
10.7	154	11.27	52		
10.7–9	66	11.28–29	182	12.17–19	122
10.7–10	103	11.28–33	178	12.18	38
10.10	xiii, 37, 39, 57, 104, 107, 109, 154	11.29–37	111	12.20	xxvii
		11.31	111, 113	12.20–22	29, 124
		11.33	66, 111, 112, 125, 146	12.20–23	164
				12.20–33	122–6
10.11	xxvi, 102, 145, 158, 178, 203			12.23–24	122
		11.35	112	12.23–26	124
		11.37	96	12.24	109
10.11–12	103	11.38	112	12.26	28, 116
10.11–15	190, 202	11.41	171	12.27	66, 105, 125, 146
10.11–18	105–6, 202	11.41–42	79, 112		
10.17–18	145	11.44	194	12.27–30	124
10.13	108	11.45–47	112	12.29	105
10.14	107, 178	11.45–52	179	12.31–36	124
10.15	145	11.47	38	12.32	125, 164, 183, 191, 201
10.15–16	163	11.50–52	164		
10.16	107, 182, 202, 204	11.53	116		
		11.54	116, 165, 179	12.32–33	176
10.17–18	194			12.33–37	131
10.18	176	11.55	109	12.42	98, 145, 164, 186
10.21	96	11.55–19.14	110		
10.22	65, 102	11.55–57	115	12.42–43	50
10.22–39	179	11.57	110	12.46	52
10.22–42	103, 106	12.1	65, 115, 116	12.47	53
10.24	165, 179			13–17	140, 171
10.25	20, 107, 160	12.1–8	83, 109, 115–19, 186	13.1	12, 118, 133–4, 143, 176
10.27	28, 182				
10.31	148	12.1–11	111	13.1–17	133, 143
10.36	52, 173	12.3	116–17	13.1–17.26	131–2
10.39	110	12.3–8	186	13.1–20	117
10.40	110	12.5	xxviii, 109, 113, 117, 142	13.1–30	131, 140, 162, 170
10.41	20			13.2	117
11–55–19.14	42	12.5–8	76	13.2–4	135
11.1–44	67	12.6	xxviii, 104, 117, 119, 142	13.3	125
11.1–45	109–13, 115			13.3–11	117
				13.4	135
11.3	194	12.7	186	13.4–6	135
11.7–37	68	12.8	xxviii, 117, 142	13.8	124, 126
11.11	115			13.12	135
11.13	118	12.9–11	115	13.12–16	117
11.14	165, 179	12.11	164	13.14–15	99, 203
11.15	178	12.12–16	121–2	13.14–16	159
11.16	147	12.12–19	61	13.15	126, 136
11.17–27	110	12.13, 15	181	13.16	136
11.19	111, 113	12.16	12, 31, 121	13.21	66, 112, 125, 146
11.24–34	67	12.16–23	191		

INDEX OF BIBLE REFERENCES

13.23–26	135	14.15–16	149	15.12	158
13.29	xxviii, 76, 113, 117, 119, 142	14.16–17	148–9, 184	15.12–13	135, 165
		14.17	24, 52, 140, 149, 168	15.12–14	134, 203
				15.12–15	159
13.31–14.31	132, 140–51, 150, 162	14.20	24, 149	15.13	xxvi, 12, 105, 116, 158, 203
		14.21	203		
		14.22	147, 148, 163		
13.31–16.33	131, 140, 145, 162, 170			15.13–14	154
		14.22–24	146	15.13–15	110
		14.23	24, 149, 152	15.14	12, 116
13.31–32	191			15.15	116, 136, 152, 157
13.31–35	141, 158	14.23–25	203		
13.34	140, 141, 143, 158, 160	14.23–29	142, 200	15.16	28, 37, 124, 125
		14.25–26	148–9		
		14.25–29	189	15.18	159
13.34–35	117, 136, 143	14.26	24, 149, 168, 197	15.18–16.4a	153, 159–60
13.35	158	14.27	112, 145–6, 149, 167, 196	15.18–25	156, 159
13.36	163			15.26	20, 152, 168, 197
13.36–38	145, 203				
13.37	158, 202, 203	14.28	146	15.26–27	149, 159–60
		14.28–29	150		
13.38	145, 202	14.29	150	15.27	20
14.1	112, 145–6, 149, 167	14.31	150	16.29–31	163
		14.36	171	16.1	165
14.1–31	144–51	15	34, 81	16.1–4a	159
14.2	28, 157	15.1	147, 153, 178	16.1–33	162–3, 166
14.2–3	146			16.2	98, 145, 164, 194
14.2–4	146–7	15.1–7	157, 158		
14.3	10	15.1–8	152–6	16.2–4	163
14.4	147, 163	15.1–11	153	16.4	165
14.5	147, 163	15.1–16.4a	132, 141, 152–61	16.4a–33	163
14.6	147, 168, 178, 182			16.4b–15	162–9, 163
		15.1–17	28, 132, 140–1	16.4b–33	132, 153
14.6–7	149			16.5	163, 165
14.8	147, 163	15.2	124, 154	16.6	112, 145
14.8–11	149	15.4	124, 154, 158	16.7	197
14.9	148			16.8	163
14.10	xxvii, 24, 28, 52, 157, 184	15.4–5	24, 202	16.8–11	165
		15.4–10	52, 149	16.12	167, 169, 189
		15.5	124, 147, 152, 153, 178		
14.10–11	150			16.12–15	162, 163, 165, 166
14.12	xxvii, 100, 137, 140, 145, 150, 170, 184, 189	15.6	155	16.13	168
		15.8	124	16.13–14	149
		15.9	143 154, 158	16.13–15	167
				16.14	168, 189
14.12–14	150	15.9–17	153, 156–7	16.15–24	163
14.13	149, 151, 168	15.10	143, 154, 158	16.17–19	163
14.15	203	15.11	37	16.21, 22	164

233

16.22	112, 145, 163	17.22	143	19.13	116
16.24	37	17.23	143, 170, 173, 174	19.14	60, 132
16.24c	162	17.23, 26	24	19.15	180
16.25	165, 179	17.24	174	19.16b–18	183
16.25–33	163	17.25	173	19.16b–37	183–6
16.27	20	17.26	172	19.16b–40	177
16.28	52, 181	18.1	183, 190	19.17	192
16.29	165, 179	18.1–11	177	19.18	196
16.29–33	165	18.1–19.16	177	19.22	180
16.30	163	18.1–19.42	176–87	19.23	135, 202, 204
16.32	163, 165	18.3	182	19.24	183
16.33	10, 196	18.3–8	178	19.25	203
17–18	178	18.3–12	178	19.25–27	36
17.1	171	18.4	178	19.26–27	184
17.1–5	171–2	18.4–6	105	19.28	xxiv, xxvii, 60, 144, 172, 184, 189
17.1–26	79, 112, 131, 162, 170	18.5	158		
		18.7	178		
		18.8	178		
17.2	172	18.10–11	178	19.28–30	105
17.3	173	18.11	178	19.30	xxiv, xxvii, 60, 125, 144, 150, 154, 172, 176, 184, 189
17.4	xxiv, 168, 170, 171	18.12	182		
		18.12–16a	177		
17.5	172	18.13–14	179		
17.6–19	171, 172, 173	18.15–17	203		
		18.15–18	179, 202		
17.6	172	18.17–18	202	19.31	132
17.8	172	18.18	182, 202	19.34	60, 87, 149, 154, 185
17.9	172, 173	18.19–23	98		
17.11	46, 143, 172	18.19–24	179	19.38	186
		18.20	xxvi, 165, 179	19.38–42	50
17.12	172, 178			19.39	186
17.12–13	172	18.21	174	19.40	186
17.13	37	18.22	179, 182	19.41	6, 183, 186, 190, 196
17.14	172	18.25–27	179, 203		
17.15	172, 173	18.28	180, 181	19.42	132
17.17	107	18.29–32	180	20.1	190, 191
17.17–19	173	18.33–38a	xxvi, 180	20.1–10	178
17.18	20, 52, 143, 172, 173	18.37	180, 182, 186	20.1–18	189, 190, 203
17.19	107, 172	18.38	147	20.1–31	189–99
17.20	60, 170, 173	18.38b–40	180	20.2	193
		19–20	148	20.3–10	203
17.20–21	189	19.1–3	180	20.5	28
17.20–26	171, 173	19.4–7	180	20.7	191
17.21	xiv, 29, 30, 143, 144, 173	19.6	182	20.8	191
		19.8–11	180	20.9	191
		19.9	48	20.10	191
17.21–23	174, 202, 204	19.11	48	20.11	191
		19.12–16a	180	20.11–18	203

INDEX OF BIBLE REFERENCES

20.14	195	21.1	201, 203, 204	21.25	135
20.15	178, 189, 190, 191, 195, 201	21.1–19	200	**Acts of the Apostles**	
		21.1–25	200–5	3.11	106
20.17	192, 201, 203	21.2	29, 36, 201, 203	5.12	106
				9.2	147
20.18	192	21.2–3	202	19.9	147
20.19	190	21.3	201	19.23	147
20.19–23	190, 195–6, 203	21.4	201	22.4	147
		21.5	201	24.14	147
20.19–29	196	21.6	125, 201	24.22	147
20.21	143	21.7	201, 202		
20.21–22	142	21.8	201	**Romans**	
20.22	24, 149, 189, 196	21.9	202	16.1	116
		21.11	125, 201, 202, 204	**1 Corinthians**	
20.24	147			2.16	xvii
20.24–25	178	21.12	83, 200, 202	10.4	185
20.24–29	190, 198, 203				
		21.13	202	**Philippians**	
20.25	198, 203	21.14	203	1.1	116
20.26–27	36	21.15	203		
20.27	116, 192	21.15–18	202	**1 Timothy**	
20.28	111, 192	21.17	202	3.8	116
20.30	38	21.19	28, 194, 203	3.12–13	116
20.30–31	135, 189, 198	21.20	28	5.10	53
20.31	21, 26–7, 56, 111, 174	21.22	28	5.25	53
		21.23	194	6.18	53
		21.20–23	204		
21	203–4	21.24–25	204		

Index of Names and Subjects

abiding 157–9
action *see lectio divina*
agriculture: bread 42, 72–83, 76, 81, 202; God as gardener 153, 155–6, 190; grain of wheat 122–6; the vineyard 33–4, 38, 152–6, 183; *see also* environment
Ahmed, Husna 144
Ahmed, Rafid 144
Allen, Ronald J., *Preaching the Gospels* (with Williamson) xix
Andrew 26, 29, 124, 202; Jesus reveals to 27, 28–9
Annas, High Priest 179–80
Anti-Human Trafficking Coalition 94
Ardern, Jacinda 144
Aristotle on friends 135, 158
Armstrong, Karen xvi; *Fields of Blood* 123
Armstrong, Neil 51–2
Artemis as saviour 61
St Augustine of Hippo 41, 90–1

Bales, Kevin, *Blood and Earth* 137
baptism: John the Baptist and 21–2; River Jordan 22
Basil of Caesarea, Spirit as Breath 24
Batsheva 91
Bauckham, Richard 34
Beaufort (Margaret) Institute of Theology xviii–xix
beggar, blind 96–100, 111
Beloved disciple 177, 184, 189–90; rivalry with Peter 204; at the tomb 203
St Benedict, Rule of, *lectio divina* xviii
Benedict XVI, Pope, on the resurrection 194–5
Biko, Steve 187
blind beggar 96–100, 111

Blood and Earth: Modern Slavery, Ecocide and the Secret to Saving the World (Bales) 137
the body: flesh 11, 172; symbol of self 193; Bonhoeffer, Dietrich 187
Boulding, Maria 93
Brackley, Dean xvi, 62
Brague, Remi 4
Braudis, Ann 13
Brodie, Thomas 99
Brooks, Geraldine, *The Secret Chord* 91
Brown, Raymond xix, 166, 168; believing in 11–12; family at the cross 184; making sense of Jesus's death 177; mercy of Jesus 90–1
Byrne, Brendan xvi, xix, 107

Caiaphas, High Priest 179–80
Cana 201, 202
Carter, Warren xix
Cassidy, Richard J. xix, 180
Charbit, Yves 93
Christians, early 164; scriptures as bond of xiv–xv; secret 47; transition from Judaism 73–4; understanding death of Jesus 177–8; *see also* Jewish people and customs
Christology 173
civic moral courage 93
Collins, Raymond 28
Comblin, José xix
consecration 107
contemplation xvi; *lectio divina* cycle xv, xvi–xviii
cosmology 12–13
creation: 'all things' 8; from the earth 125; fruitfulness 34; John's prologue cosmology 3–13; light and

INDEX OF NAMES AND SUBJECTS

darkness 96–7; resurrection and 6, 191; water 57; the Word 6–7
Culpepper, R. Alan xix, 173, 204

Daly-Denton, Margaret xix, 99; golden vine at temple 156; Jesus as gardener 5; meaning of vines 153
David, King 91
Death: Jesus responds to grief 112; Jewish customs 111–12; life/death, presence/absence 110; paradox with life 112–13
disability 96–100
disciples: abiding in Jesus 24; believing in 78; Beloved 177, 184, 189–90; at the cross 184–5; discipleship 20–1; escape of 178; farewell discourse 140–51, 145–6, 146–7; first public signs and 39; fishing and 201–2; foot washing and 136; as friends 154, 157–9; God 192; Jesus prays for 172–3; Jewish 61–2; male and female 203–4; Mary of Bethany 117; murmuring 79; resurrection and 189–92, 197–8, 200–5; to see 100; seeking/following 27–9; as servants 136
Doctors without Borders 187
the dove 24
Dysinger, Luke xvii

earth, cry of xiii, xx; *see also* environment; marginalization and poverty
Eastern Orthodox Church, *perichoresis* and 52
ecclesiology 173
Economy of Life (WWC) xiii–xiv, 174–5, 195
ecumenism xiii–xiv; receptive xiv; scriptures as Christian bond xiv–xv; spiritual 174
Edwards, Denis 24–5
Elgar, Edward, 'The Light of Life' 96
Elisha, barley loaves and 76
environment: agriculture and 156; astronauts and Earth 51–2; caring for creation 126; cry of the earth xxvi; ecumenism and xv; grain of wheat and 122–6; Green Belt Movement 160; historical context and xxix; John's Gospel and xviii–xix; justice issue xiii; Pope Francis and 13; resurrection and evolution 195; tragedy of the commons 119; transformative change and 168–9
Ephesus xxiv, 145, 164
equality, foot washing and 136
Eucharist 72, 81; Jesus and 133, 135, 202; meaning of 39; Passover and 132
evil, world and 9–10
evolution 163, 166, 194–5
Exodus 72, 75; manna in the desert 76, 82; Passover celebration 42
Ezekiel, breathes on bones 197

Faith: believing in 11–12, 38, 77–9, 79–80, 116, 146, 204; evolution of 163; opening blind eyes 96–100
family relations 35
Feast of Booths 179
Feast of Christ the King 187
Fields of Blood (Armstrong) 123
fishing: disciples and 201–2; mission task and 204
Food and Agricultural Organization 77
foot washing 131, 132, 133–7, 143, 159; equality in friendship 136
Francis, Pope: creation as common home 5; cry of earth and poor xiv; on the earth 53; God's creation and liberation 151; *Laudato Si'* 13, 175, 205; On mercy 93; on re-creation of earth 195
Freyne, Sean 29
friendship xxvi, 52; disciples and 154, 157–8; equality and 136

Gagarin, Yuri 51
Galilee 29–30, 75, 77, 123, 201
Gibler, Linda 57, 87
Gihon, fountain of 86
glory 12
God: breath of 24, 148–9, 196–7, 197–8; creation and xxv; dwelling place of 43–4, 146; as gardener 153, 155–6, 190; glory of 12, 37, 50; holiness 172–3; Jesus finishes work of xxvii; John's introduction 12;

my/our 192; redemption and 204; relationship with Jesus 147-8, 158, 167-8; sends Jesus to world 52; the temple and 42-4; vastness of 166; Word and Spirit xxvi; world and humankind 9
good works 53
Greeks looking for Jesus 124
Green Belt Movement 70, 160
Gregerson, Niels 6
Grundmann, Walter 53

A Handbook of Spiritual Ecumenism (Kasper) xiv, 174
Hanukkah 106
Hardin, Garret 119
hatred 159
Haught, John 163, 166
Herod Antipas 30
Herod the Great 156
Holy Spirit: ; as breath of God 148-9, 168, 196; guide for disciples 189; Jesus and 48-9, 159, 160, 184; Paraclete 149, 168, 197
honour, weddings and 35
human beings: self-judgement 54; water and 57-8; the world and 9

Ireneaus 24-5
Israel: ; Nathanael's view of 30-1; *see also* Jerusalem; Jewish people and customs

Jacob 58, 59, 141
Jerusalem: destruction of temple 44, 47, 113; Jesus arrives on donkey 121-2; pilgrimage to 66, 97-8, 103; Pool of Siloam 96
Jesus of Nazareth: accused of blasphemy 106-7; accused of having a demon 105; anointing of 109; appears to disciples 200-5; arrest and trial of 42, 49-50, 176-7, 179-83; belief in 78; the blind beggar and 96-100; born from above 48-9; Breath and 50, 149; calls to the thirsty 87; connection to creation xxv; context of xxiii-xxx, 75; in the cosmology 3-13; death and burial 176, 177, 183-6; declarations about the future 163-9; on a donkey 121-2; from the earth 125, 126; farewell address of 140-51, 150, 153, 156-7, 160; Father and 68-9; at Festival of Tabernacles 86; foot washing 115-16, 133-7, 143, 159; friendship xxvi; Galilee and Nazareth 29-30; as gardener 190; gathers communities 164-5; glorification 143; God sends to world 52; goes up the mountain 77; as Good Shepherd 66, 105-6, 145, 178, 202; handing out the bread 77; healing 65, 67-8, 70; before the high priests 98; his parents in Jerusalem 98; hostility towards 65, 68; 'I am the bread of life' 74-6, 80; 'I am the gate' 104; 'I am the light of the world' 86, 97-8; images xxv; John the Baptist and 20-5; as king 30-1, 181-2; Lazarus and 109-13, 112-13, 115-16, 122, 179; leaves Judea 107; life and death-resurrection 145-51; marginalization of xxvii; Mary of Bethany and 111, 115-16; meal with friends 116-17; mercy for adulterous woman 90-4; the Messiah 56, 106-7, 110-11; on the move xxv; in a new community 131; Nicodemus and 47-8, 51, 56, 57; pilgrimage to Jerusalem 66, 97-8, 103, 121-2; prayer of 170-5; reconciliation and xxvii; rejection 10; relationship with God 147-8, 158, 167-8; response to grief 112-13; resurrection of xxvi, 125, 189-99, 193-4; revealing his glory 38-9; revelation to disciples 26-9; in Samaria 58-62; Samarian woman and 58-9, 60-2; saviour of the world 61-2; sent from God 20-1; signs/mighty deeds of 38-9; Son of Man 81; in the temple 42-4; 'the word became flesh' 11; vine imagery 152-6; wedding at Cana 36-40; as Wisdom Sophia 190; women at the cross 184-5; works of God xxvii, 9-10, 99-100, 150, 151, 160, 184

INDEX OF NAMES AND SUBJECTS

Jesus Washing Peter's Feet (Madox Brown) 134, 136
Jewish people and customs: agriculture and 153–6; almsgiving 118, 142; burial and 185, 186; cast out Jesus 98; context of Jesus xxiii, 75, 131; disciples and 61–2; early Christians and 164; festivals of 65, 86–7, 103, 106, 107; 'flesh and blood' 81–2; Hebrew 'truth' and 'mercy' 182; interrogation of Jesus 197–80; leaders and common folk 96; Mary and Martha in mourning 111–12, 113; Passover 42, 109, 132; Samarians and 59; the Sanhedrin 179–80; scripture and xxv, 177; secret Christians 47; sons and fathers 68–9; stoning women 91; subjection to Pilate's rule 180–1; understanding eternal life 113; weddings 34–5
John, Gospel of: believing in 11–12; Book of Glory 131; Book of Signs 131; the coming of Jesus 10, 11; cry of the earth and marginalized 65–70; Ephesus and 164; eternal life now 54; historical context of xxiii–xxx; 'I am the light' 8; individuality of xxviii; Jesus as new temple 118; Jesus's farewell address 140–51; life and death-resurrection 145; Martha ministers 116; no narrative of Eucharist 72; perception of the world 51; prologue cosmology 3–13; relating to present Jesus 194; written after temple destroyed 113; *see also* in biblical reference index
John Paul II, Pope, sin and structures of sin 10
John the Baptist 60; on the lamb of God 44; portrayal in John's Gospel 20–5; River Jordan and 29
Johnson, Elizabeth 204
Jordan, River 29
Joseph of Arimathea 186
Josephus, Titus Flavius 41; on Pilate 181; on royal burial 186
Judas (not Iscariot) 148; questions of 150
Judas Iscariot 104; the common purse and 118, 119; hands over Jesus 178, 184; Jesus reveals to 27; leaves the supper 140, 142; objects to giving 117–18; trial of Jesus 180
Judea: division with Samaria 47; hostility to Jesus 29
Judgement: Last 53; self- 53, 54
justice *see* social justice

Karris, Robert J. xix, xxviii, 76
Kasper, Walter, *A Handbook of Spiritual Ecumenism* xiv, 174
King Jr, Martin Luther 187
Kreglinger, Giesla, *A Spirituality of Wine* 153–4

Lacugna, Catherine 52
The Last Supper 131–2; farewell 131, 132, 140–51; foot washing 131, 132, 133–7; Passover and 132; prayer of Jesus 131, 132
Laudato Si' (Pope Francis) 13, 175, 205
Lazarus of Bethany 62, 83; death of 109–13, 194; friendship of 115; Jesus reveals to 27; raised by Jesus 110, 115, 122, 146, 179
leadership, Good Shepherd and 66, 104, 105–6, 145, 178, 202
lectio divina cycle: contemplation and xv; context of scriptures xxviii–xxix; outlines of xvi–xviii
Lee, Dorothy 154, 203
Love: the disciples and 143–4; *see also* friendship
Lovell, Jim 51
Luke, Gospel of: Jesus in the temple 44; Jesus washes feet 133; Judean trial scene 106; Last Supper account 72; lost sheep and Israel 104; the newborn child 4; woman accused of adultery 90

Maathai, Wangari 70, 160
Madox Brown, Ford, *Jesus Washing Peter's Feet* 134, 136
male and female roles 35; *see also* Mary Magdalene; Mary of Bethany

Malina, Bruce 42–3
Maori xxix
marginalization and poverty 94; always with you 118; care of the poor 117; cry of xiii, xx, xxvi; ecumenism and xv; Passover and alms 142; physical disabilities 65–70; stories of xxviii
Mark, Gospel of: Jesus in the temple 44; Jesus washes feet 133; Judean trial scene 106; Last Supper account 72; lost sheep and Israel 104
Martha of Bethany 83, 178; death of Lazarus and 109–13; Jewish 62; ministers 116
Mary Magdalene 178; as disciple 191, 203, 204; Jesus appears to 27, 201, 203; Jesus as gardener 190; at the tomb 189–93
Mary, mother of Jesus: Jesus reveals to 27; role in ministry 36
Mary of Bethany 83, 178, 182; anoints body of Jesus 186; anoints Jesus's feet 115–16; death of Lazarus and 109–13; dialogue with Jesus 111; as disciple 117; Jewish 62; leadership of 115–16
Matthew (disciple) 60
Matthew, Gospel of: Jesus in the temple 44; Jesus washes feet 133; Judean trial scene 106; Last Supper account 72; lost sheep and Israel 104; Martha's faith and 111; the newborn child 4
meditation *see* contemplation
mercy: the adulterous woman 90–4; Hebrew meaning 182
Merton, Thomas 123
Messiah: John denies being 21; understanding of xxvii
migration, forced 94
miracles/signs 66–7
Miranda, José xix
missiology 173
Mitchell, Edgar 51
Moloney, Francis xix
Moses 141, 191
Motyer, Stephen xix, 5
Moxnes, Halvor 30
Mshana, Rogate xiii–xiv, 174–5

murmuring 79, 82
Murray, Paul xiv

Nathanael xxvii, 65; Cana and 36, 201; faith and 111; human Jesus 178; Jesus appears to 27, 201; Jesus as King of Israel 30; nationalist representative 164; on Nazareth 29; true Israelite 46, 56
Nazareth, place of 29–30
New Zealand: Maori life force 87; mosque massacre 144; Treaty of Waitangi xxix; water from cave 85–6
Neyrey, Jerome xix, 106
Nicodemus xxvii, 50, 65; assists in burial 112, 186; Jesus reveals to 27; 'Rabbi, we know' 46; 'ruler of the Jews' 164; secret Christian 98; at the trial 49–50; visits Jesus 47–8, 51, 56, 57

O'Day, Gail xix
O'Laughlin, Frank 73–4

'p' codes 93–4
Passover 42, 109; Eucharist and 132; food and 75–6; imagery of 72; Jesus with friends 115–16; Last Supper and 132
Peppard, Christiana 22
Peralta, Athena xiii–xiv, 174–5
Perkins, Pheme 118
Peter *see* Simon Peter
Pharisees: the adulterous woman and 90–4; arrest Jesus 49, 50; and the blind beggar 98; to the crowd 95–6; investigate Jesus 179–80; Nicodemus and 49–50; plans of 116
Philip 29; with Jesus 27, 29, 148; looking for Jesus 124; not enough bread 76, 77; questions of 150
Philo of Alexandria 6, 41; on Pilate 181; pilgrimage 41
Pilate, Pontius 179; power over the Jews 180–1; treatment of crucified 185; trial of Jesus 186
Plato 8, 135, 158
the poor *see* marginalization and poverty

Poverty, Wealth and Ecology
  Programme (WWC) 205
power and privilege 91–4
prayer: integral to spirituality 79; of
  Jesus 170–5; Oratio xviii
A Prayer for Our Earth 205
*Preaching the Gospels Without Blaming
  the Jews* (Allen and Williamson) xix

Rayan, Samuel xix, xxiv
redemption 204
Reinhartz, Adele 111
Rensberger, David xix, 182
resurrection 198–9; creation and 6; *see
  also under* Jesus of Nazareth
Revised Common Lectionary
  (RCL) xiv, xix
*Roadmap for Congregations,
  Communities, and Churches*
  (WCC) 168
Rohr, Fr. Richard 198–9
Rohrbaugh, Richard L. 42–3
Roman Catholic Church; foot washing
  and 135; Vatican II Council 163,
  174; *see also* Benedict XVI, Pope;
  Francis, Pope
Roman Empire: Artemis as saviour 61;
  burials and 185; context for
  Christians xxiii–xxiv, 164; Jesus
  and 141, 178; languages of 183;
  resistance to 184; under rule of 30,
  180–1, 186; slavery and 134, 135
Roman Lectionary (RL) xix
Romero, Oscar 187
Rossano Codex 96

Samaria 47; conflict with Judea 59;
  departure from law 58; division with
  Judea 47; Jesus in 58–62; 'living
  water' 56–61; Shechem 58
Samarian woman (Photini) 46–7, 65,
  160, 164, 178; belief in Jesus 56,
  61–2, 173; speaks to Jesus 27,
  58–62; without status 50
Schneiders, Sandra xix, 110;
  experience of glorified Jesus 193;
  good, evil, alternative worlds xxviii,
  53, 136–7; historical context xxiii;
  history, theology and spirituality 73;
  Martha and Eucharist 116; text and
  spirituality xv

Schottroff, Luise 91, 93, 184
Scripture: Jewish people and 177; the
  Word 12, 81
Scriptures: reinterpreting xxv–xxvi, 47
The Secret Chord (Brooks) 91
Sepphoris 75
Seven Rivers (documentary) 22
sheep and shepherds 23, 183; the
  Good Shepherd 66, 102–8, 104–6,
  145, 178, 202; lamb of God 28–9;
  pastoral task and 204
Shepard, Alan 51
Simon of Cyrene 183
Simon Peter: abiding with Jesus 28;
  approaches Jesus 26; Beloved
  Disciple and 204; Bethsaida and 29;
  denials of 179, 202–3; dialogue with
  Jesus 145; faith and 111; follows
  Jesus 60; Jesus rebukes 178; Jesus
  reveals to 27, 28–9; portrayal of 27;
  presentation in John's Gospel 203–4;
  renamed 202–3; risen Jesus appears
  to 201; 'To whom shall we go?' 82;
  at the tomb 189–90, 191
sin 99–100; 'Who sinned?' 99–100
slavery: global threat of 137; position
  of slaves 134, 135
smell 119
social justice: context of
  scriptures xxix; *see also*
  environment; marginalization and
  poverty
spirituality xv
A Spirituality of Wine
  (Kreglinger) 153–4
Stang, Dorothy 187
Stoic philosophy 8
stoning women 91–2
Swetman, James 184

Teilhard de Chardin, Pierre 9, 166
temple: ; destruction of 44, 47, 113;
  Jesus as 43–4, 118; Jesus in 43;
  meanings within 42–3
Thomas 178; absence of 190; faith
  and 111; Jesus appears to 27, 192,
  193, 201, 203; Jesus reassures 147;
  questions of 150; will not
  believe 198
Tiberias 75, 78
Tiberius, Emperor 181

Traditional Ecological Knowledge 87
Trafficking in Persons report (US Dept of State) 137
Trinity relationship 52
truth, Hebrew meaning of 182

United Nations IPBES document 168
Uriah 91

Water: ; current situations 62; pool of Bethesda 66; springs 85–7; woman at the well 85
Watson, Sir Robert 168
Weddings: at Cana 34, 36–40; social and cultural context 34–5
Westcott, B. F. xix
wilderness, meaning of 21
Williams, Rowan xiv, 174
Williamson, Clark, *Preaching the Gospels* (with Allen) xix
Wisdom Sophia xxvi, 72; abiding and friendship 157; becomes flesh 11, 12; bread and 76, 80; consecration and 107; creation and 5, 190; cries out for justice 179; gathers friends 82, 165; Jesus and 75–6, 183; provisions for all 78; Spirit and 24–5; the Word and 7, 24
woman accused of adultery: Jesus and forgiving words 90–4
the world: choosing light or darkness 10; 'coming into' 8–9; evil, good, alternative 53; meaning of 8–10
World Council of Churches (WCC): ecological commons 119; *Economy of Life* xiii–xiv, 100, 174–5, 195; Greed Line Study Group 108; on inequality 13; Philippine people and 187; PWE Programme 205; Roadmap 168

Zebedee, sons of 201
Zechariah 21

www.ingramcontent.com/pod-product-compliance
Lightning Source LLC
Chambersburg PA
CBHW021939290426
44108CB00012B/891